Publisher 97

Made Simple

Publisher 97 Made Simple

Moira Stephen

MADE SIMPLE
BOOKS

Made Simple
An imprint of Butterworth-Heinemann
Linacre House, Jordan Hill, Oxford OX2 8DP
A division of Reed Educational and Professional Publishing Ltd

Ɋ   A member of the Reed Elsevier plc group

OXFORD   BOSTON   JOHANNESBURG
MELBOURNE   NEW DELHI   SINGAPORE

First published 1998

TRADEMARKS/REGISTERED TRADEMARKS
Computer hardware and software brand names mentioned in this book are protected
by their respective trademarks and are acknowledged.

British Library Cataloguing in Publication Data
A catalogue record for this book is available from the British Library

ISBN 0 7506 3943 1

Typeset by P.K.McBride, Southampton

Archtype, Bash Casual, Cotswold and Gravity fonts from Advanced Graphics Ltd
Icons designed by Sarah Ward © 1994
Printed and bound in Great Britain by Scotprint Ltd, Musselburgh, Scotland

FOR EVERY TITLE THAT WE PUBLISH, BUTTERWORTH-HEINEMANN
WILL PAY FOR BTCV TO PLANT AND CARE FOR A TREE.

Contents

Preface

Welcome to Publisher 97 Made Simple.

This book starts off by giving you an overview of the package and some ideas on the kind of documents that you can produce from Publisher 97 - you'll be creating newsletters, booklets, flyers, forms, mailshots and Web pages in no time!

Chapters 3 – 6 cover the features that you'll find useful for any type of publication you create. Page layout, inserting and formatting text plus inserting and formatting graphics are all discussed.

In Chapters 7 and 8 we consider some of the more specialist areas that will help you design good-looking forms and produce effective mailings.

Chapter 9 provides information on some shortcuts for formatting text, saving and applying design elements and laying out your page. The features discussed can help you give your publications a consistent look (important for a company image) and could also save you a considerable amount of time. Styles, the Design Gallery and templates are all discussed.

Do you want to create your own Web site? Do you want to create hyperlinks to other pages and Web sites? And just how do you get a Web site from your computer onto the Web? Find out in Chapter 10.

1 Getting started

What is Publisher?

Publisher is an easy to use, flexible, fun DTP (DeskTop Publishing) package.

You can use Publisher to create:

- ◆ Newsletters
- ◆ Invitations
- ◆ Brochures
- ◆ Booklets
- ◆ Flyers
- ◆ Web pages
- ◆ Forms
- ◆ Cards
- ◆ Certificates

the list goes on and on!

Publisher gives you the tools you need to create your own professional-looking publications – so you may be able to produce many of your own without the services of a designer! Using Publisher could save you money!

However, to get the best results from Publisher you have to start thinking like a designer yourself. This chapter will give you some tips on points to consider when designing your publications – then it's over to you to experiment and try things out.

Keywords for successful publications:

- ◆ Simplicity
- ◆ Consistency
- ◆ Contrast

We'll discuss these in more detail later in this chapter.

Publisher has several PageWizard design assistants that can help you create your publication. The wizards do most of the work for you – all you need to add is your own text and pictures. It's the easiest place to start! We'll use a PageWizard design assistant to create your first publication, in Chapter 3.

If you work through this book, you'll also find out how to design your own publications from scratch – giving you total control and flexibility!

Take note

Publisher is fun to use! Don't be scared to experiment with it.

Publisher terminology

As you work with Publisher, you'll become familiar with the specialised terminology it uses. Brief definitions of some of the main words and phrases are listed here.

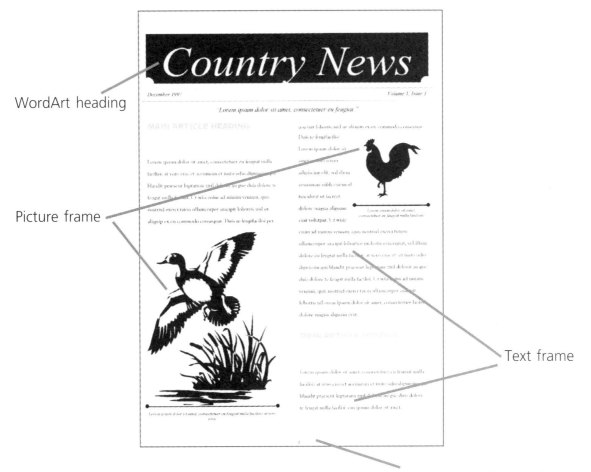

WordArt heading

Picture frame

Text frame

Page number on background

Design element

A design element is a text frame, picture frame or any object you place on a page in your publication. Try not to have too many elements on any one page – it will give a cluttered effect.

Object

An object is an element that is created in another program and is inserted into your Publisher file. The object maintains its connection to the *source* program and the fuctions and features of that program are used when you create and edit the object.

You therefore have access to the power of the package providing the object, as well as the design and layout capabilities of Publisher at your disposal!

Frames

Each object you position on the page is placed within a frame. Frames may contain text, pictures, tables, WordArt or any other object you insert.

Text frames

The text that you type into your publication is entered into a text frame (see page 46). The edges of the frame work like margins do in a word-processing file – text will wrap within the frame. If the text you enter into a frame is more than the frame can accommodate you will have to consider how you can make it fit. You could reword your article (so that it takes up less space), increase the size of the frame or link the text frame to another text frame so that the text will flow from one frame to another.

Picture frames

Pictures – Clip Art, logos, or other images – are placed within picture frames in your publication.

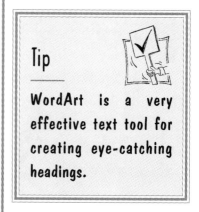

Tip

WordArt is a very effective text tool for creating eye-catching headings.

Page layout

When working in Publisher, the layout of your page is very important. It helps ensure the message you want to convey is communicated effectively. You determine your page layout by deciding where you want your text and pictures to go and what size the frames should be.

Foreground

Text, pictures, tables, etc. that make up the articles in your publication are placed on the page foreground.

Background

Page numbers, headers, footers or any elements that you want repeated on each page of your publication are entered onto the page background. The background in Publisher is similar in concept to header and footer areas in a word-processing package (see page 66).

White space

Don't be tempted to crowd too much information onto a page (unless the publication is meant for a specialist group who will appreciate it).

White space is the term given to the blank areas on your page – those with no text or pictures. The white space can be in the margins or between items on your page. Effective use of white space can have a positive effect – don't try to fill up every last bit of the page!

Font (Typeface)

You can vary the font, font size or font attributes (bold, italic, etc.) used on a page to draw attention to your text - but don't overdo it.

On most pages in this book you'll find 4 variations in the font used - the headings use one font, in 2 different sizes - one for the page heading, one for sub-headings – Basic steps, Take note, Tip. The text within a Take note or Tip box is bold, and the main text uses a font that is easy on the eye and comfortable to read. Fonts are discussed in more detail in Chapter 4.

Margins

A margin is the white space between the edge of the page and the area that your objects are placed within.

Columns and rows

The information on your page will be displayed in columns and rows. You can specify the number of columns and rows you wish to have on each page. You specify the number of columns and rows required in the Layout Guides dialog box (see page 37).

Boundaries and guides

Boundaries and guides are non-printing lines that can be displayed on your page to show where the margins, column and row boundaries, and edges of frames are. They can be very are useful in helping you to position your objects on the page.

Before you start to set up your publication in Publisher, give some thought to its *design*. There are no hard and fast rules for design, but you want to end up with a publication that gets your message across to your target audience.

What message do you want to convey?

● Match the design to your audience, e.g. something eye-catching and amusing for a young audience.

● Are you trying to pass on lots of information, or is the message short and sharp?

● Does your publication convey a serious message, or something light-hearted?

Collect ideas

● Take a look at some other similar publications – get an idea of what you think does and doesn't work.

● Use the designs in Publisher.

● Sketch your ideas out on paper.

● Ask friends and colleagues if they think your design will attract attention and get your message across.

Remember the three basic rules

● Keep it simple.

● Be consistent.

● Use contrast to draw attention to your message.

Watch your budget

Check the paper, printing and binding costs *before* finalising your design. You may want to change things if it is going to work out too expensive.

Paper

Things that might influence the type of paper you use:

● Printing and copying methods. Some papers are made specifically for commercial printing machines. Others are ideal for photocopiers and desktop printers. Some papers are more suitable for ink-jet printing.

● Cost! Some types of paper are much more expensive than others. Your budget will usually narrow down the range of papers available to you, considerably.

● Type of publication. A glossy newsletter or magazine with high quality colour photographs will look better on a glossy coated paper than on an uncoated one.

● Function and shelf life of publication.

Business Hours

Monday	9.00-5.30
Tuesday	9.00-5.30
Wednesday	9.00-1.30
Thursday	9.00-6.00
Friday	9.00-8.00
Saturday	9.00-5.00
Sunday	Closed

Colour

Consider using colour to add emphasis to your publication. You can use:

● Full Colour. You have access to up to 16 million colours when using full colour. The main limiting factor in the number and sharpness of colours is the printer you are using. You can print a full colour publication on your desktop printer, or send it to a commercial printer.

● Spot Colour. This allows you to add up to 2 colours to your publication (in addition to black). It's useful for highlighting areas.

● Coloured paper. Cheap, easy and effective!

Basic steps

1 Click the **Start** button on the Task Bar.

2 Select **Programs**.

3 Choose **Microsoft Publisher**.

❑ The Microsoft Publisher copyright screen appears for a few seconds followed by the Startup dialog box.

4 For the time being, click the **Cancel** button in this dialog box, and have a look at the Publisher window.

Starting Publisher is similar to starting any other Windows 95 application.

At the Startup dialog box, you can create a new publication, in two ways:

● Use one of the PageWizard design assistants from the PageWizard tab (see Chapter 3).

● Create a publication from a blank page, by selecting a layout from the Blank Page tab.

Or you can open an existing publication:

● Select the Existing Publication tab, and locate the file required (see Chapter 3).

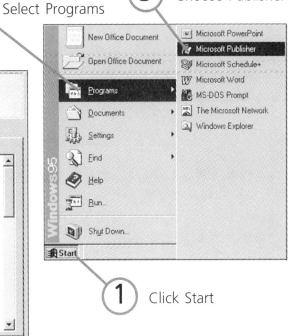

③ Choose Publisher

② Select Programs

① Click Start

④ Cancel for now

Publisher window

The main areas in the Publisher window are identified on the diagram below.

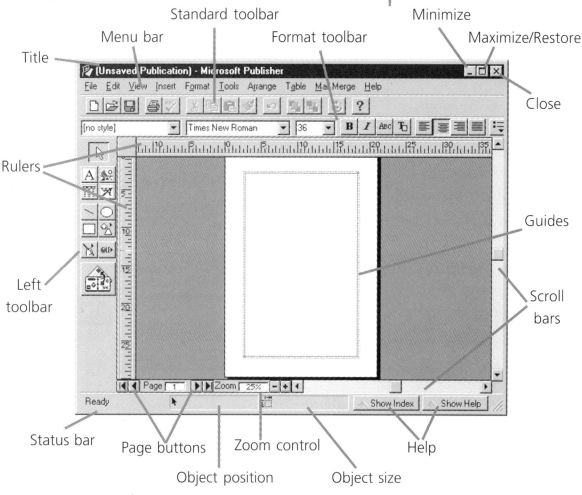

Standard toolbar

Menu bar

Format toolbar

Minimize

Maximize/Restore

Title

Close

Rulers

Guides

Left toolbar

Scroll bars

Status bar

Page buttons

Zoom control

Help

Object position

Object size

Take note

The toolbars provide shortcuts to many of the most regularly used commands.

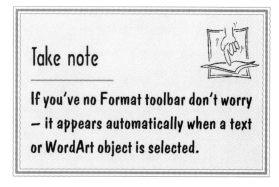

Take note

If you've no Format toolbar don't worry – it appears automatically when a text or WordArt object is selected.

Basic steps

1 Open the **File** menu.

2 Choose **Exit Publisher**.

Or

3 Hold down the **[Alt]** key on your keyboard.

4 Press **[F4]**.

Or

5 Click the **Close** button in the top right of the Publisher window.

 Click Close

Exiting Publisher

When you've finished working with Publisher you should exit the package *before* closing down your computer and switching off.

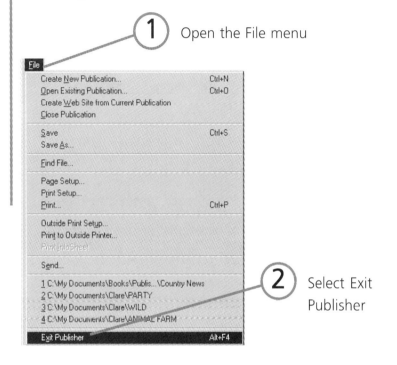

(1) Open the File menu

(2) Select Exit Publisher

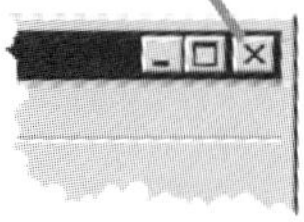

Tip

If you have finished with Publisher, it is a good idea to close it before moving on to another application. This frees up memory so your other application will perform better.

Take note

If you've entered any objects onto your publication, you will be prompted to save before exiting – see Chapter 3 for information on saving.

11

Summary

- Publisher is a flexible, fun to use, desktop publishing package.

- Desktop publishing packages use different **terminology** to that found in other packages – learn the new jargon as you go along.

- There are no hard and fast rules about **design** – experiment and have fun.

- Useful **keywords** – simplicity, consistency, contrast.

- Know your **target audience**.

- **Pitch the publication** to suit your target audience.

- You can create new publications, or open existing ones from the Publisher **Startup dialog box**.

- The **Publisher window** contains toolbars and buttons to help you work efficiently.

- Remember to **exit Publisher** *before* switching off your computer.

2 Help

Introduction to Publisher

There's lots of Help available within Publisher to get you up and running as quickly as possible.

If you have never used any version of Publisher before, you may find the **Introduction to Publisher** a good place to start to give you an overview of the package.

1 Open the **Help** menu.

2 Choose **Introduction to Publisher**.

3 Select **Introduction to Publisher** at the dialog box.

4 Click **OK**.

5 Work through the introduction to get an overview of the package.

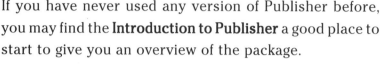

(1) Open the Help menu

(2) Select Introduction to Publisher

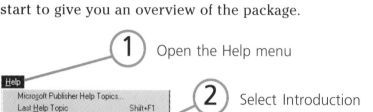

(3) Select Introduction

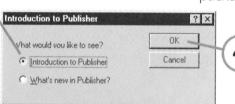

(4) Click OK

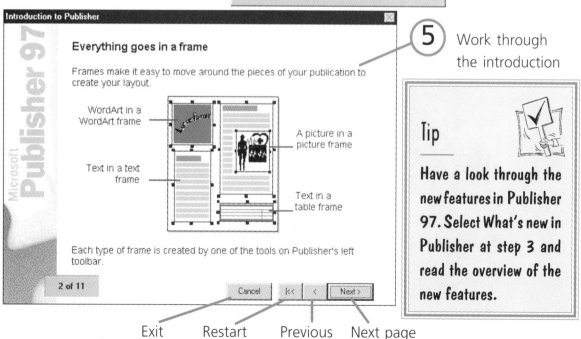

(5) Work through the introduction

Exit   Restart   Previous   Next page

Tip

Have a look through the new features in Publisher 97. Select What's new in Publisher at step 3 and read the overview of the new features.

Basic steps

1 Open the **Help** menu.
2 Select **Quick Demos...**
3 Choose a demo from the list in the **Publisher Demos** dialog box.
4 Click **OK**.
5 Work through the demo you have selected.

Quick Demos

You may also find it useful to work through some of the mini demonstrations that have been set up as part of Publisher's Help system. Most of these are on topics we haven't discussed yet, but have a look to see what's there – you can return to any that you feel would be useful.

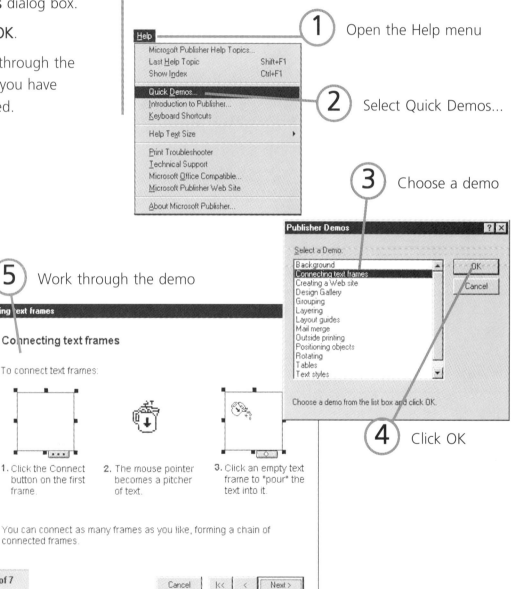

Show Help

At the bottom right of the Status Bar you will notice the Show Help button. You can open and close the main Help files from here. Once you've opened the Help files, you can work through the pages until you find the Help you need.

1 Click the ▢ Show Help button.

2 Select a topic you want Help on from the list displayed – click on it.

3 Repeat step 2 until you reach the Help required.

4 Read the **How To** tab to find out how to do the task.

5 If there is a **More Info** tab, select it to find out more about your topic.

6 Click the ▢ Hide Help button to close the Help files.

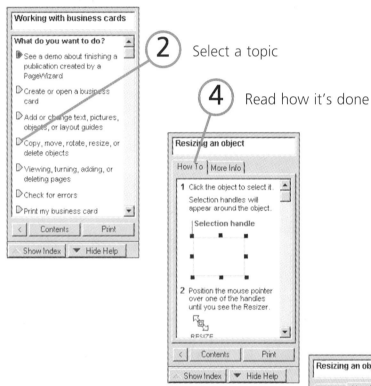

② Select a topic

④ Read how it's done

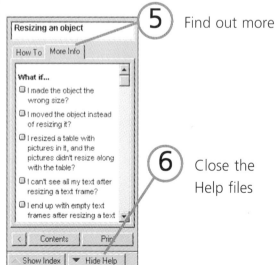

⑤ Find out more

⑥ Close the Help files

Take note

You can also toggle the display of the Help pages by clicking the Help tool ? on the Standard toolbar, or by pressing [Shift]- [F1].

16

Basic steps

1 Click the `Show Index` button.

2 Start typing the word or phrase you are looking for into the index entry box.

❑ A list of possible Help pages will be displayed.

3 Select a topic.

❑ The Help page for that topic will be displayed.

4 Work through the Help pages until you find the answers you need.

5 Click the `▼ Hide Index` button when you're finished.

Show Index

If you want to search for help on a particular word or phrase you could try using the index. Once you have become familiar with Publisher's terminology and you know what you want Help on, the index will often prove to be the quickest way of locating the Help you require.

2 Enter the word(s)

4 Work through the Help

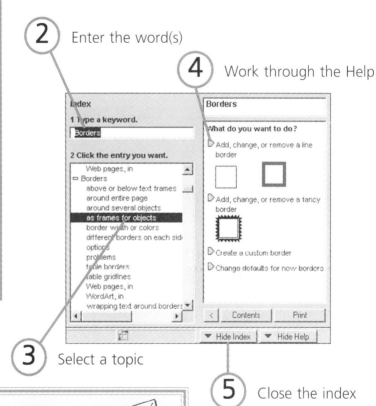

3 Select a topic

5 Close the index

Tip

Once you've found the Help page that tells you what to do, you can leave it open as you work on your publication. Just click on your publication and continue working, following the instructions on the Help page if necessary. You can hide the Help page when you've finished with it.

Instant Help

Tooltips

When you rest the cursor on a tool in a toolbar, a tooltip appears to tell you about it.

If the tooltips do not appear, you may need to switch the option on in the Toolbars and Rulers dialog box.

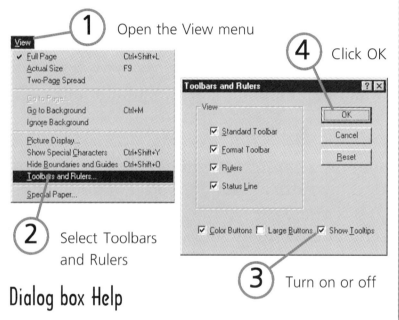

Open the View menu

Click OK

Select Toolbars and Rulers

Turn on or off

Dialog box Help

If you are in a dialog box, and want to know the purpose of an option you can use the dialog box help button to find out. Only dialog boxes offer this kind of Help.

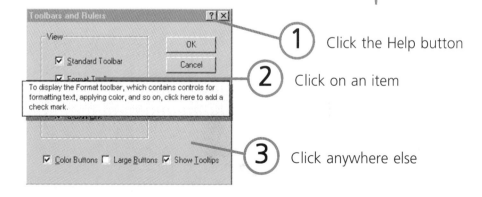

Click the Help button

Click on an item

Click anywhere else

- ❑ **Tooltips**
- **1** Open the **View** menu.
- **2** Choose **Toolbars and Rulers...**
- **3** Click the **Show Tooltips** checkbox to turn the option on or off.
- **4** Click **OK**.
- ❑ **Dialog box help**
- **1** Click the **Help** button ? in the top right hand of the dialog box.
- **2** Click on the item you want to find out about.
- ❑ A brief description of the item is displayed.
- **3** Click anywhere within the dialog box to cancel the definition.

Basic steps

1 Right click on an object you want Help on.

2 Select **Help on this Object** from the pop-up menu.

3 Work through the Help pages until you find the Help you need.

4 Click ▼ Hide Help when you've finished.

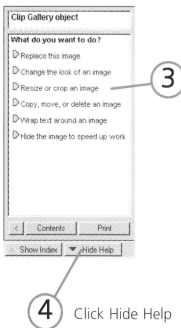

④ Click Hide Help

Object help

As you create a publication in Publisher, you add objects to your page. These objects may be text frames, WordArt, ClipArt, tables, etc. You can get help on any object in your publication at any time.

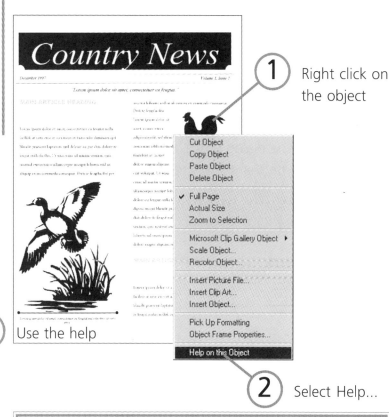

① Right click on the object

Use the help

② Select Help...

Take note

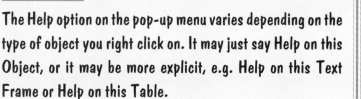

The Help option on the pop-up menu varies depending on the type of object you right click on. It may just say Help on this Object, or it may be more explicit, e.g. Help on this Text Frame or Help on this Table.

Summary

- **Introduction to Publisher** in the on-line Help gives a brief overview of the package.

- The **Quick Demos** in the on-line Help will step you through some of the features in Publisher.

- The main **Help pages** can be accessed at any time.

- You can use the **Index** to take you directly to the Help page for any topic listed in the index.

- **Tooltips** are useful reminders to prompt you on the purpose of any tool on the toolbars.

- In many of the **dialog boxes**, you can open a brief explanation on the items listed.

- You can access the Help system if you **right click on an object** in your publication.

3 Your first publication

PageWizards

The easiest way to start using Publisher is to use one of the PageWizard Design Assistants to help you create your publication. The Wizards do most of the hard work for you – all you need do is enter your own text and pictures into the layout created.

You can create a new publication as you start Publisher, or you can create a new publication from within Publisher.

Basic steps

❑ **From within Publisher**

1 Open the **File** menu.

2 Choose **Create New Publication...** and continue from step 4.

❑ **At start up**

3 At the **Startup** dialog box, select the **PageWizard** tab.

4 Choose the type of publication.

5 Click **OK**.

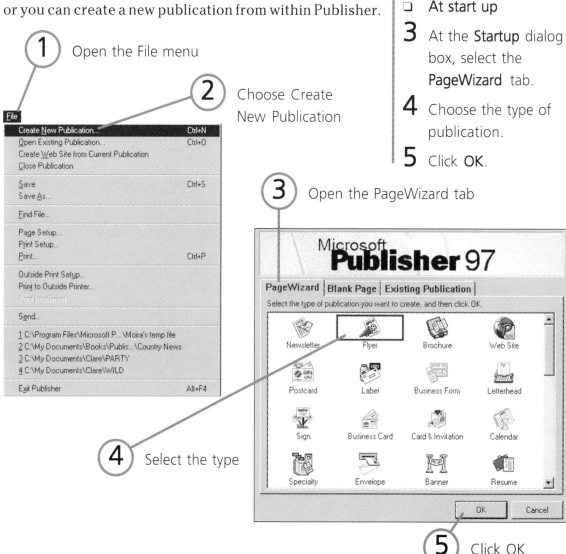

① Open the File menu

② Choose Create New Publication

③ Open the PageWizard tab

④ Select the type

⑤ Click OK

Basic steps

1 Select the category from the options listed.
2 Click **Next**.
3 Choose the style.
4 Click **Next**.
5 Click **Create It!**

Using a PageWizard

Exactly what happens next depends on the PageWizard you have selected. I chose the Flyer, with a view to creating a publication to advertise a school football event.

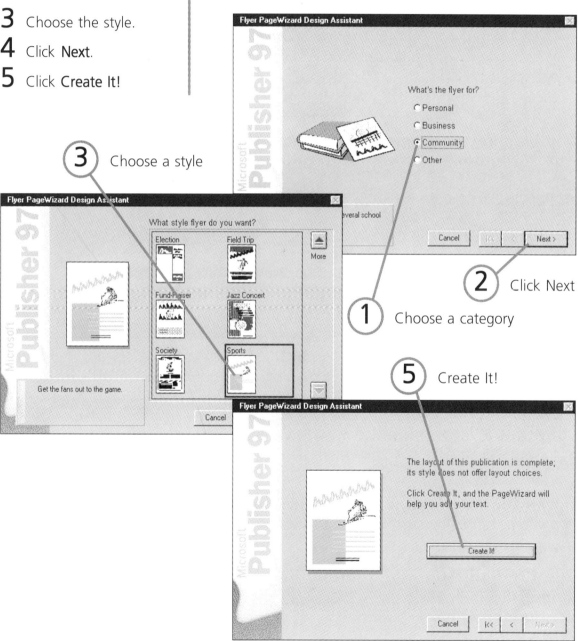

③ Choose a style

② Click Next

① Choose a category

⑤ Create It!

Providing the detail

You will most probably be asked for additional information, depending on the type of publication you are creating. Work through the steps, completing the fields as necessary.

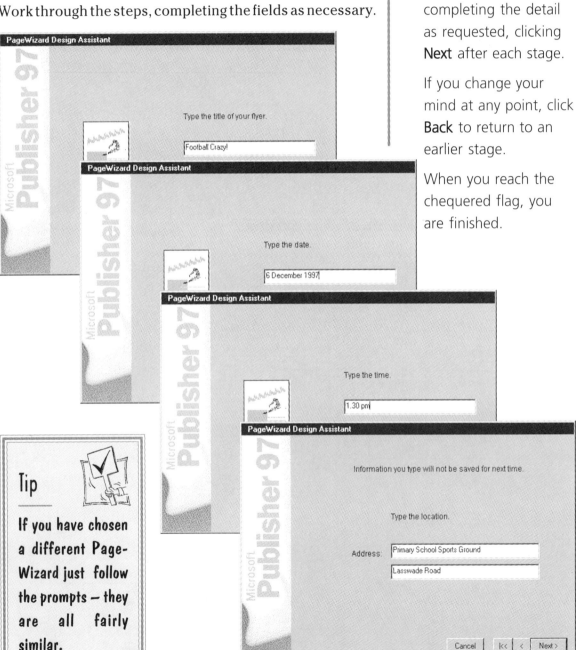

Tip

If you have chosen a different Page-Wizard just follow the prompts — they are all fairly similar.

Using Wizards

❑ Work through the steps in the wizard, completing the detail as requested, clicking **Next** after each stage.

If you change your mind at any point, click **Back** to return to an earlier stage.

When you reach the chequered flag, you are finished.

Completing the publication

☐ **To replace dummy text**

1 Click on the Text frame – the dummy text becomes selected.

2 Press the [Delete] key.

3 Press [F9] to zoom in – if you don't, you can't read your typing!

4 Enter your text.

5 Press [F9] to zoom out again.

Once you've worked through the wizard, check out the publication and make any final amendments to it. The details you provided in the wizard are displayed in the appropriate areas of your publication. In this example, there is an area for some more text if required. There is also a picture that isn't really suitable! (See Chapter 6.)

Boundaries and guides – these don't print out

Picture frame – we need a more appropriate picture

Text frame with dummy text

1 Select the Text frame

3 Zoom in – [F9]

4 Type new text   **5** Zoom out – [F9]

Take note

Select the text frame, zoom in if necessary, then click the Spelling tool 🔍 on the Standard toolbar to check your spelling. Check your text after spell-checking! If, for instance, you type 'alter' when you mean 'later', the spell-checker won't complain.

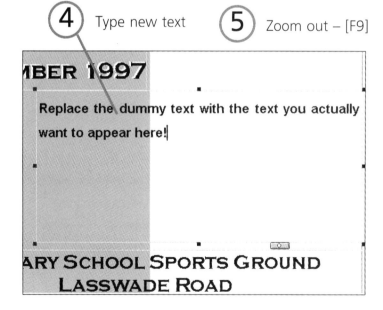

Saving the publication

You can save your file at any time – you don't need to wait until you've set it all up! If your computer crashes before you save, you'll lose your work! Save your file regularly.

Basic steps

1 Click the **Save** tool 🖫.

Or

2 Open the **File** menu and choose **Save**.

3 Locate the folder you want to save into.

4 Enter a name for it into the **File Name** slot.

5 Click **Save**.

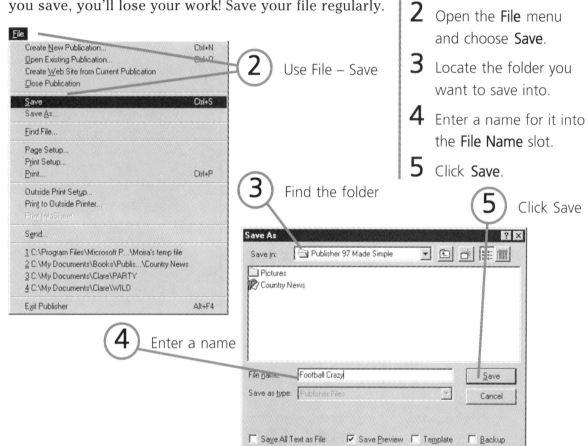

② Use File – Save

③ Find the folder

④ Enter a name

⑤ Click Save

Take note

Publisher will remind you to save your publication every 15 minutes (unless this option is switched off). You can set the time between the reminders on the Editing and User Assistance tab of the Options... dialog box – reach this from the Tools menu.

Tip

If you edit an existing publication and wish to keep the new version plus the original, choose Save As and save it with a new name.

Previewing the publication

1 Open the **View** menu.

2 Choose **Full Page**.

3 Select **Hide Boundaries and Guides** from the **View** menu.

4 Choose **Hide Special Characters** from the **View** menu.

❑ A full page preview of your publication will appear on screen.

Before printing your publication, you can preview it on your screen to see how it will look.

If your publication contains important details , e.g. date, time, place, get someone to check them – it's easy to make a mistake!

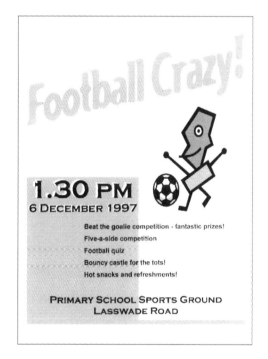

Tip

To redisplay the boundaries and guides or special characters (space, [Enter] and [Tab] keypresses), choose **Show Boundaries and Guides** and **Show Special Characters** from the View menu.

Take note

You must close your publication properly at the end of a session – open the File menu and choose Close Publication.

If you have changed your publication since you last saved it, a prompt will appear asking if you want to save the changes.

Printing the publication

If you're happy with the preview, it's time to print. You can either use your own desktop printer, or you can send your file to an outside printer and get them to print it for you.

Using your own desktop printer has several advantages:

- You can print what you want, when you want.
- You can double-check it after printing, fix any errors, then print again if necessary.

Basic steps

1 Open the **File** menu.

2 Choose **Print...**

Or

3 Click the **Print** tool ⬚.

4 Complete the **Print** dialog box as required.

5 Click **OK**.

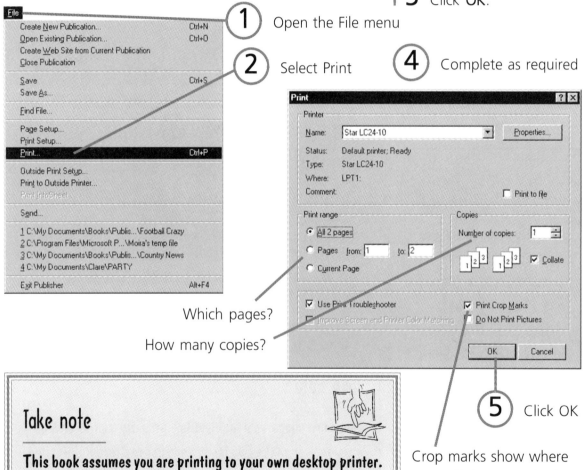

1 Open the File menu

2 Select Print

4 Complete as required

Which pages?

How many copies?

5 Click OK

Crop marks show where to cut if the page size is smaller than your paper

Take note

This book assumes you are printing to your own desktop printer. If you want to use an outside printer, look up 'Setting up outside printing' in the Help index and read the associated Help pages.

Basic steps

1 Open the **File** menu.

2 Choose **Open Existing Publication**.

Or

3 Click the **Open** tool 🗁.

4 Select the publication from the lists displayed.

5 Click **OK**.

Or

6 If the file is not listed, click 🏠 to access the **Open Publication** dialog box.

7 Browse through your folders and locate the file you want.

8 Click **Open**.

Opening a publication

If you have an existing publication on disk that you want to work on, you must open it before you can do so.

The preview panel helps to identify the file

4 Select from the lists

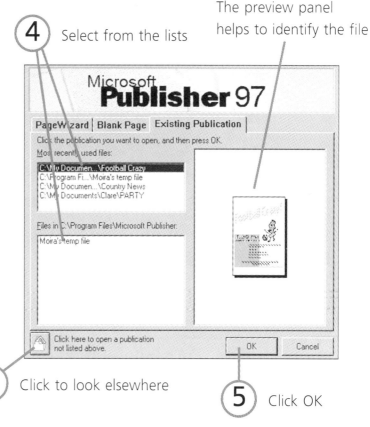

6 Click to look elsewhere

5 Click OK

7 Browse for the file

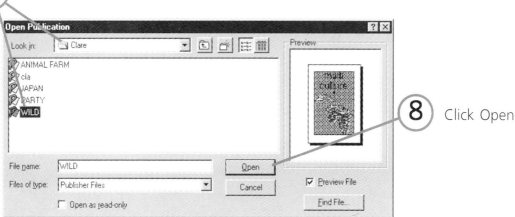

8 Click Open

Summary

- Publisher has a number of **PageWizard design assistants** to help you produce professional looking publications easily.

- You can **add your own text** to the publications you create using a PageWizard.

- **Zoom in on your Text frames** so you can see what you're typing.

- The **spell checker** can be used to check and correct most of the spelling errors in your publication.

- If you want to keep your publication, you must **save** it.

- **Preview** your publication to check that it looks good before printing.

- **Printing** can be done on your desktop printer, or you can send your file to an outside printer.

- **Close your publication** when you've finished working on it.

- **Existing publications** must be opened before you can work on them again.

4 Layout

Drawing up the design

Although the Page Wizard Design Assistants are useful, other people will most likely be using them as well, so you may find that your publications look similar to many other publications you see. Instead of using a Design Assistant you can design your own publication from scratch.

Sketch out the design before you start to set it up in Publisher. This will help you think through your ideas and decide where you want headings, text, pictures, etc.

Flyer

Below is a possible layout for a flyer, advertising a community event (e.g. BBQ or picnic). It has:

- A large heading.

- Pictures to make it eye-catching.

- An area for important information – date, time and place.

- An area for additional information – attractions, price, etc.

Take note

Planning your design doesn't mean you can't change the design once you start to set your publication up – but it does help you think your ideas through and note the important things you want to include.

Tip

You can always modify your original plan as you see how the publication develops.

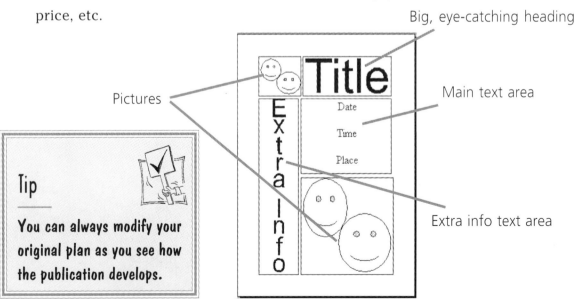

Big, eye-catching heading

Pictures

Main text area

Extra info text area

Booklets

If you are designing a booklet, you will have to consider the number of pages. It must be a multiple of 4 – you can set up a 4, 8, 12, 16, etc. page booklet. You should also think about any items that you will want to repeat on each page, e.g. page numbers or headers or footers. These items would be placed on the publication background.

Newsletter

If you are designing a newsletter, you may want to consider using some other design elements:

- A newsletter may be laid out in several columns – 3 in this example. Headers and/or footers may be repeated on all pages or, as here, on pages 2 – 4 only.

- The position of the main story, second story, etc. could also be shown.

- *Sidebars* (see page 68)can hold information that is not included in the main stories, but that may interest your readers.

- *Pull-quotes* can be used to draw attention to an exciting piece of information (see page 70).

Take note

The amount of detail on your design is up to you. It could be a sketch showing where the headings, text and pictures will go or you can include details of fonts and font sizes, the size of the frames, etc.

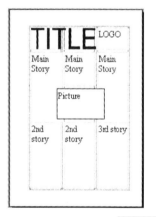

1

2 & 3

4

Choosing the page layout

Now that you've got some idea about how you want your publication to look, you can start to set it up.

To create a flyer or A4 size poster, select the Full Page option. If you are creating a booklet choose Book Fold.

Basic steps

1 Choose **Create New Publication** from the **File** menu.

2 Select the **Blank Page** tab in the **Startup** dialog box.

3 Pick page layout.

4 Click **OK**.

❑ A new, blank publication will appear.

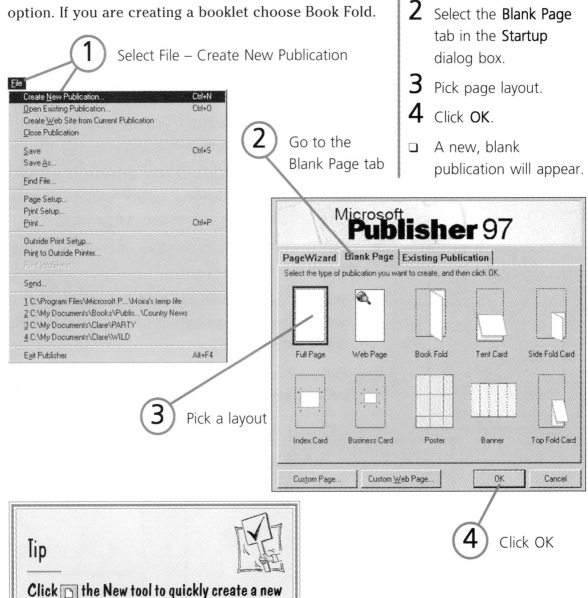

① Select File – Create New Publication

② Go to the Blank Page tab

③ Pick a layout

④ Click OK

Tip

Click 🗋 the New tool to quickly create a new blank publication using the Full Page option.

Basic steps

1 Open the **File** menu and choose **Page Setup...**

2 Select the **Choose a Publication Layout** option required.

3 Select **Portrait** or **Landscape** in the **Orientation** options.

4 Click **OK**.

Page setup

If you need to change the publication layout, orientation (whether the page is portrait - tall, or landscape - wide) or page size once you've created your publication you can access the Page Setup dialog box from your publication.

(2) Select a layout

(4) Click OK

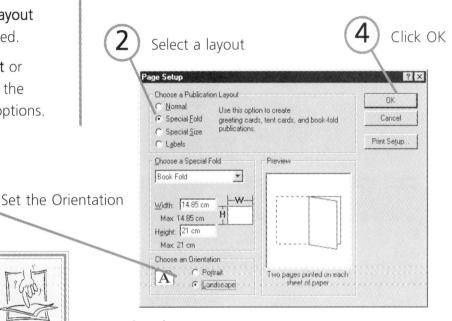

(3) Set the Orientation

Layout options

Normal	Most publications including newsletters, brochures, flyers.
Special Fold	Greeting cards, tent cards and bookfold publications – with this option, you select the special fold option you want to use from the drop-down box.
Special Size	Banners, posters, index cards, business cards – with this option you can select the publication size from a list of options.
Labels	Mailing labels and full-page labels.

Paper size

By default, Publisher will print your publication onto A4 size sheets of paper (210 by 297mm). If your publication will be bigger than A4 – a banner or poster for example – Publisher will print the file on a series of A4 sheets, which you can then assemble to give you the final publication.

You can change the paper size that Publisher will print onto in the Print Setup dialog box.

If you want to set a default paper size other than A4, you must do so by changing the printer properties in Windows.

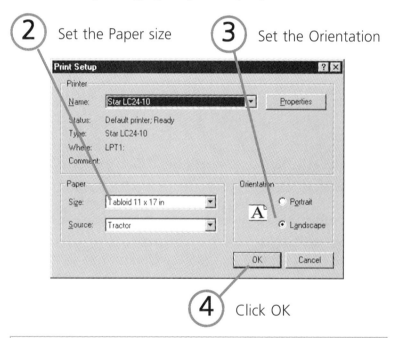

2 Set the Paper size   3 Set the Orientation

4 Click OK

Take note

With a folded booklet, the paper must be double the size of each page. A booklet with a page size of 148 by 210mm (an A5 page) will be printed on paper 210 by 297 (A4 paper).

Basic steps

1 From the **File** menu choose **Print Setup...**

Or

Click the **Print Setup...** button in the **Page Setup** dialog box

2 Set the **Paper Size**.

3 Select the **Orientation**.

4 Click **OK**

5 If you get the **Update embedded object** prompt, click **Yes**.

❑ **To set the default paper size**

6 Click **Start** on the **Taskbar**, select **Settings**, then **Printers**.

7 Right click on the printer you want to adjust and choose **Properties** from the pop-up menu

8 Select the **Paper** tab.

9 Choose the paper size and click **OK**.

❑ All new publications will use the new default paper size.

Layout guides

Take note

If you want to preview your publication before printing it, you can easily hide the layout guides to give you a clearer view of the page (see page 27).

Layout guides are used to help you position your text and pictures on each page of your publication. They do not print out, regardless of whether they are displayed or not.

There are margin layout guides and grid layout guides.

- The margin layout guides are pink, and show the position of the top, bottom, left and right margins.
- The grid layout guides are blue, and show the top, bottom, right and left edges of rows and columns.

If you select Full Page when creating your publication, the margin and grid layout guides appear together. This is because your page consists of a work area that is one column across and one row high.

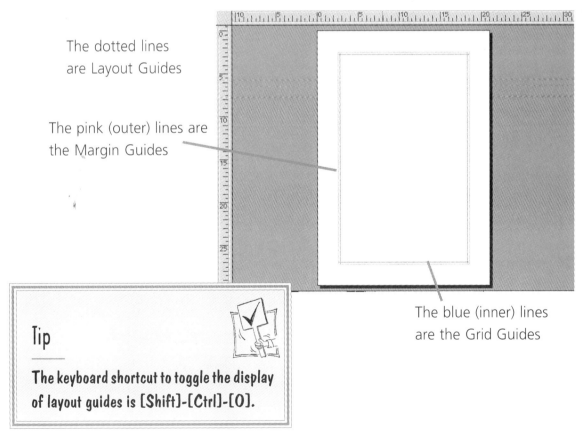

The dotted lines are Layout Guides

The pink (outer) lines are the Margin Guides

The blue (inner) lines are the Grid Guides

Tip

The keyboard shortcut to toggle the display of layout guides is [Shift]-[Ctrl]-[O].

Foreground/Background

Every page has 2 levels – a foreground and a background.

● The text, headings, pictures etc that you want on a page are entered onto the *foreground*.

● Layout guides are placed on the page *background*.

Any object that you want to repeat on every page, such as headers, footers or page numbers must also be placed on the *background* . (See page 66.)

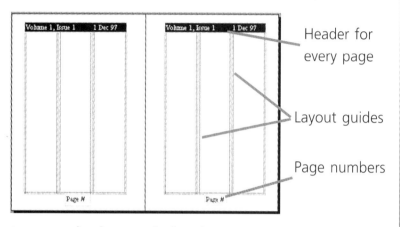

Header for every page

Layout guides

Page numbers

Ignoring background objects

If you do not want your background objects on all the pages – for example you may not want the header or footer on the first page – you can get Publisher to ignore them.

1 Display the page you don't want to display the background objects on.

2 Open the **View** menu.

3 Choose **Ignore Background**.

4 If you have 2 pages displayed, you will be asked which page you want the background objects ignored on. Select the page(s) and click **OK**.

❑ If you want the background objects displayed again, repeat steps 1–3.

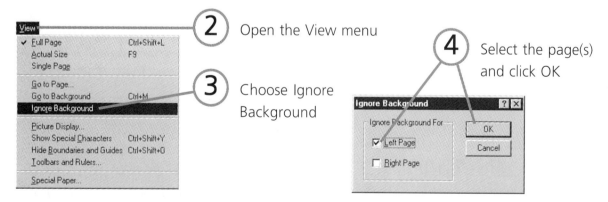

2 Open the View menu

3 Choose Ignore Background

4 Select the page(s) and click OK

Basic steps

Rows and Columns

1 Open the **Arrange** menu.

2 Choose **Layout Guides…**

3 Set the number of columns and rows in the **Grid Guide** options.

4 Click **OK**.

❑ You should now have the basic layout.

In the flyer design drawn up earlier in the chapter, the basic page layout consisted of 2 columns and 3 rows. To help position the text and graphics accurately on the page, we can add more grid guides to show where the column and row boundaries will be.

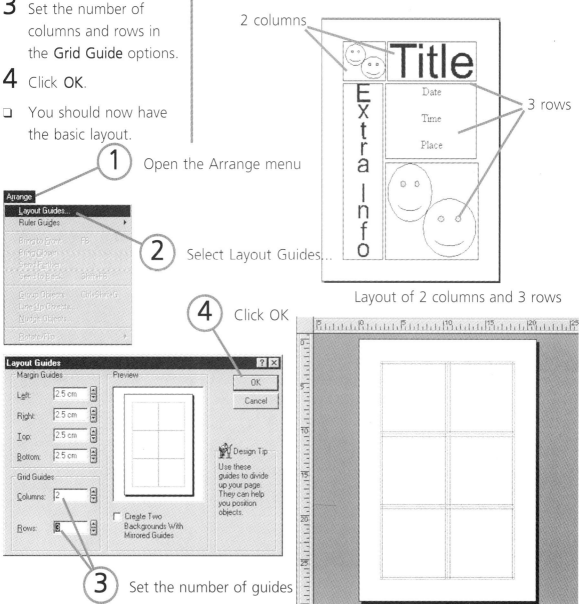

① Open the Arrange menu

② Select Layout Guides…

Layout of 2 columns and 3 rows

④ Click OK

③ Set the number of guides

Adjusting the guides

The guides split the page up into the number of rows and columns requested, with the rows and columns all the same height and width.

If you don't want all your rows and columns the same size, you can easily adjust the position of the guides to make the rows and columns the size you require.

The guides appear on the page *background*, so you must go there to adjust them.

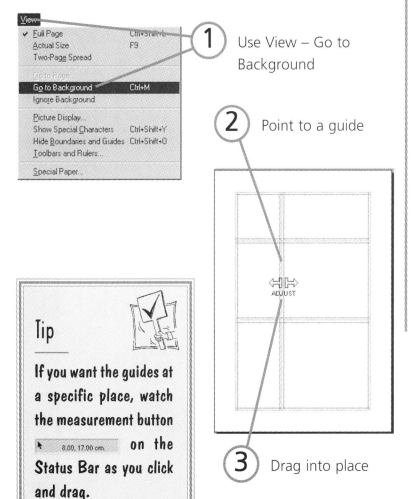

① Use View – Go to Background

② Point to a guide

③ Drag into place

1 Open the **View** menu and choose **Go to Background**.

❑ The [🗇] button replaces the page buttons on the Status Bar to show you are in the page background.

2 Hold down **[Shift]** and point to a guide that you want to move.

❑ The pointer becomes a handle – ◁⊞⊡▷ over a ADJUST vertical or ↕ over a ADJUST horizontal guide.

3 Keeping **[Shift]** held down, drag the guide to its new position.

4 Choose **Go to Foreground** from the **View** menu.

Basic steps

1 Open the **Arrange** menu.

2 Choose **Layout Guides**...

3 Select the **Create Two Backgrounds with Mirror Guides** checkbox.

4 Set the Inside and Outside margins required.

5 Specify the number of columns – e.g. 3 in this example

6 Click OK.

Mirrored guides

If a publication is going to be printed with facing pages and then bound, you will probably find that you need extra space down the inside edge of the page for the binding.

You can specify the amount of space required for the inside margin in the Layout Guides dialog box.

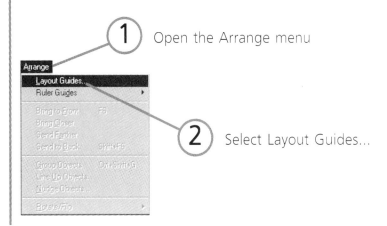

① Open the Arrange menu

② Select Layout Guides...

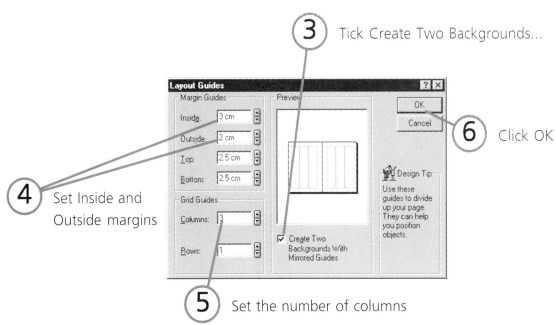

③ Tick Create Two Backgrounds...

⑥ Click OK

④ Set Inside and Outside margins

⑤ Set the number of columns

Ruler guides

The margin and grid guides appear on every page in your publication. If you are creating a multi-page publication, and some pages have a different layout, you may find *ruler* guides useful. These can be applied to the foreground of individual pages.

● You can add vertical or horizontal ruler guides.

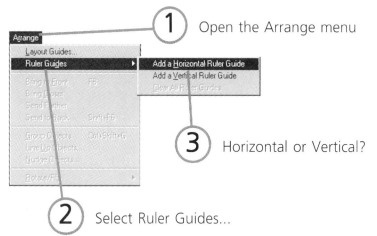

① Open the Arrange menu

③ Horizontal or Vertical?

② Select Ruler Guides...

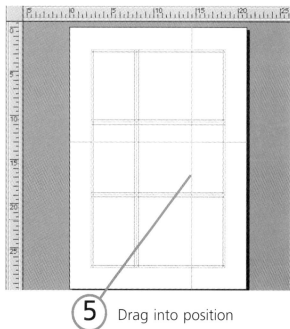

⑤ Drag into position

Basic steps

❏ **To add ruler guides**

1 Open the **Arrange** menu.

2 Choose **Ruler Guides...**

3 Select the **Horizontal** or **Vertical Guide** option.

❏ . Repeat steps 2 and 3 for each new guide.

❏ **To adjust ruler guides**

4 Hold down [Shift] and point to the guide.

5 Drag the ruler guide to its new position.

❏ **To remove ruler guides**

6 Open the **Arrange** menu and choose **Ruler Guides...**

7 Select **Clear All Ruler Guides**.

Take note

You can add ruler guides by holding down [Shift] and dragging in from the horizontal or vertical ruler.

Basic steps

1 Open the **Tools** menu.

2 If the **Snap to Guides** option is not ticked, click on it to turn it on.

3 If the **Snap to Ruler Marks** option is not ticked, click on it to turn it on.

Snap to guides

Once you have set up your guides, check that the snap to guides option is switched on. With this on, your objects will automatically line themselves up with the guides, making it easy to get them in the correct position.

If you have Ruler guides on your page, you should also check that the Snap to Ruler Marks option is switched on.

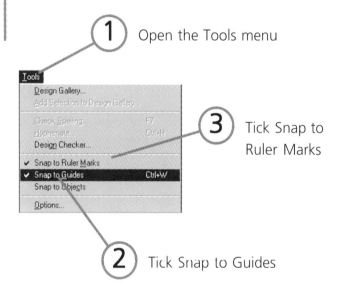

1 Open the Tools menu

3 Tick Snap to Ruler Marks

2 Tick Snap to Guides

Tip

You can toggle **Snap to Guides** on and off by pressing **[Ctrl]-[W]**.

Tip

To remove a single ruler guide, hold down [Shift] and drag the unwanted guide off the page.

Take note

It is usually easier to line your objects up with each other if these options are switched on. However, if you need to position objects and you don't want them lined up with the guides and ruler marks automatically, you can switch the Snap to ... options off in the Tools menu.

Summary

- **Plan** your publication before you start.

- **Choose the paper layout** required from the Blank Page tab in the Startup dialog box.

- If required, you can **change the layout** of a publication through the Page Setup dialog box.

- You can use **margin** and **grid guides** to help you arrange your objects on the page.

- Margin and grid guides are placed on the publication **background**.

- **Objects** placed on the publication background **can be ignored** on specific pages if required.

- The **position of guides** can be adjusted as necessary.

- **Mirrored guides** are useful for publications that will be printed and bound with facing pages.

- **Ruler guides** are placed on the publication foreground.

- Objects can easily be lined up relative to each other if the **Snap to Guides** option is switched on.

5 Working with text

Inserting text frames

Most of the text you enter onto a page will be placed in a series of text frames on the publication *foreground.* Text frames are like mini documents on your page. Text entered into a text frame will wrap between the left and right edge of the frame.

1 Click the **Text** tool in the toolbar down the left side.

2 Drag over an area in your publication to insert a Text frame.

3 Press the **[F9]** key to zoom in on the frame.

4 Type in your text.

5 Press **[F9]** to zoom out when you've finished.

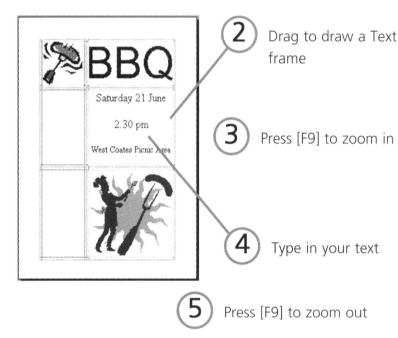

BBQ

Saturday 21 June

2.30 pm

West Coates Picnic Area

2 Drag to draw a Text frame

3 Press [F9] to zoom in

4 Type in your text

5 Press [F9] to zoom out

Take note

You can easily move, resize or delete any objects you place in your publication. See page 57.

Take note

In this chapter we discuss *text* objects — other objects will be discussed in the chapters that follow.

Tip

You can add as many Text frames as you require to enable you to position the text exactly where you want it.

Line spacing

Basic steps

1 Select the paragraph(s) whose line spacing you want to change.

2 Open the **Format** menu.

3 Choose **Line Spacing**.

4 Increase or decrease the **Line Spacing** as required.

5 Click **OK**.

When entering text into Text frames, you may need to alter the space between the lines of text within a paragraph, or between the paragraphs, to get the effect you want.

The term *leading* (pronounced 'ledding') is used to describe the amount of spacing between lines of text.

By default, Publisher leaves one space (sp) between lines of text. The size of the space depends on the font size.

You can also use centimetres (cm), inches (in) points (pt) or picas (pi) when specifying the spacing between your lines. Simply enter the number followed by the abbreviation for the measurement, e.g. 2 pi, 1 in, 2 pt or 3 cm.

2 Open the Format menu

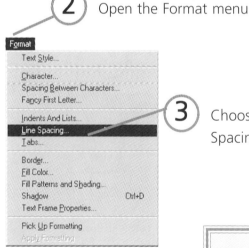

3 Choose Line Spacing

4 Set the spacing between lines...

6 Click OK

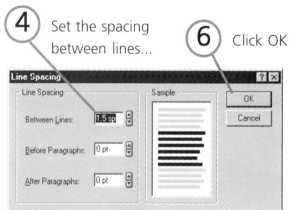

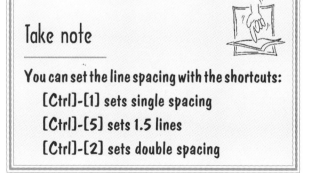

Take note

You can set the line spacing with the shortcuts:

[Ctrl]-[1] sets single spacing

[Ctrl]-[5] sets 1.5 lines

[Ctrl]-[2] sets double spacing

Character spacing

You can also specify the amount of spacing you want to have between the characters in your words. There are two types of character spacing:

Tracking

Also known as 'track kerning', this is the adjustment of spacing between all characters. You can adjust the tracking to squeeze letters closer together so that they will fit inside a frame or spread the letters out to create a special effect.

❑ **To adjust Tracking**

1 Select the paragraph or text you want to adjust the tracking for.

2 Open the **Format** menu.

3 Choose **Spacing Between Characters...**

4 Specify the tracking options required.

5 Click **OK**.

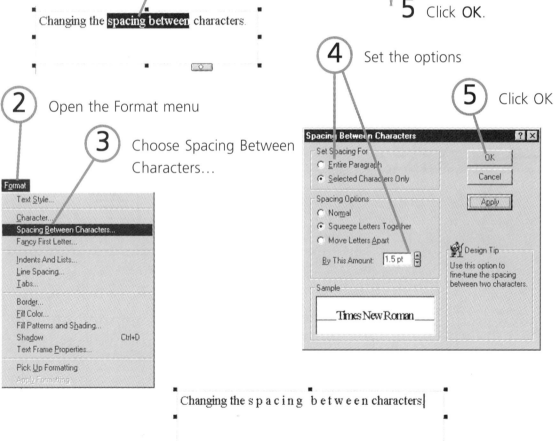

1 Select the text to adjust

Changing the spacing between characters.

2 Open the Format menu

3 Choose Spacing Between Characters...

4 Set the options

5 Click OK

Changing the s p a c i n g b e t w e e n characters

Basic steps

Kerning

□ **To adjust kerning**

1 Open the **Tools** menu

2 Choose **Options...**

3 Select the **Editing and User Assistance** tab.

4 Increase or decrease the **Kern character pairs above:** field as required.

5 Click **OK**.

Also known as 'letter kerning', this is the adjustment of space between certain pairs of letters in a word. Kerning is used to improve the appearance of specific character pairs that would otherwise appear to be squeezed too closely together, or spread too far apart. Letters with a font size above 15 pt are automatically kerned in Publisher.

Notice how the white space between kerned letters is closed up.

Letters not kerned:- W A V

Kerned letters:- WAV

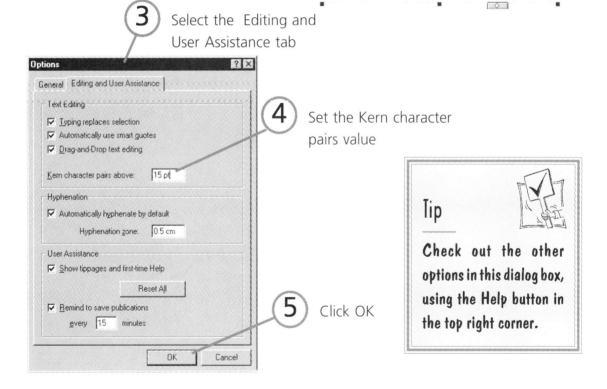

③ Select the Editing and User Assistance tab

④ Set the Kern character pairs value

⑤ Click OK

49

Formatting text

You can format the text you enter into a Text frame using the tools on the Format toolbar, or through the Character dialog box.

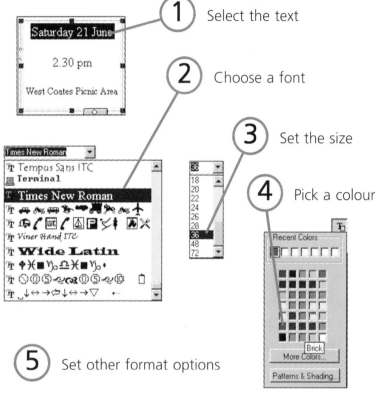

① Select the text

② Choose a font

③ Set the size

④ Pick a colour

⑤ Set other format options

❑ **Using the Toolbar**

1 Select the text – anything from a single character to the whole frame.

2 Change the font using the **Font** list.

3 Select the size required from the **Font size** list.

4 Click the **Font Color** tool and select a different colour.

5 Apply other format options if wanted.

6 De-select your text – click anywhere off the text.

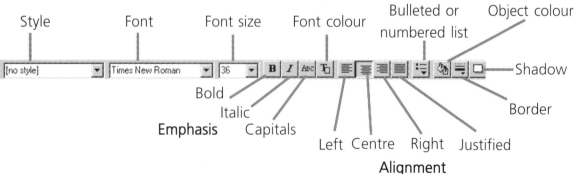

| Style | Font | Font size | Font colour | Bulleted or numbered list | Object colour |

Shadow
Border

Bold
Italic
Emphasis   Capitals

Left Centre Right Justified

Alignment

Font size. You can change the size of individual characters within words to create unusual effects!

Basic steps

❑ **Using the dialog box**

1 Select the text you want to format.

2 Open the **Format** menu.

3 Choose **Character...**

4 Select the options in the dialog box.

5 Click **OK**.

6 De-select your text.

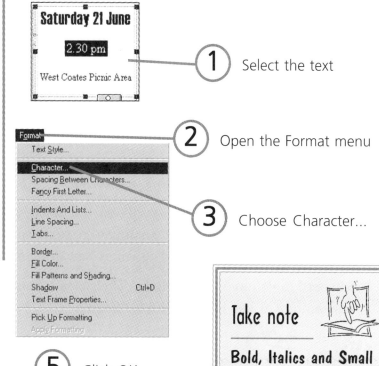

① Select the text

② Open the Format menu

③ Choose Character...

④ Set the options

⑤ Click OK

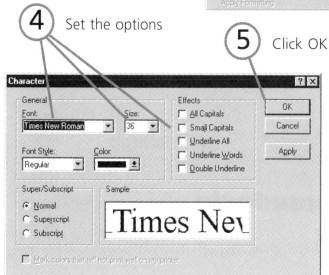

Take note

Bold, Italics and Small Capitals are toggles. Click the tool to switch the option on, then click the tool to switch the option off again.

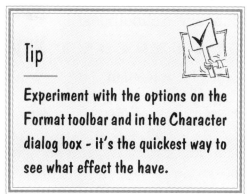

Tip

Experiment with the options on the Format toolbar and in the Character dialog box - it's the quickest way to see what effect the have.

Fonts

There are a large number of fonts to choose from in Publisher – Windows and the CD version of Publisher give you access to over 150 fonts (the disk version of Publisher comes with about 50 different fonts).

Fonts come in families. If you look down the font list you'll find several from the Arial family, Bookshelf, Eras, Lucida family etc.

Publisher groups its text fonts into 3 categories:

- **Serif** fonts have a little tail (serif) on the straight lines of charactrers. For large amounts of text, use a serif font that's easy to read eg Times New Roman.

- **San serif** fonts have simpler lines. Their clean, bold appearance makes them useful for headings.

- **Script** fonts give a hand-written look to your text – attractive on invitations, but some fonts can be difficult to read if used for big blocks of text.

Examples of some of the fonts available are displayed here.

Take note

Publisher's categories are not standard. Fonts are normally divided into serif, sans serif and display – with all the fancier fonts, including scipts, being grouped under display.

Serif fonts

Baskerville Old Face

Century Schoolbook

GOUDYSTOUT

Times New Roman

Sans serif fonts

Arial

Braggadocio

Impact

Script fonts

Lucida Blackletter

Monotype Corsiva

Viner Hand ITC

Basic steps

Tabs

1 Select the Text frame where you want to set your tabs.

2 Open the **Format** menu.

3 Choose **Tabs...**

4 Enter the tab position required.

5 Set the alignment.

6 Click **Set**.

7 Repeat steps 4–6 for each tab required.

8 Click **OK**.

Tabs can be useful when you need to align text at a specific point on your line, within a Text frame. Tabs can be left, centre, right or decimal aligned.

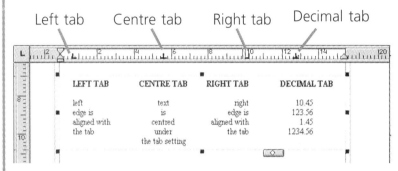

Left tab   Centre tab   Right tab   Decimal tab

By default, tabs are set every 10 cm along your ruler. When you are in a Text frame, you can jump along the line to the next tab stop by pressing **[Tab]** on your keyboard.

If you want to set a tab at a specific position on the line, you can do so using the Tab dialog box.

The tab position is relative to the left edge of the Text frame, e.g. a tab position of 3 is 3 cm from the left edge.

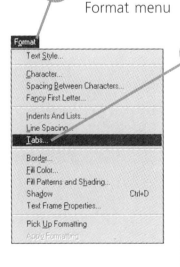

② Open the Format menu

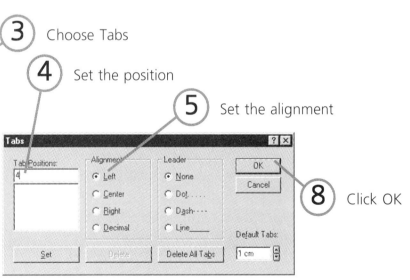

③ Choose Tabs

④ Set the position

⑤ Set the alignment

⑧ Click OK

Tabs from the Ruler

You can set tabs directly on to the ruler if you prefer.

The left and right indents can also be set here.

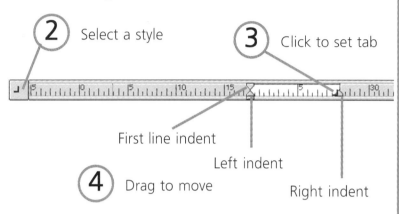

Select a style

Click to set tab

First line indent

Left indent

Drag to move

Right indent

Basic steps

1 Select a Text frame.

2 Click the tab style box at the left of the ruler until you get the tab style required.

3 Click on the ruler to set your tab.

❑ **To move a tab or indent marker**

4 Drag it along the ruler.

❑ **To delete a tab**

5 Drag it off the ruler.

Line spacing set at 1.5

Right tabs set

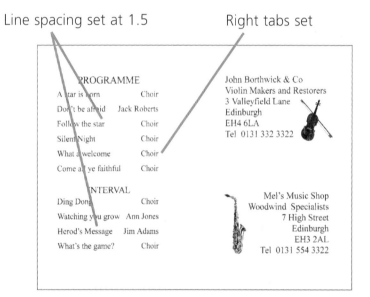

Tip

Double click on the ruler to open the Tabs dialog box.

On page 3 of this booklet, a right tab was set to help align the names of the performers. The line spacing was set to 1.5 for the lists of items to be performed in each part of the show.

Basic steps

1 Select a Text frame.

2 Place the insertion point where you want the list to start.

3 Click the **Bulleted or Numbered List** tool on the Format toolbar.

4 Select the bullet you want to use.

5 Enter your item and press **[Enter]**. A bullet appears ready for your next item.

6 Repeat step 5 until you've completed your list.

7 Click the bullet tool and choose **None** to switch the bullets off.

Bullets

If you are listing items, you may find bullets useful to draw attention to each entry in your list.

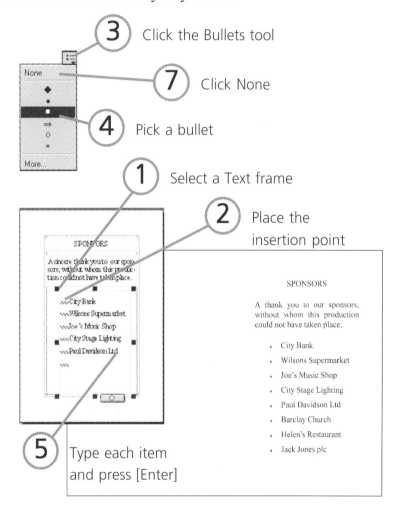

③ Click the Bullets tool

⑦ Click None

④ Pick a bullet

① Select a Text frame

② Place the insertion point

SPONSORS

A thank you to our sponsors, without whom this production could not have taken place.

- City Bank
- Wilsons Supermarket
- Joe's Music Shop
- City Stage Lighting
- Paul Davidson Ltd
- Barclay Church
- Helen's Restaurant
- Jack Jones plc

⑤ Type each item and press [Enter]

Take note

If you already have a list keyed in, and then decide you want to add bullets to it, select the list then apply the bullets.

Tip

Explore the Indents and Lists dialog box. You can use it to produce numbered lists as well as bulletted lists if you wish.

Bullet characters

You can use any character you want as a bullet character.

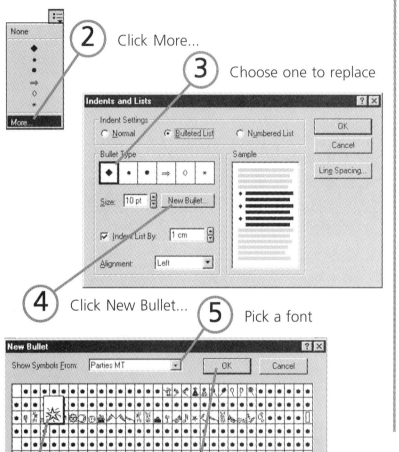

② Click More...

③ Choose one to replace

④ Click New Bullet...

⑤ Pick a font

⑥ Select a character

⑦ Click OK

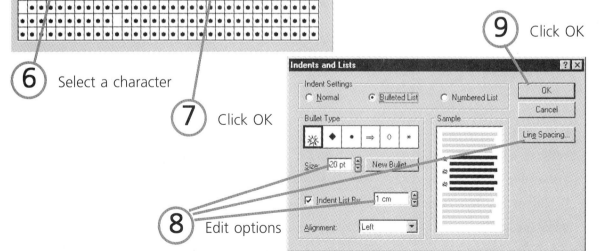

⑧ Edit options

⑨ Click OK

1 Place the insertion point where you want to start the list.

2 Click the **Bulleted or Numbered List** tool and choose **More...**

3 In the **Indents and Lists** dialog box choose the bullet to replace.

4 Click **New Bullet...**

5 At the **New Bullet** dialog box pick a font.

6 Select a character.

7 Click **OK**.

8 Edit other options as required in the **Indents and Lists** dialog box.

9 Click **OK**.

56

Working with frames

1 Select the frame. The selection handles appear on the frame.

❏ **To resize**

Point to a handle. The pointer becomes the resizer . Drag to resize.

❏ **To Move or copy**

Point to its edge. The pointer becomes the mover . Drag the frame to move it.

Or

Hold down [Ctrl] and drag to copy it.

❏ **To delete text frames**

Choose **Delete Text Frame** from the menu.

❏ **To delete non-text frames** simply press the [Delete] key.

Text frames do not automatically expand to accommodate the text you enter. If this happened, the arrangement of the frames on your page would change and you may not end up with the effect you desire. If you want to enter more text into a text frame than there is room for you could:

● Edit the text so that it fits inside the frame.

● Use a smaller font size.

● Enlarge the frame to fit the text you are entering.

● Connect the text frame to another (see page 58).

You mau need to move, copy or delete a frame to get the effect your require.

A frame must be *selected* before you can resize, move, copy or delete it – just click within the frame to select it.

① Select the frame

Tip

If you want to move a frame (or any object) a small amount, you can *nudge* it into position. Select it, hold down [Alt] and press [←], [↑], [→] or [↓] until it is exactly where you want it. The object will move one *pixel* (screen dot) at a time.

Connecting text frames

Text frames can be connected, so that the text flows automatically from one frame to another as you enter and edit the text. This feature is essential if you want a story spread over different areas or pages in your publication.

You can connect frames that are on the same page or different pages. Once frames are connected the Connect Frame button changes it guise to indicate it is linked to another frame. A Next Frame or Previous Frame button also appears so you can easily jump between connected frames.

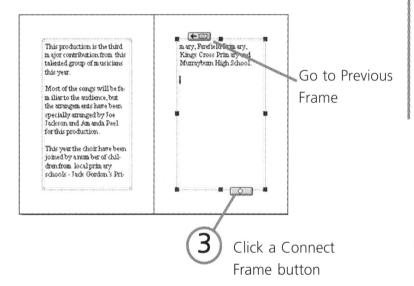

Go to Previous Frame

3 Click a Connect Frame button

Take note

If the Connect Frame button looks like ▭ it means that there is no text in the current frame, or that the text fits okay. If it looks like ▭ it means that there is text in the frame and it doesn't fit in (see page 57).

Basic steps

1 Create your first text frame.

2 Create your second text frame.

3 Select the first frame.

4 Click the **Connect Frame** button ▭ or ▭ at the bottom right of the first frame.

❑ Note the pitcher 🖈 mouse pointer.

5 Click on the frame that you want to connect the first one to.

Tip

If you accidentally delete a frame, use Edit – Undo or click ↺ the Undo tool. If this has no effect, it will be because you performed another action after you deleted, and some actions cannot be undone.

The keyboard shortcut for Undo is [Ctrl]-[Z].

58

Basic steps

1 Right click on the frame where you want a "Continued on..." or "Continued from..." prompt.

2 Choose **Text Frame Properties** from the list.

3 Select the **Include "Continued On Page..."** or **Include "Continued From Page..."** checkbox.

4 Click **OK**.

Continued on...Continued from

If you have stories that are continued on other pages, it is often a good idea to add a "Continued on..." or "Continued from..." prompt to the frames.

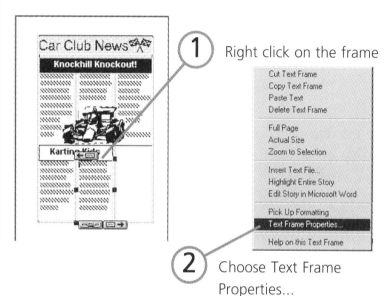

① Right click on the frame

② Choose Text Frame Properties...

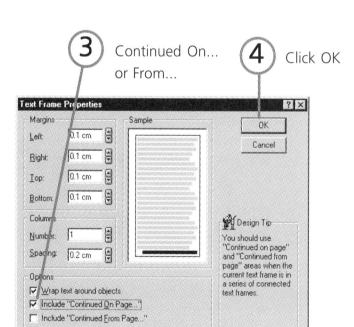

③ Continued On... or From...

④ Click OK

Karting Kids

Wednesday 17 December will be the first meeting for a group of enthusiastic karting youngsters (between 9 and 14 years of age). The meeting will take place in the Tranent

(Continued on page 2)

Tip

Check that the story does continue on the page if you say it does.

Importing text files

In addition to adding text to text frames within Publisher, you may want to bring text into your publication from a file created on a word processing package, e.g. Word.

If the file you are entering will not fit inside the frame, Publisher will ask if you want the text to flow automatically into any connected frames. If there are no frames to flow into, it will ask if you want new frames created.

Publisher can convert text files from many different word-processing packages. In most cases the character and paragraph formatting of the text will be preserved. Formats that can be converted include:

- Word for Windows versions 2.0, 6.0 and 7.0
- Works for Windows version 3.0 and Windows 95
- Write for Windows version 3.1 and Windows 95
- Word Perfect for DOS versions 5.0, 5.1 and 6.0
- Plain Text
- Rich Text Format

Basic steps

1 Select the text frame into which you want to import the text.

2 Open the **Insert** menu.

3 Choose **Text File...**

4 Locate the file you want to import – you may have to change folders or drives.

5 Select the file.

6 Click **OK**.

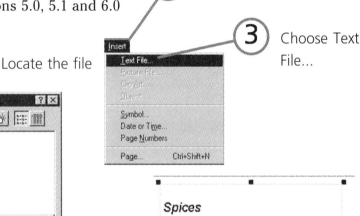

④ Locate the file

② Open the Insert menu

③ Choose Text File...

⑤ Select the file ⑥ Click OK

The text from the file will appear in the selected frame.

Basic steps

1 Create a text frame.

2 Place your insertion point where you want your text to appear.

3 Open the **Edit** menu.

4 Choose **Edit Story in Microsoft Word**.

5 Enter and edit your story using Word features and functions.

6 Close the Word document when you've finished – your story will be inserted into the text frame in Publisher.

Edit Story in Microsoft Word

If you have Microsoft Word installed on your computer, you can insert and edit your text using Word rather than doing so in Publisher, if you prefer.

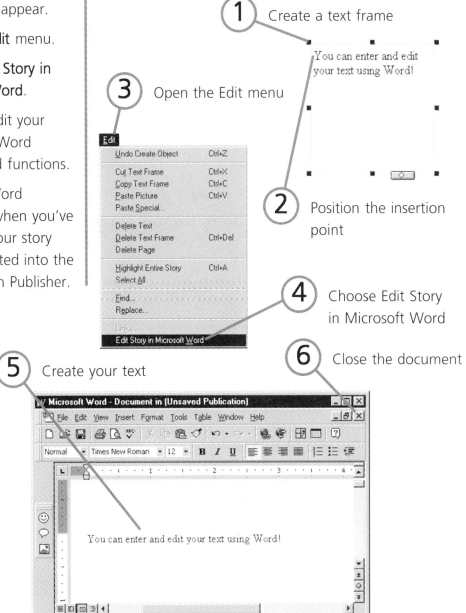

1 Create a text frame

3 Open the Edit menu

2 Position the insertion point

4 Choose Edit Story in Microsoft Word

5 Create your text

6 Close the document

Borders

Borders can be used to draw attention to any of the objects in your publication. You can either use the main options available through the Border tool on the Format toolbar, or if you want to change the colour of the border, or add a top and bottom border only, for example, you can use the BorderArt dialog box.

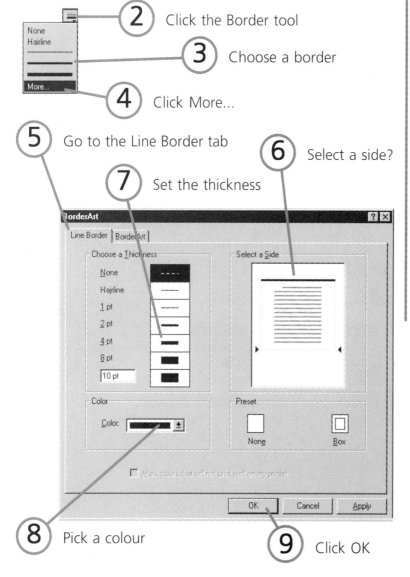

② Click the Border tool

③ Choose a border

④ Click More...

⑤ Go to the Line Border tab

⑥ Select a side?

⑦ Set the thickness

⑧ Pick a colour

⑨ Click OK

1 Select the object.

2 Click the **Border** tool on the Format toolbar.

3 Select the border.

Or

4 Click **More....**

5 Select the **Line Border** tab.

6 If you want to apply the effect to one side only, click on it in the Select a Side window.

7 Pick a thickness.

8 Choose a colour.

If you are setting sides separately. repeat steps 6 to 8 for each side.

9 Click **OK**.

Basic steps

Colours and shading

1 Select the object.

2 Click the **Object Color** tool.

3 Select the colour.

Or

4 Click **More Colors**.... or **Patterns and Shading**...

5 Select the option.

6 Click **OK**.

A range of fill patterns and shading options can be applied to your objects.

(1) Select the object

(2) Click the Object Color tool

(3) Choose a colour

(6) Click OK

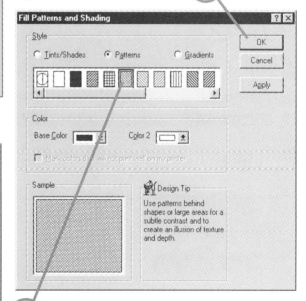

(4) Get more options

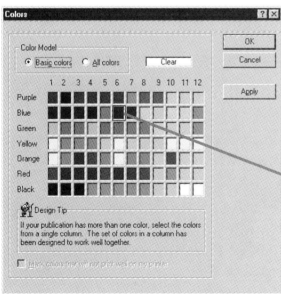

(5) Set the options

Fill Colour or Shading

Tip

To add (or remove) a Shadow, click the Add/Remove Shadow tool ▢ or press [Ctrl]–[D].

BorderArt

If you want to be a bit more adventurous, you could have a look through the BorderArt to see if there is anything suitable. BorderArt applies a box border to an object – it can be very useful for menus, invitations, etc.

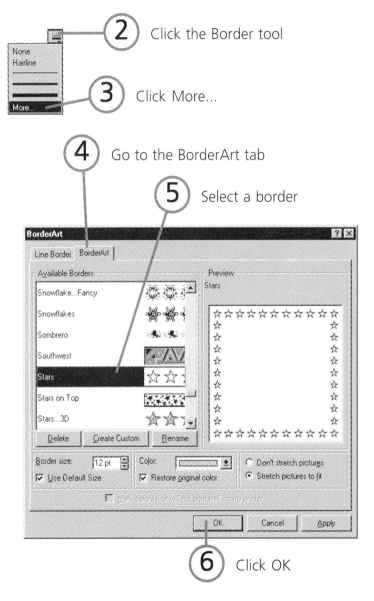

② Click the Border tool

③ Click More...

④ Go to the BorderArt tab

⑤ Select a border

⑥ Click OK

Basic steps

1 Select the object you want to apply a border to.

2 Click the **Border** tool.

3 Choose **More...**

4 Select the **BorderArt** tab in the BorderArt dialog box.

5 Scroll through the list and select a border you want to use.

6 Click **OK**.

Top and bottom borders

Box border

64

Adding pages

Basic steps

1 Display the page you want to add the new pages after.

2 Open the **Insert** menu.

3 Choose **Page**...

4 Enter the **Number of Pages** required.

5 Specify where the pages should go.

6 Select the **Insert Blank Pages** option.

7 Click **OK**.

Many of your publications will run to several pages. If you create a publication using the Full Page layout, your file will consist of 1 page to begin with, if you chose a book fold layout, your file will initially have 4 pages.

You can add pages at any position within your publication (as long as you're on the foreground).

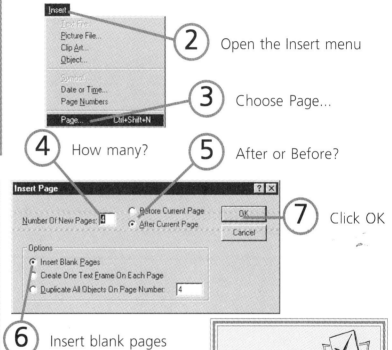

(2) Open the Insert menu

(3) Choose Page...

(4) How many?   (5) After or Before?

(7) Click OK

(6) Insert blank pages

Take note

To Delete a page, display it and choose Delete Page... from the Edit menu.

Take note

If you view 2 pages, when you access the Insert Page dialog box, the options for the position of the new pages are Before left page, After right page or Between Pages.

Tip

You can add pages easily at the end. View the last page, then click **Next Page**. You will be asked if you want to add more pages – just click OK.

Background objects

Headers, footers and page numbers that you want repeated on every page of your publication are placed within text frames on the *background* of your publication.

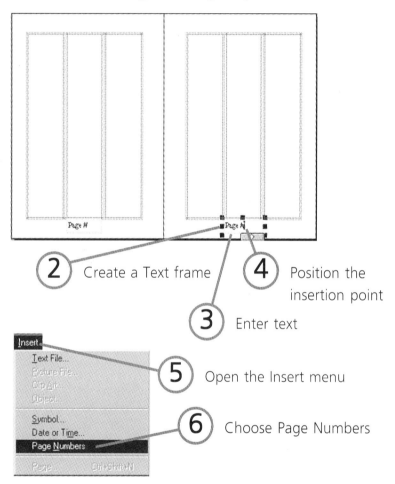

(2) Create a Text frame

(4) Position the insertion point

(3) Enter text

(5) Open the Insert menu

(6) Choose Page Numbers

❏ **Page numbering**

1 Press [Ctrl]-[M] to go into Background view.

2 Create a Text frame where you want the page numbering to appear.

3 If you want 'Page', or any other text, to appear before your number, enter it into the Text frame.

4 Position the insertion point where you want the number to appear.

5 Open the **Insert** menu.

6 Choose **Page Numbers**.

7 Press [Ctrl]-[M] to return to Foreground view.

❏ A # sign will appear on your page background – when you return to the foreground the actual page number will be displayed.

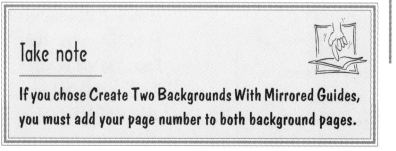

Take note

If you chose **Create Two Backgrounds With Mirrored Guides**, you must add your page number to both background pages.

Basic steps

Headers and footers

❏ **Page header or footer**

1 Press [Ctrl]–[M] to go into Background view if necessary.

2 Create a Text frame where you want your page header/footer to go and type your text.

❏ **To insert the date**

3 Choose **Date or Time...** from the **Insert** menu.

4 Select the date format – to insert a specific date, e.g. the first of next month, type it in manually.

5 Click **OK**.

6 Complete the header/footer as required.

7 Press [Ctrl]-[M] to return to Foreground view.

Publisher does not have the special Headers and Footers that word-processors do, but you can still achieve the same effect by placing text at the top and/or bottom of the background.

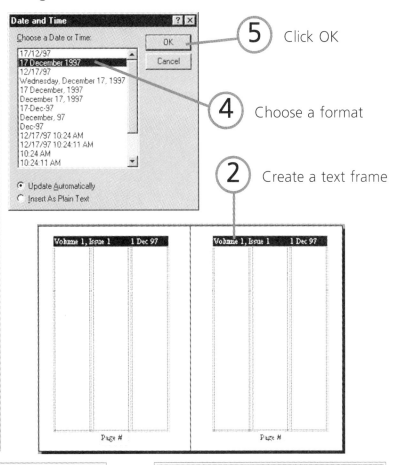

⑤ Click OK

④ Choose a format

② Create a text frame

Sidebars

Text frames can be used to create special effects on your page. You can use a text frame to create a *sidebar* that runs down the side of your page. It is a useful place to put additional information that will be of interest to your reader, but is not essential to the understanding of the main text in your publication. Try to put your sidebar either on the same page, or within a page or two, of the text it is related to.

You can either create a sidebar from scratch, or use one from the Design Gallery.

❑ **To create a sidebar**

1 Insert a Text frame where you want the sidebar – down the left or right side of a page.

2 Enter your text.

3 Format the text.

4 Add a border and/or shading if required.

5 Insert a picture if you wish (see Chapter 6).

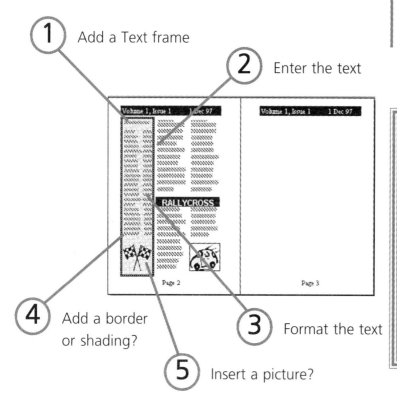

① Add a Text frame

② Enter the text

④ Add a border or shading?

③ Format the text

⑤ Insert a picture?

Take note

A 'sidebar' is a text frame that runs down the side of the page. It can provide an effective way of presenting information not in the main stories, but of interest to your readers.

Basic steps

❏ **The Design Gallery**

1 Display the page that you want a sidebar on.

2 Click the **Design Gallery** tool .

3 Select **Sidebars** in the category list.

4 Choose a design.

5 If you can't find one you want, click **More Designs** and try the other categories.

6 Click **Insert Object**.

7 Move or resize the sidebar as necessary.

8 Click inside the sidebar – the text becomes selected – and type in your text.

Take note

There is no **Sidebars** category in the **CD Deluxe** design sets in the Design Gallery.

③ Select Sidebars ⑥ Click Insert Object

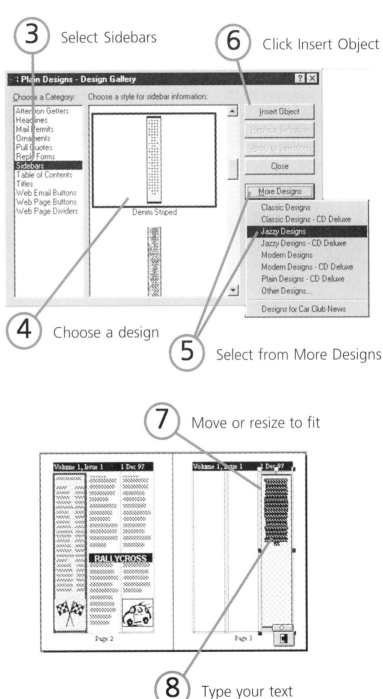

④ Choose a design

⑤ Select from More Designs

⑦ Move or resize to fit

⑧ Type your text

Pull quote

Another special effect you can create using a text frame is a *pull quote*. A pull quote is an excerpt from the main story that adds interest to the page and gets the reader's attention.

You would usually use a larger font for the text in the pull quote (to make it stand out from the rest of the text), and you can also use borders or shading for the same reason (see Chapter 6).

You can create pull quotes from scratch, or use one from the Design Gallery in the same way as when creating sidebars.

❑ **Starting from scratch**

1 Insert a text frame where you want the pull quote to appear.

2 Copy or type in your text.

3 Format the text as required – use a larger font than the main story text to draw attention to the quote.

4 Apply shading and borders if required.

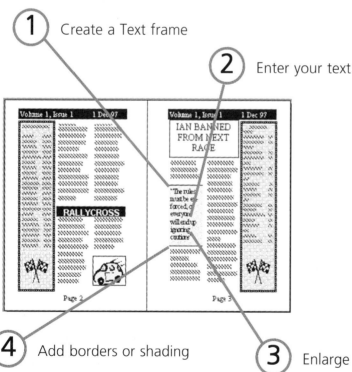

① Create a Text frame

② Enter your text

④ Add borders or shading

③ Enlarge the font size

Take note

There is no 'link' between the text in the story and that in the pull quote. If you edit the text in the story, remember to update it in the pull quote too!

Basic steps

❑ **Using the Design Gallery**

1 Display the page you want to place a pull quote on.

2 Click the **Design Gallery** tool 🔲.

3 Select **Pull Quotes** in the category list.

4 Choose a design

5 If you can't find one you want, click **More Designs** and browse through the options.

6 Click **Insert Object**.

7 Move or resize the Pull Quote as necessary.

8 Click inside the Pull Quote – the text becomes selected.

9 Delete the dummy text and copy the text required from the main story.

③ Select Pull Quotes

⑥ Click Insert Object

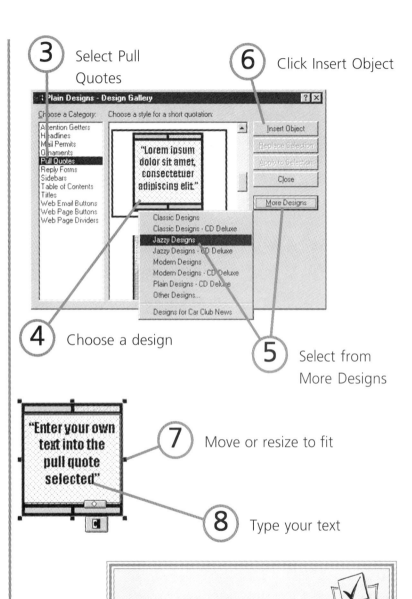

④ Choose a design

⑤ Select from More Designs

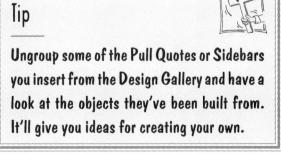

⑦ Move or resize to fit

⑧ Type your text

Tip

Ungroup some of the Pull Quotes or Sidebars you insert from the Design Gallery and have a look at the objects they've been built from. It'll give you ideas for creating your own.

Summary

- Text is entered into **text frames** on your page.

- The **line spacing** can be changed as required.

- **Tracking** and **kerning** refer to the amount of spacing between characters.

- Text can be **formatted** using the Format toolbar or the dialog boxes.

- Publisher has many **fonts** to choose from.

- **Tabs** are used to align text and figures.

- **Bullets** can be used to add emphasis.

- Frames can be **copied, moved** and **deleted**.

- Text will flow from one text frame to another provided the frames are **connected**.

- You can link a story through several connected frames using the **Continued on...Continued from** prompts.

- Text can be **imported from other applications**, and you can enter and edit text using Word if you wish.

- Emphasis can be added to frames using **borders, shading** and **shadow**.

- **BorderArt** can be used to add special border effects.

- **Extra pages** can be added at any point.

- Any object you want repeated on every page should be placed on the page **background**.

- **Sidebars** can be used to hold information that your readers will be interested in.

- **Pull quotes** are used to draw attention to something that is said in a story.

6 Using graphics

Using the Clip Gallery

The Clip Gallery contains a large selection of Clip Art and pictures that you can use – especially if you have the CD version of Publisher. Try adding some clips to your publication.

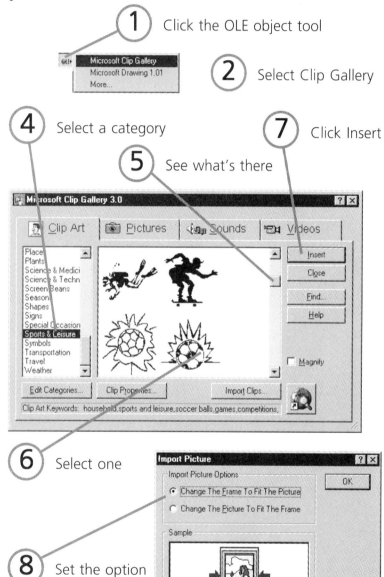

(1) Click the OLE object tool

(2) Select Clip Gallery

(4) Select a category

(7) Click Insert

(5) See what's there

(6) Select one

(8) Set the option

1 Click the **OLE Object** tool on the toolbar down the left side.

2 Choose **Microsoft Clip Gallery**.

3 Drag over the area where you want to insert your clip.

4 Select a **Category** that you think will hold suitable clips.

5 Scroll through the Clip Art available.

6 Select the one you want to use.

7 Click **Insert**.

8 Respond to the prompt.

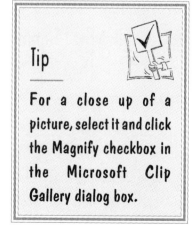

Tip

For a close up of a picture, select it and click the Magnify checkbox in the Microsoft Clip Gallery dialog box.

Basic steps

1 Click the **Find** button in the Clip Gallery.

2 Enter a keyword you are looking for.

3 Click **Find Now**.

❑ Any pictures that have the keyword you specified will be displayed.

4 Select a clip and insert it in the usual way.

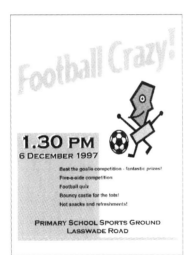

Take note

To replace an existing picture, double click on it then insert a new one from the Clip Gallery.

Searching for clips

You can search for clips that might be suitable for your publication, rather than hunt through each category. The search looks through the *keywords* that have been set up for the clips, and displays any that have the keyword you specify. The keywords are displayed at the bottom of the Clip Gallery dialog box when a clip is selected.

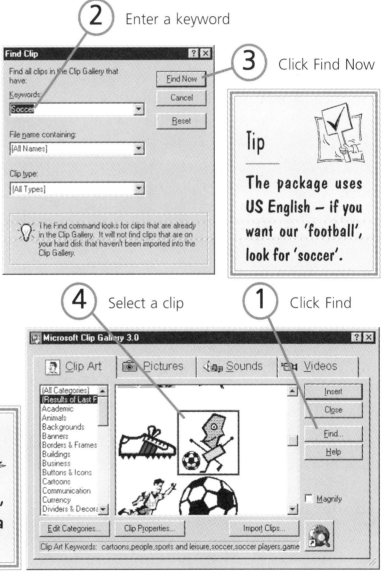

② Enter a keyword

③ Click Find Now

Tip

The package uses US English – if you want our 'football', look for 'soccer'.

④ Select a clip

① Click Find

Formatting Clip Art

When a Clip Art object is selected, a new set of tools appears under the Standard toolbar. You can use these tools to format the pictures you insert.

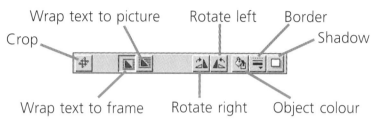

Wrap text to picture   Rotate left   Border
Crop   Shadow
Wrap text to frame   Rotate right   Object colour

Cropping

If you don't want to use all of a picture you can chop bits off to leave only the area you want to use. This is cropping.

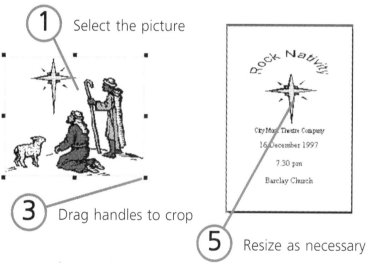

① Select the picture

③ Drag handles to crop

⑤ Resize as necessary

Wrap Text

If text wraps around your picture, you have a choice of whether the text wraps to the *frame* of the picture, or whether it wraps to the picture itself. The default option is to wrap text to the frame.

Click theSelect the picture and use the **Wrap Text to Frame** tool 🖼, or **Wrap Text to Picture** tool 🖼 .

❑ Cropping

1 Select the picture.

2 Click the **Crop** tool ⊞.

3 Drag a selection handle inwards to crop.

4 When you've finished, click ⊞ again.

5 Resize your picture as necessary.

❑ If you trim too much off, select the **Crop** tool and drag the handle out again.

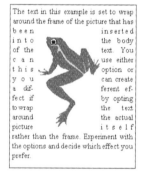

Text wrapped to frame

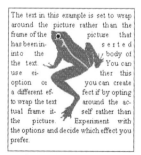

Text wrapped to picture

Basic steps

Rotate picture

- ❑ **Rotate picture**

1 Select your picture.

2 Click the **Rotate Right** tool 🔄 or the **Rotate Left** tool 🔄 to get the effect you want.

Or

3 Open the **Arrange** menu.

4 Choose **Rotate/Flip** then **Custom Rotate...**

5 Click a rotate button until the object is in the position required (the angle changes by 5 degrees for each click).

Or

6 Set the number of degrees in the **Angle** field.

7 Click **Close**.

If you want to rotate your picture to the left or right, then use the rotate tools on the Format toolbar.

If you want to rotate your object by a specific amount, you can use the Rotate dialog box.

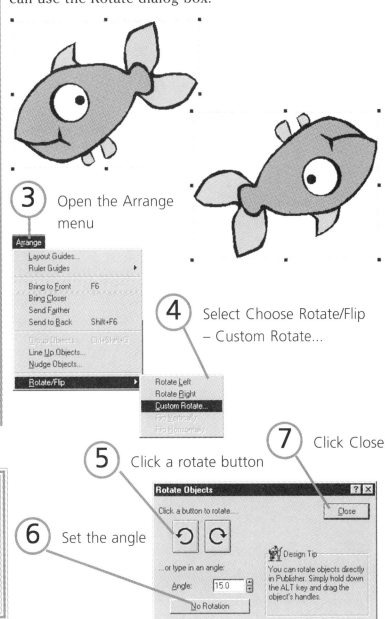

③ Open the Arrange menu

④ Select Choose Rotate/Flip – Custom Rotate...

⑦ Click Close

⑤ Click a rotate button

⑥ Set the angle

Tip

You can also rotate an object by holding [Alt] down and dragging a select handle.

The drawing tools

You can use the drawing tools to create your own pictures or to add different effects to your publication. The drawing tools are located on the left-hand toolbar.

Line, Oval and Box

You can use these tools to draw basic lines and shapes.

Arrows

You can add an arrow head at either or both ends of a line.

Custom Shapes

In addition to the basic line, box and oval shapes, there are several custom shapes you can choose from. The custom shapes make it very easy to draw stars, arrows, triangles and many other shapes.

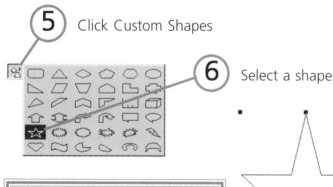

5 Click Custom Shapes

6 Select a shape

Tip

Use the object position and size fields on the Status bar to check the measurements of an object.

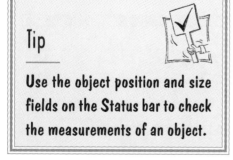

7 Drag to draw the shape

To draw a shape

1 Click a tool – **Line** ⬚, **Oval** ⬚ or **Box** ⬚.

2 Click where you want the shape to start and and drag to draw it.

❑ To get a perfect square or circle, hold **[Shift]** down as you drag.

❑ **Arrowheads**

3 Draw or select a line.

4 Click the **Add/Remove Arrow** ⬚ ⬚ ⬚ tools on the Format toolbar.

❑ The arrow heads are very small – zoom in **[F9]** to view them.

❑ **Custom Shapes**

5 Click the **Custom Shapes** tool ⬚.

6 Select a shape.

7 Drag on the page to draw the shape.

Basic steps

1 Select the object.

2 Open the **Arrange** menu.

3 Choose an option to change the position of the object relative to the others.

❏ **Bring to Front** and **Send to Back** move the object to the top or bottom layer.

❏ **Bring Closer** and **Send Farther** move the object one layer up or down at a time.

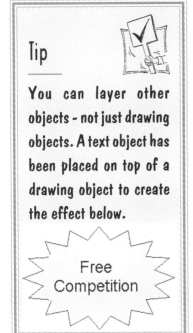

Tip

You can layer other objects - not just drawing objects. A text object has been placed on top of a drawing object to create the effect below.

Free Competition

The objects you place on your page can be layered on top of each other to create an effect. When you draw your objects on top of each other, the first one you draw is on the lowest layer, the second one is on a layer above the first one, the third one on the next layer and so on.

If you end up with your objects on the wrong layer relative to each other, you can move them backwards and forwards through the layers as necessary.

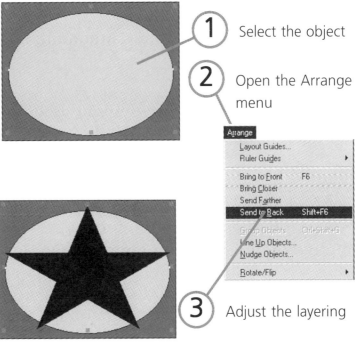

(1) Select the object

(2) Open the Arrange menu

(3) Adjust the layering

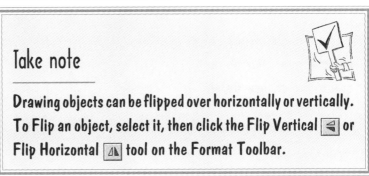

Take note

Drawing objects can be flipped over horizontally or vertically. To Flip an object, select it, then click the Flip Vertical ◁ or Flip Horizontal △ tool on the Format Toolbar.

Grouping objects

If you are drawing a picture using different drawing objects, you will find the final picture easier to resize and move if you *Group* the objects together. The objects are grouped into one object and can then be resized, moved or deleted as one. If you need to work on an individual object that has been grouped, you can ungroup the object again.

Before you can group objects, you must select them.

(4) Select all the objects

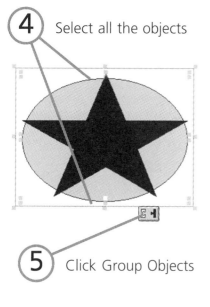

(5) Click Group Objects

(6) Select the grouped object

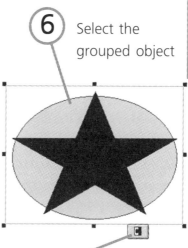

(7) Click Ungroup Objects

❑ **To select multiple objects**

1 Select the first object.

2 Hold down **[Shift]** and click on each of the other objects.

Or

3 Select the **Pointer** tool and click and drag over the objects.

❑ **To group objects**

4 Select the required objects.

5 Click the **Group Objects** button.

❑ **To ungroup objects**

6 Select the object.

7 Click the **Ungroup Objects** button.

Tip

To delete a group of objects, right click on the group and choose Delete Group from the menu.

Text frame and Clip Art grouped to form a sidebar

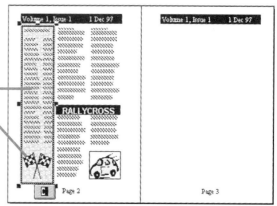

Basic steps

1 Click the WordArt tool 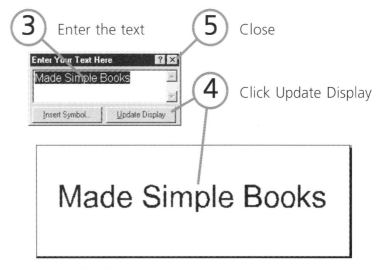 on the left toolbar.

2 Drag to draw the WordArt object.

3 Enter the text required in the **Enter Your Text Here** dialog box.

4 Click **Update Display** to update the object in your publication.

5 Click the **Close** button.

Take note

To modify an existing WordArt object, double click on it to take it back into WordArt.

There are many options available for formatting text – you can use different fonts, font sizes, colours, bold, italic, etc. For unusual text effects, you can insert a WordArt object – explore the options available and experiment. WortArt is very useful for eye-catching headings.

3 Enter the text

5 Close

Enter Your Text Here

Made Simple Books

Insert Symbol...   Update Display

4 Click Update Display

Made Simple Books

The WordArt toolbar

When you are in WordArt, a special toolbar appears and you can use this to change the appearance of your WordArt object. Some of the tools are fairly self-explanatory, others may need a bit of experimenting with!

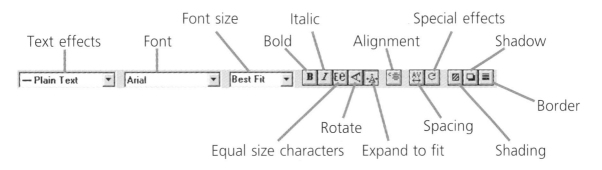

Text effects   Font   Font size   Bold   Italic   Alignment   Special effects   Shadow

— Plain Text   Arial   Best Fit

Equal size characters   Rotate   Expand to fit   Spacing   Shading   Border

Text effects

There are 36 different text effects to choose from. You can have your text going straight across, or you can slant it, curve it, create buttons with it, make it go in a wavy line – it's up to you!

Some of the effects are very easy to create – simply enter your text into the **Enter Your Text Here** dialog box, display the Text Effects and choose the one you want to use.

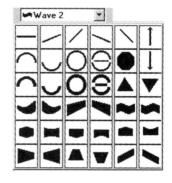

Made Simple Books   Made Simple Books

If you opt to use a button style (the fourth effect on the second and third rows), press **[Enter]** between each line you type in the **Enter Your Text Here** dialog box. Each line will be displayed on a different line in the button.

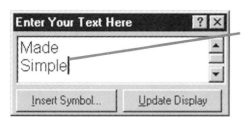

Press [Enter] after each line if you are using a button effect

Font, font size, bold and italic

These work in the same way as normal text format tools.

Ee   Makes upper and lower case letters the same height. It is a toggle – it switches the effect on and off.

Rotates text from horizontal to vertical (and back).

Stretches your text to fill the object size. The tool is used to switch the effect on or off.

Displays the **Alignment** options for your text.

The Alignment options

✓ Center
Left
Right
Stretch Justify
Letter Justify
Word Justify

WordArt dialog boxes

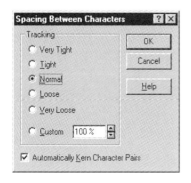

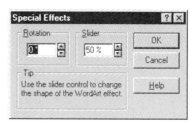

Displays the **Spacing Between Characters** dialog box where you can set the tracking (see page 48).

Opens the **Special Effects** dialog box. You can specify the number of degrees to rotate your text, or slant it to the right or left using the Slider field.

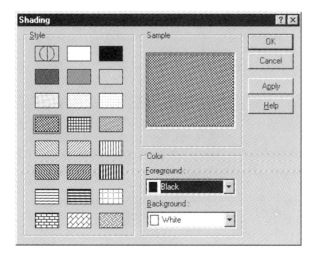

Opens the **Shading** dialog box, where you can select a variety of shading options for your letters.

Made Simple Books

Displays the **Shadow** dialog box, where you can choose a shadow effect and colour for your text.

Opens the **Border** dialog box where you can select a border thickness and colour for your letters.

Tip

Experiment! WordArt can be very effective!

Summary

- There are lots of Clip Art objects and pictures in the Microsoft Clip Gallery.

- The clips are arranged into categories, to help you locate something suitable.

- You can search for appropriate clips using key words.

- Clip Art can be adjusted to give the effect you require.

- The drawing tools allow you to create your own images.

- Objects can be arranged on top of each other in layers.

- Several objects can be grouped together to make one object.

- WordArt offers many options for eye-catching headings.

7 Tables and forms

Inserting a table

If you have a list of items you want to display in columns, tables can be very useful. Tables enable you to arrange your information neatly in rows and columns very easily.

If you've used tables in Word or if you use Excel, you'll find them very easy to work with. If you're new to tables, here's an introduction to some of the terminology.

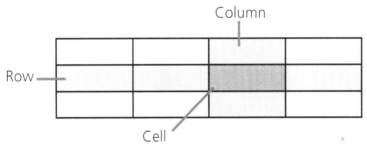

A table consists of **rows** and **columns**. Where a row and column intersect, you get a **cell** (the individual rectangular shapes on the illustration). You can enter text or figures into the cells to display lists of information.

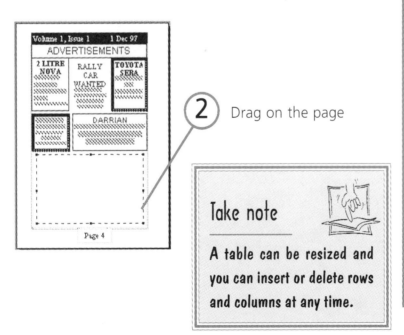

(2) Drag on the page

Take note

A table can be resized and you can insert or delete rows and columns at any time.

1 Click the **Table** tool 🎞 on the left-hand toolbar.

2 Drag on your page to indicate the position for the table.

3 Edit the number of rows and/or columns.

4 Choose a format from the **Table Format** list.

5 Click **OK**.

❑ An empty table will appear on your page.

6 If the table area is too small for the number of rows and columns, you will be asked if you want to resize the table. Click **Yes** to get Publisher to resize it.

7 Click in the first cell in your table.

8 Enter your information.

9 Press [Tab] to move on to the next cell.

❑ Repeat steps 8 and 9 until you've filled in all your information.

(3) Set the number of rows and columns

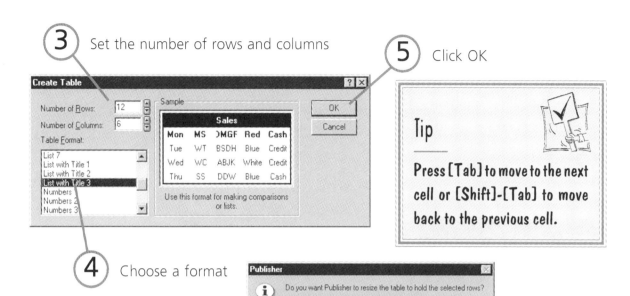

(5) Click OK

(4) Choose a format

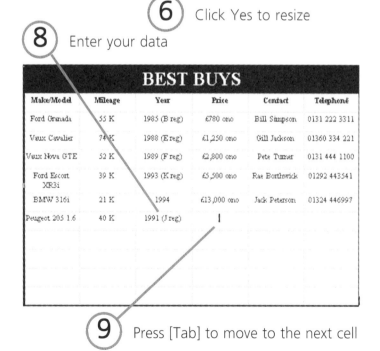

(6) Click Yes to resize

(8) Enter your data

(9) Press [Tab] to move to the next cell

Selection techniques

Tables are arranged in rows and columns. When working with tables you will need to be able to select cells, rows and columns so that you can format your table.

When a table is selected, the row, column and table selectors appear on it automatically.

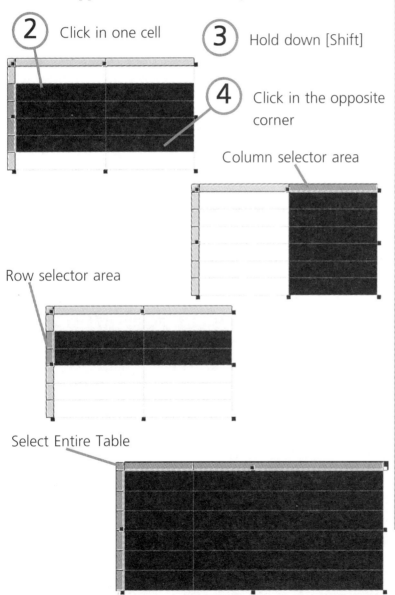

2 Click in one cell

3 Hold down [Shift]

4 Click in the opposite corner

Column selector area

Row selector area

Select Entire Table

- ❑ **A range of cells**
- **1** Click and drag over the range of cells.

Or

- **2** Click in a corner cell.
- **3** Hold down [**Shift**].
- **4** Click in the corner cell diagonally opposite.

- ❑ **One column or row**

  Click in the selector area above the column/ to the left of the rows.

- ❑ **Several columns/rows**

  Click and drag in the selector area.

- ❑ **The whole table**

  Click the **Select Entire Table** button.

- ❑ **Text within a cell**

  Click and drag over the text required.

- ❑ **All the text within a cell**

  Click inside the cell and press [**Ctrl**]-[**A**].

Adjusting the column width

1 Select the table and press [F9] to zoom in.

❏ **To resize the table as you adjust the column**

2 In the selector area, point to the dark line to the right of the column. The pointer becomes an adjust handle ⬌ADJUST.

3 Drag to set the width.

❏ **To keep the table the original size**

4 Point at the vertical bar in the header area *between* the columns you want to adjust.

5 Hold down [Shift] and drag until the columns to the right and left are the width you require.

When you insert a table into your file, the columns are all of equal width. You can easily adjust the column widths if you wish. When you adjust the width of a column, you may or may not want the overall width of the table to change.

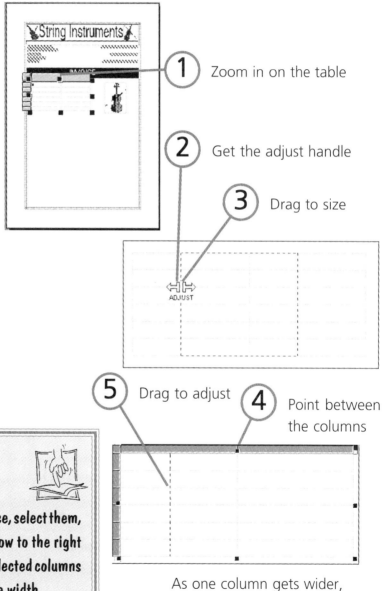

1 Zoom in on the table

2 Get the adjust handle

3 Drag to size

5 Drag to adjust

4 Point between the columns

As one column gets wider, the other gets narrower

Take note

To adjust several columns at once, select them, then drag a bar in the header row to the right of one of the columns. All the selected columns will adjust and end up the same width.

Adjusting the row height

The heights of the rows in your table can be adjusted in a similar way to the columns. However, there is a **Grow to Fit** option for the row heights that allows the rows to deepen automatically to accommodate the contents of the cell. When turned on, this applies to the whole table.

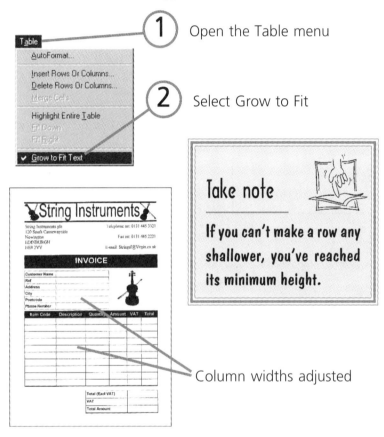

(1) Open the Table menu

(2) Select Grow to Fit

Column widths adjusted

Take note

If you can't make a row any shallower, you've reached its minimum height.

Take note

If your table must remain a specific size, and not adjust automatically to accommodate the data you enter, switch the Grow to Fit Text option off.

❏ **Grow to Fit Text**

1 Open the **Table** menu.

2 Click **Grow to Fit Text** to turn the option on.

❏ **To adjust manually**

3 Point to the line in the selector area below the row you want to adjust. The pointer becomes an adjust handle .

4 Drag to set the height.

❏ **To adjust without affecting the table size**

5 Point to the horizontal line *between* the rows you want to resize.

6 Hold down [Shift].

7 Drag to set the heights – as one row deepens the other narrows.

Merge and split cells

Basic steps

❏ **To merge cells**

1 Select the cells you want to merge.

2 Open the **Table** menu.

3 Choose **Merge Cells**.

❏ **To split cells**

4 Click in the cell that has been merged.

5 Open the **Table** menu.

6 Choose **Split Cells**.

You can merge the cells in a table *horizontally*, to allow you to enter headings that span several columns. If you change your mind later, and don't want the cells merged, you can easily split them again.

Cells that have previously been merged can be split again. If you have adjusted the column width in the meantime, the cells will automatically take up the new column widths when you split them.

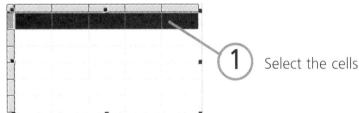

① Select the cells

② Open the Table menu

③ Choose Merge Cells

Cells merged into one

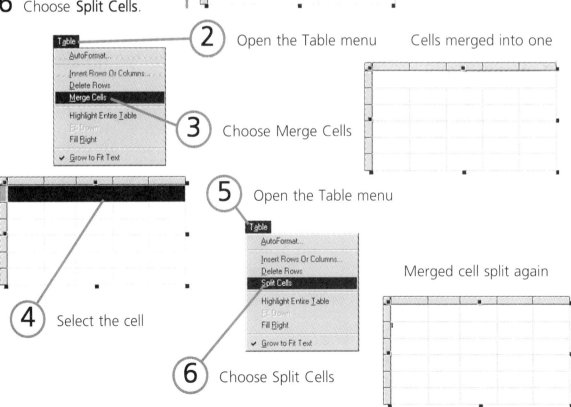

④ Select the cell

⑤ Open the Table menu

⑥ Choose Split Cells

Merged cell split again

Adjusting the table size

Deleting rows or columns

If you discover that you have too many rows or columns in your table, you can delete those you don't need.

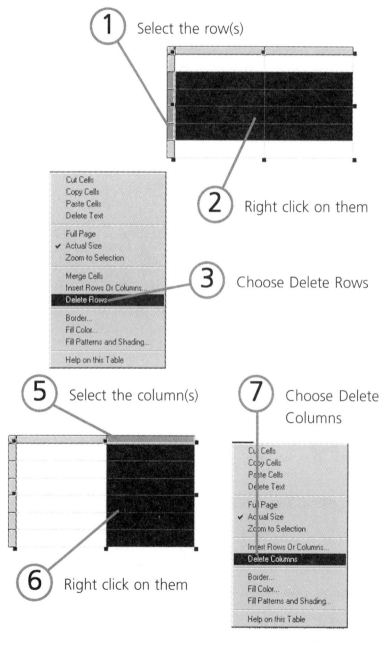

1. Select the row(s)

2. Right click on them

   Cut Cells
   Copy Cells
   Paste Cells
   Delete Text
   Full Page
   ✓ Actual Size
   Zoom to Selection
   Merge Cells
   Insert Rows Or Columns...
   Delete Rows
   Border...
   Fill Color...
   Fill Patterns and Shading...
   Help on this Table

3. Choose Delete Rows

5. Select the column(s)

6. Right click on them

7. Choose Delete Columns

   Cut Cells
   Copy Cells
   Paste Cells
   Delete Text
   Full Page
   ✓ Actual Size
   Zoom to Selection
   Insert Rows Or Columns...
   Delete Columns
   Border...
   Fill Color...
   Fill Patterns and Shading...
   Help on this Table

Basic steps

❑ **To delete rows**

1 Select the unwanted row(s).

2 Right click within the selected area.

3 Choose **Delete Rows** from the pop-up menu.

Or

4 Open the **Table** menu and choose **Delete Rows**.

❑ **To delete columns**

5 Select the unwanted column(s).

6 Right click within the selected area.

7 Choose **Delete Columns** from the pop-up menu.

Or

8 Open the **Table** menu and choose **Delete Columns**.

Basic steps

Inserting rows or columns

1 Click inside a cell where you want to insert a row or column.

2 Right click to display the pop-up menu.

Or

3 Open the **Table** menu.

4 Choose **Insert Rows Or Columns...**

5 Select either **Rows(s)** or **Column(s)** in the **Insert** option.

6 Specify the **Number of rows** or **columns**.

7 Does the row or column go **Before** or **After Selected Cells**?

8 Click **Apply** to carry out your instructions but leave the dialog box open (if you want to insert *both* rows and columns you might want to do this).

Or

9 Click **OK** to apply and close the dialog box.

You can also add extra rows or columns anywhere within your table.

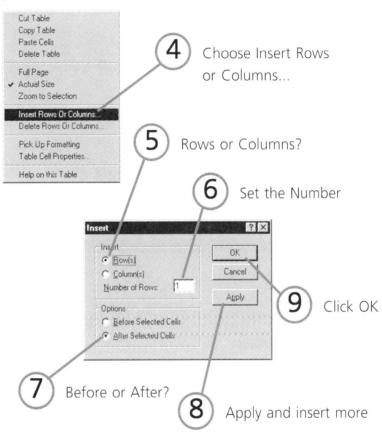

④ Choose Insert Rows or Columns...

⑤ Rows or Columns?

⑥ Set the Number

⑨ Click OK

⑦ Before or After?

⑧ Apply and insert more

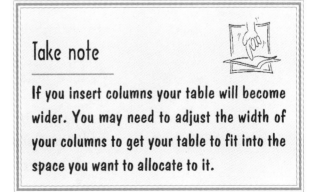

Take note

If you insert columns your table will become wider. You may need to adjust the width of your columns to get your table to fit into the space you want to allocate to it.

Formatting your table

If you created a table using the default option you may decide it needs some formatting to bring it to life. You can either format the table using the AutoFormat, or you can format it manually.

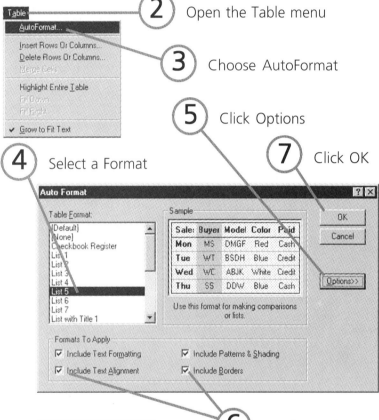

(2) Open the Table menu

(3) Choose AutoFormat

(5) Click Options

(7) Click OK

(4) Select a Format

(6) Set the options

❏ **AutoFormat**

1 Click within the table you want to format.

2 Open the **Table** menu

3 Choose **AutoFormat...**

4 Select a **Format**.

5 Click **Options** to open the options area.

6 Set your options.

7 Click **OK**.

❏ **Manual formatting**

Select the cells, row or column and use the tools on the Formatting toolbar.

Take note

You can also set formats from the Border, Fill Color or Fill Patterns and Shading... dialog boxes. To open them, right click on the selected area and choose from the pop-up menu.

Basic steps

1 Open the **File** menu and choose **Create New Publication...**

2 Select the **PageWizard** tab.

3 Choose **Business Form**.

4 Click **OK**.

5 Work through the Wizard, setting options and giving your own or your company's details.

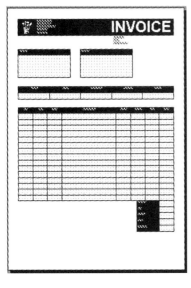

A form created using the Business Form wizard, with added text boxes and tables

Tables are particularly useful when it comes to creating forms. You can create your own forms using text frames, tables, WordArt, Clip Art etc. This form has 3 tables on it:

● The top table has 2 columns and 6 rows;

● The middle one has 6 columns and 9 rows;

● The bottom one has 2 columns and 3 rows.

Forms from PageWizard

You can also use the Page Wizard Design Assistant to help you create a form – try it.

2 Select the PageWizard tab

3 Choose Business Form

4 Click OK

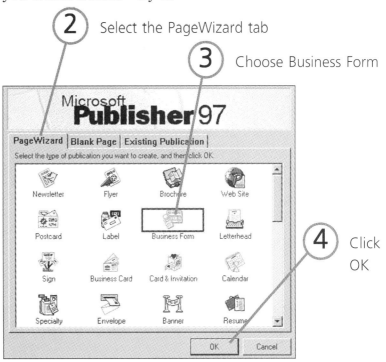

Summary

- You can **select rows, columns, cells or an entire table** when editing and formatting your table.

- **Column widths** can be adjusted to suit your requirements.

- **Row heights** can be fixed, or they can **grow to fit** the text entered.

- **Cells can be merged** together – useful if you want to enter headings that span several columns.

- Merged **cells can be split up again** if you change your mind.

- **Unwanted rows and columns** can be deleted.

- **Rows and columns can be added** if you need more than you first thought.

- **AutoFormat** allows you to quickly format your table using a pre-set design.

- You can **manually format** your table using any of the normal formatting options.

- **Tables** are useful if you are creating a form.

- You can create **professional-looking forms** quickly using the PageWizard design assistant.

8 Mail Merge

An overview

You can use mail merge to create personalised documents – advertising letters, address labels, certificates, etc.

Mail merge terminology

Data source – The file containing the names and addresses (or other details) you want to combine with your publication file. The data source may be created in Publisher or in a different application – e.g. Word, Excel or Access.

Entry – All the information on each item in your data source file, e.g. a customer's name, address, phone number, etc., is held in an entry. If you are used to working with database packages, or mail merge in Word, an entry in Publisher is a record in Access or Word.

Field – Each piece of detail in an entry is called a field. You might have a first name field, last name field, address field, town field, etc. Each field is identified by a field name.

Main document – The main document is the Publisher file that you are going to combine with your data source.

Merge – This is the process where the information in the data source file is combined with the main document.

The mail merge process

1 Create or open the data source file.

2 Create or open the publication file.

3 Link the data source and publication files.

4 Insert the fields from the data source file into the publication.

5 Merge the detail from the data source file into the publication.

6 Print the final document.

❑ We'll consider each of these steps in this chapter.

The main document in this example holds the certificate's design and all its text apart from the name. Names are held in the data source file, and each one is merged with the main document to produce a new printed certificate.

Basic steps

1 Open the **Mail Merge** menu.

2 Choose **Create Publisher Address List...** The New Address List dialog box appears.

3 Click the **Customize** button to open the **Customize Address** List dialog box (next page).

Tip

If the ready-made field list will meet your needs, you can go straight to entering your data.

Creating an address list

You can easily create and manage a simple name and address list in Publisher. The name and address list you create could be one containing details of existing customers or it could be a list of potential customers you want to send an advertising leaflet or brochure to.

Publisher does all the hard work for you in creating an address list, though you will probably have to spend a little time customising your new list.

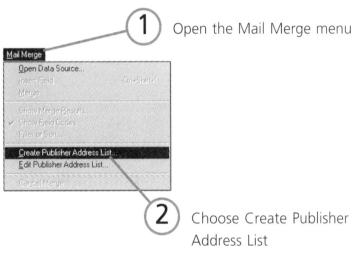

① Open the Mail Merge menu

② Choose Create Publisher Address List

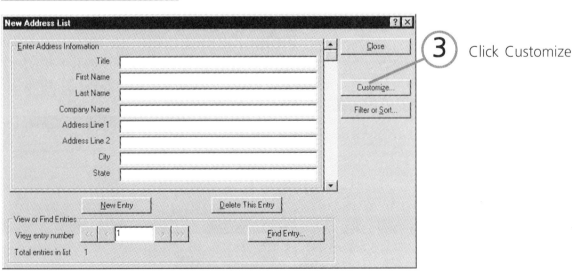

③ Click Customize

Customising the field list

The Field names used in the Address list follow American conventions – there are 'States' and 'Zip codes' instead of counties or regions and post codes. You can easily customise the fields.

Basic steps

1 Select the field from the field name list.

❑ **To delete a field**

2 Click **Delete Field**.

3 Confirm at the prompt.

Or

❑ **To rename a field**

4 Click **Rename Field...**

5 Enter the new name and click **OK**.

Or

❑ **To add a field**

6 Click **Add New Field...**

7 Enter a name for the new field.

8 Choose whether to insert **Before** or **After** the selected one.

9 Click **OK**.

⑥ Click Add New Field   ① Select the field

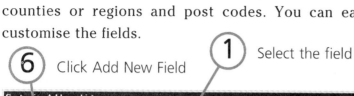

② Click Delete Field

④ Click Rename Field

Use these to change a field's position

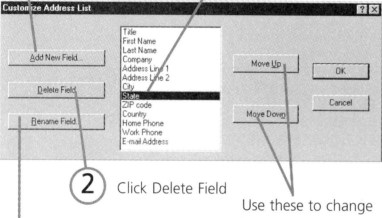

③ Confirm with Yes

⑦ Type a name   ⑨ Click OK

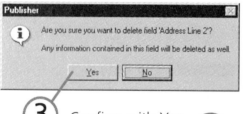

⑤ Enter the new name

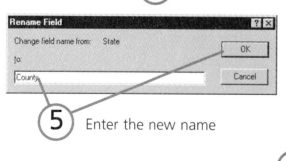

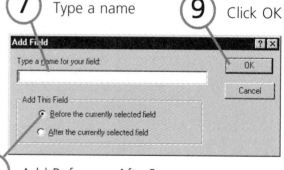

⑧ Add Before or After?

Basic steps

1 Type the detail in the first field.

2 Press **[Tab]** to move to the next field.

3 Enter your data.

4 Repeat steps 2 and 3 until the entry is complete.

5 Click the **New Entry** button to enter your next set of detail.

Entering your data

Once you've got the list of field names you want to use, you can start adding your records.

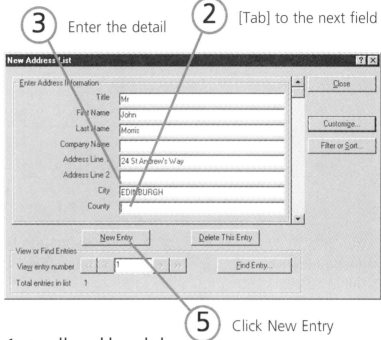

3 Enter the detail   **2** [Tab] to the next field

5 Click New Entry

Saving the address list

Once you've entered your data, close your address list – click Close in the New Address List dialog box. You will be taken into the Save As dialog box. Locate the folder, enter a file name and click Save, as normal.

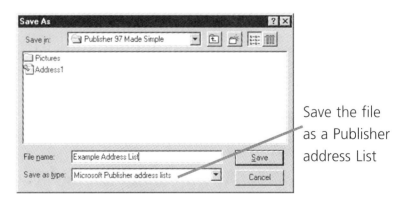

Save the file as a Publisher address List

Moving between entries

At some stage you will need to move from one entry to another – perhaps to check some data. You can move between the entries using the View or Find Entries panel.

You can use the arrow buttons to move through the entries in your address list.

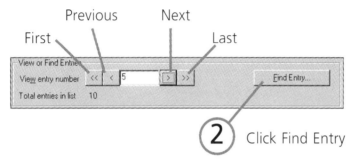

If you want to go to a specific entry, you can jump to it, using its number, or find an entry that contains specific detail in a field.

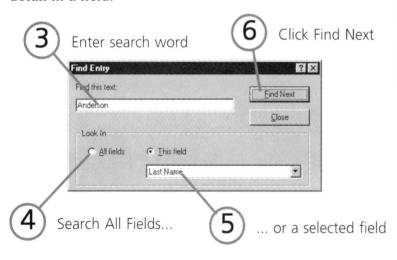

③ Enter search word

⑥ Click Find Next

④ Search All Fields...

⑤ ... or a selected field

□ **Find Entry**

1 Click **Find Entry**...

2 Type in the data you are looking for.

3 Select **All fields**.

Or

4 Select **This field** (if you know which to look in) and pick the field from the drop-down list.

5 Click **Find Next** to locate the data.

□ If the first entry found is not the one required, click **Find Next** again until you reach the entry you want.

Tip

To go to a specific entry, double-click on the entry number field, type the number and press [Enter].

When there are no more matching entries, this prompt appears to let you know.

Editing an address list

1 Open the address list and display the **Mail Merge** menu.

2 Choose **Edit Publisher Address List...**

3 Locate the folder and select the file.

4 Click **Open**.

❑ **To edit an entry**

5 Move to the entry.

6 Edit as necessary.

Or

❑ **To add a new entry**

7 Click **New Entry**.

Or

❑ **To delete an entry**

8 Display the entry.

9 Click **Delete This Entry** and confirm at the prompt.

You can edit an address list file at any time. You may need to add or delete entries, or amend some of the details held within an entry.

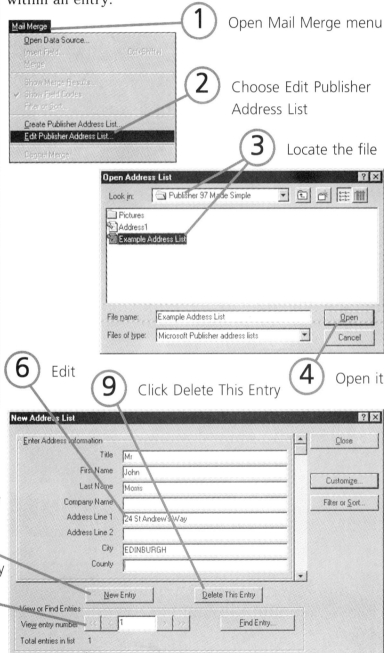

① Open Mail Merge menu

② Choose Edit Publisher Address List

③ Locate the file

④ Open it

⑥ Edit

⑨ Click Delete This Entry

⑦ Click New Entry

⑤ Move to the entry

Creating labels

The main document may be a file you have already created, or you might need to set one up for a specific purpose.

We are going to produce some mailing labels, so we'll create a main document with this in mind. A PageWizard will help us set up some labels. Start up a Wizard, and work through its steps, selecting the options that your require.

(2) Open the PageWizards tab

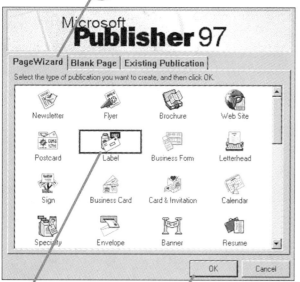

(3) Choose Label

(4) Click OK

(5) Select Address Bulk Mailing

Basic steps

1 Open the **File** menu and choose **Create New Publication...**

2 Select the **PageWizard** tab.

3 Choose **Label**.

4 Click **OK**.

5 Select **Address Bulk Mailing** and click **Next**.

6 Choose a **Label style** and click **Next**.

7 As we are going to prepare our merge, select **Yes** at the next step and click **Next**.

8 Click **Create It!**

9 At the chequered flag, pick **No** and click **OK**.

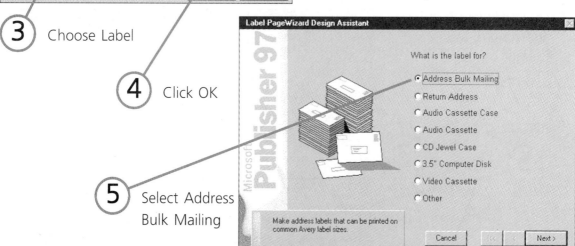

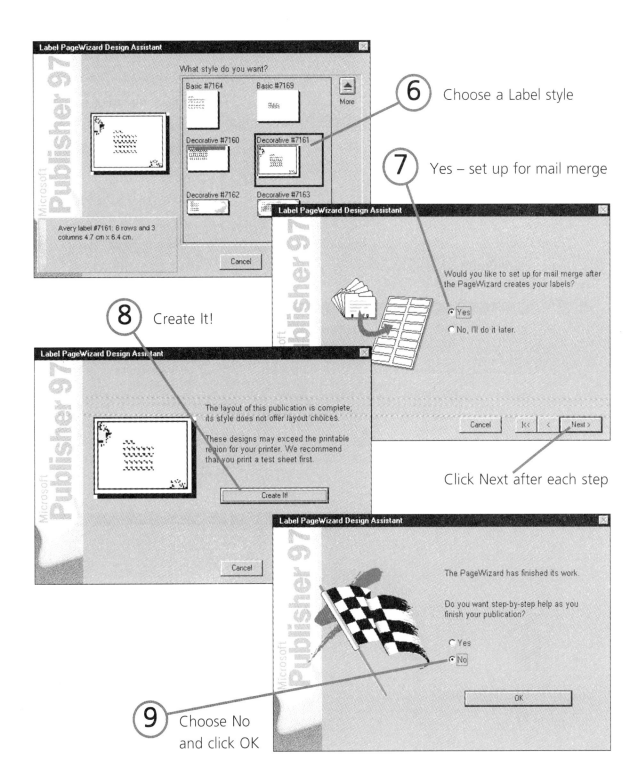

6 Choose a Label style

7 Yes – set up for mail merge

Click Next after each step

8 Create It!

9 Choose No and click OK

Opening the data source

Once your main document has been set up, you must open the data source that contains the information you want to merge into it.

- If you selected *Yes* at the prompt to set up for mail merge once the Wizard had created the labels (at step 3), Publisher automatically moves on to the Open Data Source dialog box.

- If you selected *No, I'll do it later*, you must choose Open Data Source... from the Mail Merge menu to display the dialog box.

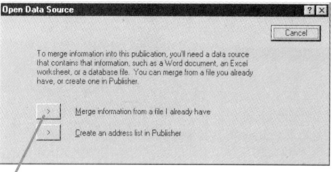

③ Click Merge information from a file...

Basic steps

1 Display your main document on screen.

2 Open the **Mail Merge** menu and choose **Open Data Source** (if necessary).

3 Click **Merge information from a file I already have** (we've set up our address list file).

4 Locate the folder and select the file you want to use.

5 Click **Open**.

④ Locate the file

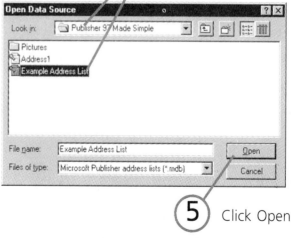

⑤ Click Open

Tip

You can open a file by double clicking on its name.

1 Click inside your label.

2 Select the field from the **Fields** list in the **Insert Field** dialog box.

3 Click **Insert**.

4 Type spaces, or press **[Enter]** to set the insertion point for the next field.

5 Repeat steps 2 to 4 to insert the other fields.

6 Click **Close**.

7 Save your main document if you want to re-use it in future.

Tip

To display the field list again, use Mail Merge — Insert Field...

Take note

Publisher closes up any spaces that may result from having no data in a field in the source file.

The main document

You must now insert the fields required from the data source file. The list of fields is displayed. The main document, created by the Page Wizard, is also displayed.

A prompt tell you what to do at the Insert Fields dialog box.

> Click the place in the text frame where you want to insert a field code, then click to select a field from the list and click Insert.

Name
Address line 1
Address line 2
Address line 3
Address line 4

① Click inside the label

② Select a field

③ Click Insert

Insert Fields

Choose Insert to add the selected fields to your publication.

Insert
Close

«Title» «First Name»
«Address Line 1»
«Address Line 2»
«City»

Fields:
Address Line 2
City
County
Post code
Country
Home Phone
Work Phone

⑥ Click Close

④ Position the insertion point

Merging the files

The next step is to combine the detail in the data source document with the main document.

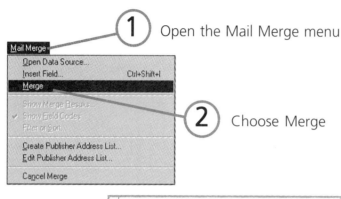

① Open the Mail Merge menu

② Choose Merge

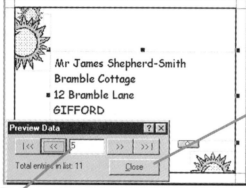

④ Click Close

③ Preview your labels

Take note

If you want to display the merged results again later, open the Mail Merge menu and choose Show Merge Results...

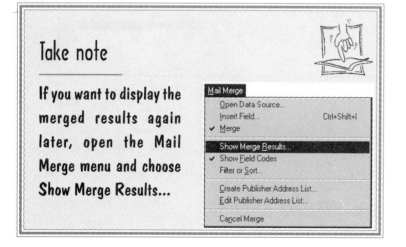

Basic steps

1 Open the **Mail Merge** menu.

2 Choose **Merge**.

3 Preview your labels to check the layout (drag the Preview Data dialog box out of the way if necessary).

4 Click **Close** to close the Preview Data window when you're done.

Tip

Work through enough of your labels to be sure that the layout will work for different length names, addresses, etc.

Basic steps

Printing

1 Open the **File** menu.

2 Choose **Print Merge...**

3 Complete the dialog box as required.

4 Click **OK**.

Finally, you need to print out your merged publication.

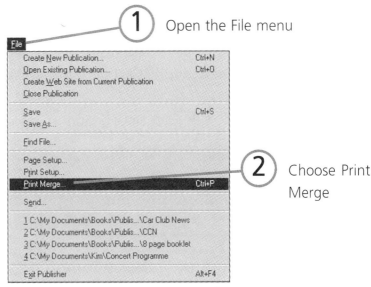

① Open the File menu

② Choose Print Merge

③ Complete as required

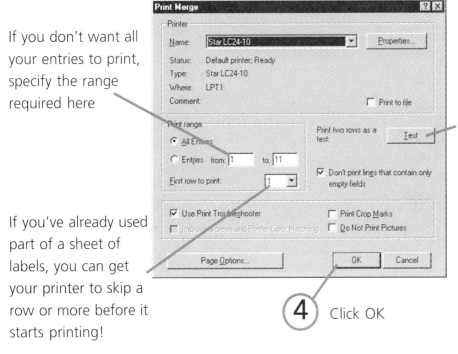

If you don't want all your entries to print, specify the range required here

A useful option if you're printing labels – check how they will look before committing yourself!

If you've already used part of a sheet of labels, you can get your printer to skip a row or more before it starts printing!

④ Click OK

109

Sorting entries

There may be times when you want to organise your entries into a specific order (an order other than that in which they were entered).

You can set the sort order in the Filter and Sort dialog box. You can access this from the address list file, or from the Mail Merge menu.

① Click FIlter or Sort...

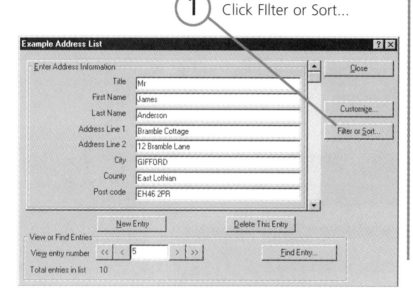

❑ **From the address list**

1 Click the **Filter or Sort...** button.

❑ **From the main document**

2 Open the **Mail Merge** menu and choose **Filter or Sort...**

3 Select the **Sort** tab.

4 Specify the sort order required – you can sort on up to three fields.

5 Click **OK**.

❑ Your entries will be re-arranged in the order requested.

② Use Mail Merge – Filter or Sort...

Tip

If you choose **Show Merge Results** from the Mail Merge menu, you should find that your entries are in the order requested.

❏ To remove the sort criteria

6 Display the **Filtering and Sorting** dialog box.

7 Click the **Remove Sort** button.

8 Click **OK**.

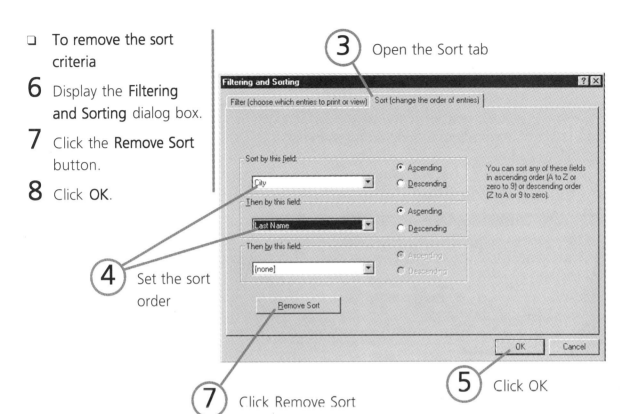

③ Open the Sort tab

④ Set the sort order

⑦ Click Remove Sort

⑤ Click OK

Tip

You must remove the Sort criteria to restore the original order of the entries. If you are doing a new sort, it is sometimes quicker to remove the old criteria and start from scratch.

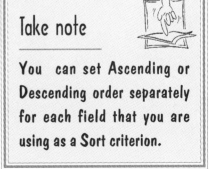

Take note

You can set Ascending or Descending order separately for each field that you are using as a Sort criterion.

Filtering entries

There may be times when you want to merge only entries that meet specific criteria. You can use the Filtering tab in the Filtering and Sorting dialog box to specify your filter criteria.

(1) Open the Filtering and Sorting dialog box

(2) Select the Filter tab

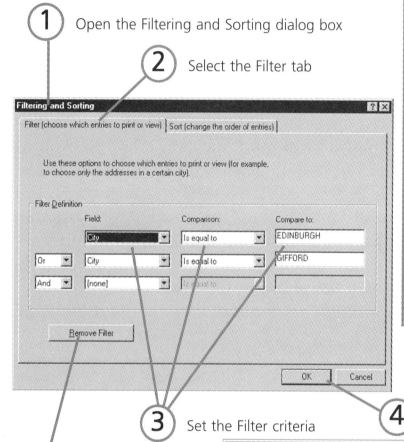

(3) Set the Filter criteria

(4) Click OK

(6) Click Remove Filter

Basic steps

1 Access the **Filtering and Sorting** dialog box.

2 Select the **Filter** tab.

3 Set up your filter criteria.

4 Click **OK**.

❏ Only the entries that meet the criteria specified will be displayed or printed.

❏ **To remove the filter**

5 Display the **Filtering and Sorting** dialog box.

6 Click the **Remove Filter** button.

7 Click **OK**.

Take note

The match between the text that you enter into the Compare to: field and the data in your records is not case sensitive. In this example, City is equal to **Edinburgh**, **EDINBURGH** or **edinburgh** – all will give the same result.

Comparisons

The comparison options are:

Is equal to   Is not equal to   Is less than   Is greater than

You can use **Is greater than**, **Is less than** to filter out a range of entries. In the example below, this will find all records where the surname begins with N, O, P, Q or R.

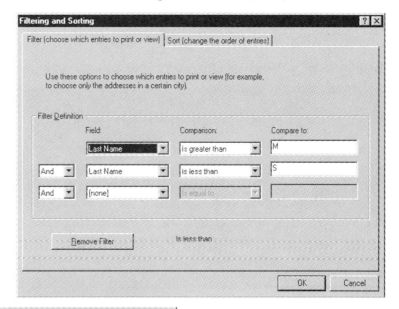

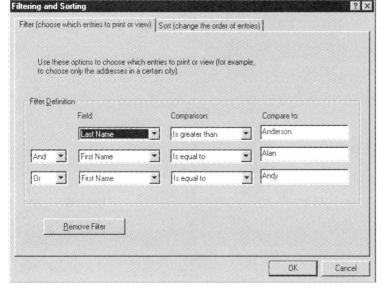

Experiment with the filter definition fields. This would return the following records:

Alan Anderson

Andy Anderson

Andy Morris

Andy Watson

E.g. Alan Anderson and anyone with Andy in the First name field.

Summary

- Publisher can be used to produce **personalised documents** – labels, invitations, greetings cards, etc.

- The **data source file** can either be set up in Publisher or it can be created in another application, e.g. Word, Access, Excel.

- You can choose **which fields you want to set up** in a Publisher address list file.

- Publisher displays an **entry form** that you can use to input and edit your data.

- It is easy to **move from one entry to another** in an address list file.

- **Close and save the address list file** once you've entered your data.

- You can **add, delete or edit the entries** in your address list file.

- **Labels** can be created using the labels PageWizard.

- The **data source must be open** before you can set up the main publication.

- **Merge** combines the entries in the data source with the main publication.

- The result publication can be **printed** once the files have been merged.

- **Sort** allows you to arrange the entries in a specific order.

- **Filter** allows you to extract entries that meet the criteria you specify.

9 Styles and Templates

Creating styles

You can use styles to record the text formatting options you wish to apply to your text.

There are two main advantages to using styles:

Consistency. By applying a style to your text, you automatically apply all the formatting options that are set up within it – it doesn't matter if you forget which font size you used, or whether you used italic or underline on it.

Speed. If you are applying more than a couple of formatting options to text it is *quicker* to apply a style than it is to apply the formats individually. All the formatting options are applied in one go!

The options that you can record into a style are:

- ◆ Character type and size   ◆ Indents and lists
- ◆ Spacing between characters   ◆ Line spacing
- ◆ Tabs

You can create a style from text that has been formatted within your publication (create by example) or you can use the Format Text Style dialog box to set up your styles.

Basic steps

❑ **Create by example**

1 Select some text that has the formatting you wish to record into a style.

2 Click in the **Style** box on the **Format** toolbar.

3 Type a name for the style and press [Enter].

4 Click **OK** at the **Create Style By Example** dialog box to confirm.

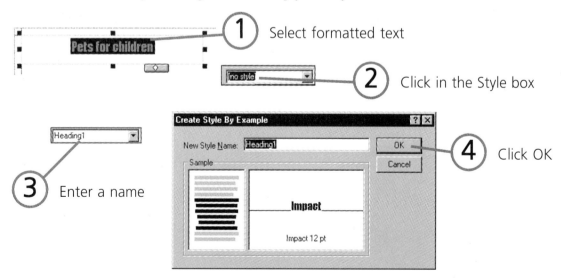

① Select formatted text

Pets for children

no style   ② Click in the Style box

Create Style By Example

Heading1

3 Enter a name

New Style Name: Heading1   OK   ④ Click OK

Cancel

Sample

Impact

Impact 12 pt

Basic steps

❏ **Using the dialog box**

1 From the **Format** menu choose **Text Style...**

2 Click **Create A New Style**.

3 Enter a name.

4 Select an option.

5 Format as required and click **OK** to close the dialog box.

6 Repeat steps 4 and 5 as necessary.

7 Click **OK** to close the Create New Style dialog box.

8 Click **Close** to close the Text Styles dialog box.

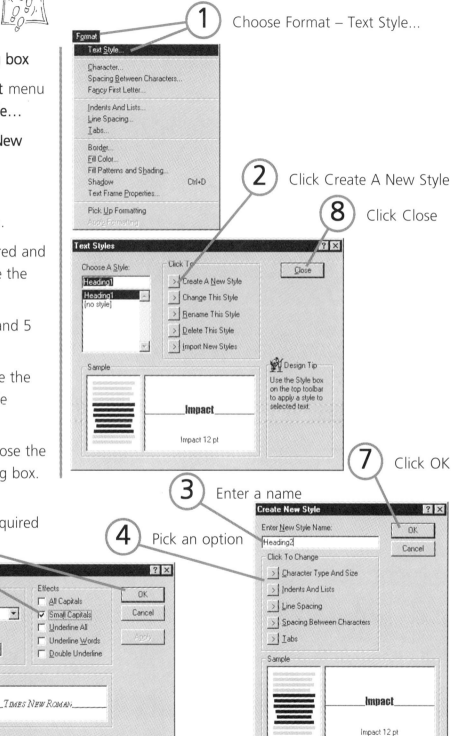

Choose Format – Text Style...

Click Create A New Style

Click Close

Click OK

Enter a name

Format as required

Pick an option

Applying styles

Once you've created your styles, using either of the methods described, you can apply the styles to any text you wish within your publication.

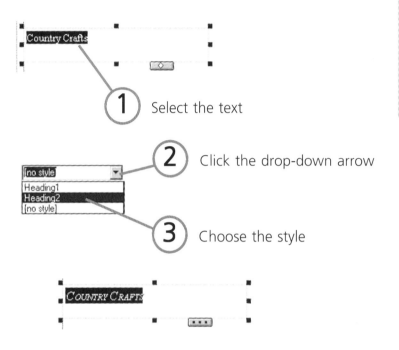

① Select the text

② Click the drop-down arrow

③ Choose the style

Text with style applied

1 Select the text to which you want to apply a style.

2 Click the drop-down arrow to the right of the **Style** box.

3 Choose the style required from the list.

Tip

Try using styles – they can save you time and frustration, especially with longer publications where you need to use the same formatting on different pieces of text.

Take note

If you change the formatting of a style that has already been applied to some text, the formatted text would automatically update to reflect the changes made to the style.

Take note

If you accidently change the formatting of a style click Undo – before you do anything else!

Basic steps

1 From the **Format** menu choose **Text Style…**

2 Select the style.

❏ **To edit a style**

3 Click **Change This Style** and continue as for creating a new style.

Or

❏ **To rename a Style**

4 Click the **Rename This Style** button.

5 Enter the new name and click **OK**.

Or

❏ **To delete a Style**

6 Click the **Delete This Style** button.

7 Click **Yes** to confirm.

Styles are stored within the publication file, so any time you open a publication you have access to the styles set up within it. Once you've set a style up, you may change your mind about it and want to make changes to it. You can easily edit, rename or delete any style you create.

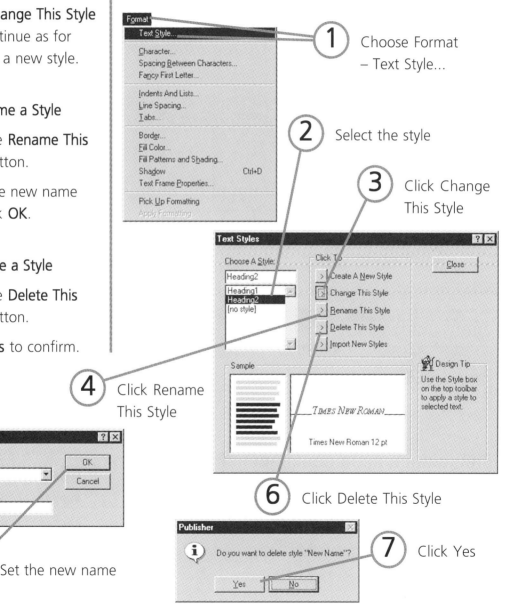

① Choose Format – Text Style…

② Select the style

③ Click Change This Style

④ Click Rename This Style

⑤ Set the new name

⑥ Click Delete This Style

⑦ Click Yes

Importing styles

Styles are stored with the publication in which they were created. If you want to use a style from another publication, you can import it rather then set it up again.

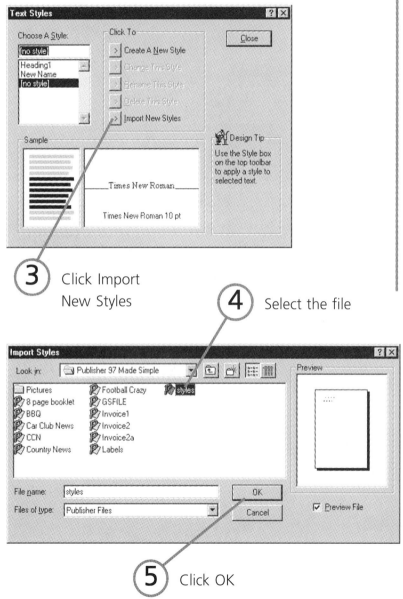

3 Click Import New Styles

4 Select the file

5 Click OK

1 Open the publication you want to import styles into.

2 Choose **Text Style...** from the **Format** menu.

3 Click **Import New Styles**.

4 At the Import Styles dialog box, select the file that contains the styles you want.

5 Click **OK**.

❑ The styles are added to those listed in the Text Styles dialog box.

Take note

If the publication already has styles with the same names as those you are importing, a **Duplicate style name** prompt will appear, giving you the chance to cancel the import.

120

Adding to the Design Gallery

1 Open the publication that contains the item you want to add to the Design Gallery.

2 Select the object.

3 Click the Design Gallery tool

4 If the designs for the current publication are not displayed, click **More Designs** and choose **Designs for** the current publication – 'Car Club News' in this example.

5 Click **More Designs** again and choose **Add Selection to Design Gallery…**

cont…

We have already used some of the designs in the design gallery to add interest to our publications. You can also add your own designs to the design gallery if your wish.

(1) Open the publication

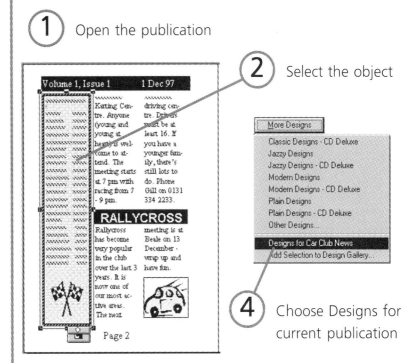

(2) Select the object

(4) Choose Designs for current publication

(5) Choose Add selection to Design Gallery

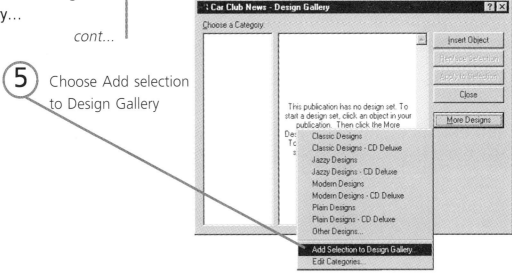

6 Enter a name and category

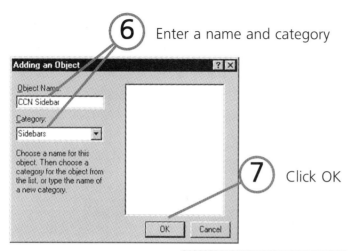

7 Click OK

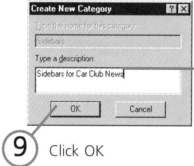

9 Click OK

The description is shown here when you
view the object in the Design Gallery

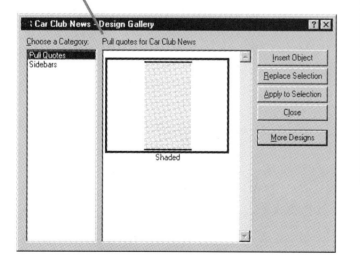

...cont

6 Give the object a **Name**
and specify a **Category**
for the entry, e.g.
Sidebar, Pull quote,
etc.

7 Click **OK**.

8 If it's a new category,
enter a **description**.

9 Click **OK**.

8 Enter a description

Take note

Your entries in the Design Gallery
are available within the publication
you have created them in.

To import a design set from an
existing publication, select Other
Designs... from the More Designs
list and access the file that contains
the set required.

122

Basic steps

1 Click the **Design Gallery** tool to access the Design Gallery.

2 Click **More Designs** and choose **Edit Categories**.

3 In the **Edit Categories** dialog box, select the category.

Or

❑ **To delete a Category**

4 Click **Delete Category**.

5 Confirm at the prompt.

Or

❑ **To rename a Category**

6 Click **Rename Category**.

7 Give a new name at the dialog box.

Or

❑ **To create a Category**

8 Click **New Category**.

9 Enter a name and description.

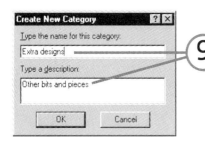

Editing the Design Gallery categories

Once you've set up some categories in the Design Gallery, you can edit them as necessary. You can add new categories, rename existing ones or delete ones you no longer require.

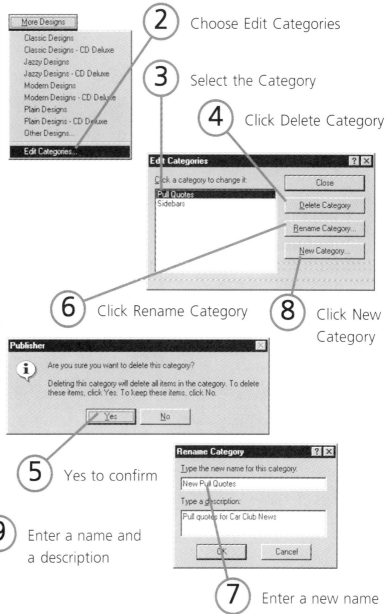

② Choose Edit Categories

③ Select the Category

④ Click Delete Category

⑥ Click Rename Category

⑧ Click New Category

⑤ Yes to confirm

⑨ Enter a name and a description

⑦ Enter a new name

Templates

Templates are patterns on which your publications are based. You can easily set up templates for any publication you design to a specific layout – your newsletter for example. The template would hold the basic layout for your publication – the page setup, the number of columns and rows, gridlines, ruler lines, frames for text, WordArt, Clip Art, etc.

In addition to the basic layout of your design, a template can hold the styles you will be using and any entries you've made to the Design Gallery.

Basic steps

1 Set up the basic layout for your publication.

2 Create any styles you intend to use.

3 Add any design elements required to the Design Gallery.

4 Click the **Save** tool 🖫 on the Standard toolbar.

5 Enter a name for your template.

6 Select the **Template** checkbox.

7 Click **Save**.

8 Close your file.

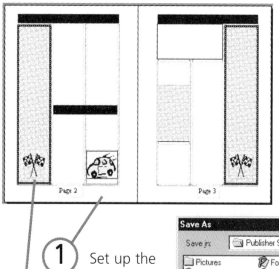

① Set up the basic layout

③ Add to the Design Gallery?

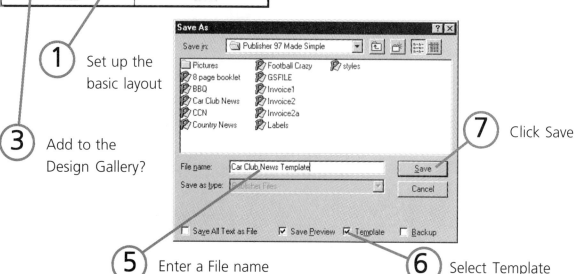

⑦ Click Save

⑤ Enter a File name

⑥ Select Template

124

Basic steps

1 Open the **File** menu and choose **Create New Publication...**

2 Select the **Templates** tab (this tab only appears once you've saved a file as a template).

3 Choose the template you want to base your new publication on.

4 Click **OK**.

Using your template

Once you've set up and saved your Template you can easily create new publications based on its pattern at any time.

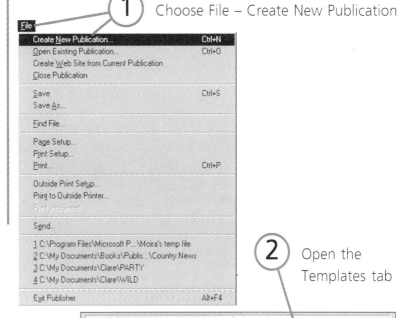

① Choose File – Create New Publication

② Open the Templates tab

③ Select a template

④ Click OK

Take note

If you created styles in the template file, or added objects to the Design Gallery, you will find that they are available to you in any publication you create based on the template.

Summary

- **Styles** are used to record text formatting commands.

- The main benefits of styles are **speed** and **consistency**.

- Existing **styles can be edited** if necessary.

- Styles can be **renamed** if you wish.

- Styles that you no longer use can be **deleted**.

- Styles can be **imported from other publications** if necessary.

- You can **add** your own sidebars, pull quotes, eye catching designs, etc. **to the Design Gallery.**

- The **Design Gallery categories** you create can be added to, renamed or deleted.

- **Templates** are patterns that you can create for your publications.

- Templates can contain **the basic layout** for your publication, styles and design elements.

- When you **save a publication as a Template** a **Templates tab** is added to the Microsoft Publisher 97 Startup dialog box.

10 The Internet

Web publishing

If you feel that you can reach your target audience over the Internet, you could set up a Web site. This may contain information about your company, club, school or yourself.

Before you start to set up a Web site, spend some time viewing other people's sites. Find out what you like or don't like about the way some of the pages are presented.

Web jargon

Service provider: A company that provides access to the Internet.

Web or WWW: World Wide Web. A vast collection of pages, stored on computers throughout the world, and joined to each other using **hypertext links**.

Browser: A piece of software that allows you to view pages on the WWW. Netscape and Microsoft Explorer are the browsers most often used.

Home page: The front (or main) page of a multi-page site.

HTML: The language used for creating Web pages. When you publish to the Web, Publisher converts *pure* text to Hypertext Markup Language (HTML) files.

URL: (Uniform Resource Locator) – the unique address of a page, or other file, on the Internet. The URL tells you what a page is called, where to find it and how to get to it!

Surfing: Exploring and reading web pages.

Download: Transfer a file from another, often distant, computer to your own. Text files are much smaller than graphic files and therefore download quicker.

Upload: Transfer a file from your computer to a remote one, e.g. your service provider's.

Tip

Don't try to put everything you want to say on one page. Use the first page (the home page) of your site to give your visitor an overview of your site and point them to other information that they may be interested in.

Take note

You can install Internet Explorer 2.0 from your Publisher CD. Look under 'Web Browsers' in the on-line help for more information.

Tip

Visit the Publisher Web site at www.microsoft.com/publisher/ for tips, updates, Clip Art, etc.

Take note

WordArt, BorderArt, fancy first letters, rotated text and text frames filled with colour, etc. will be converted to GIF files.

FTP: File Transfer Protocol – used for transferring files from one computer to another over the Internet. The special software necessary is easily obtainable – your service provider can usually supply it.

Fonts

Try to use these standard fonts for your Web pages: Arial, Courier New, Times New Roman, Symbol and Wingdings.

If you use a font that is not installed on a computer which is viewing your Web site, the font will be converted to one that is available, and your pages may not look so good.

Graphics formats

Publisher can import all the main picture formats, including bitmap (BMP), Graphics Interchange Format (GIF), JEPG Picture Format (JPG), PC Paintbrush (.PCX), Tagged Image Format (TIF), Kodak Photo CD (PCD), DrawPerfect (WPG), CorelDraw (CDR), Windows Metafile (WMF) and Encapsulated Postscript (EPS)

Regardless of the picture format your image originally had, it will be converted to a GIF file when published to the Web. GIF is the most frequently used graphics format on Web pages, as it is very compact. A typical GIF is a fraction of the size of a BitMap version of the same image.

A Web page that contains a lot of graphics will take longer to download than one that doesn't have many pictures. This leads to a couple of possible problems:

● Page that are slow to download can deter visitors.

● You may run out of the free space allocated to you on your service provider's machine.

Creating a Web site

The techniques are much the same as for any publication. Start with **File – Create New Publication**, selecting **Web Site** from the **Blank** tab.

Insert text frames and Clip Art to get the layout you want. Either follow the example here, or set up your own site.

The site I am creating here consists of 4 pages:

- Home Page
- Books I Have Written
- Made Simple
- Edinburgh

Tip

Aim for a good balance of text and graphics on your Web page.

Home Page

Hi! Welcome to Moira's home page.

Books I Have Written   Edinburgh

Books I Have Written

Over the past few years I have written a number of computer books, aimed at the new, occasional or student user. I have contributed to the:

- Made Simple series published by Butterworth Heinemann
- Step by step series published by Butterworth Heinemann and PC Plus

Return to Home Page

Made Simple

The first Made Simple computing books were published in 1994. Since then, the number of titles in the series has increased dramatically. The books are:

- Easy to follow
- Jargon free
- Task based
- Practical

I have contributed the following titles to the series: -

- Publisher 97
- Access 2
- Access 7
- Access 97

- PowerPoint 4
- PowerPoint 7
- PowerPoint 97
- WordPro
- Ami Pro

For a full listing of the books in the series, visit the Web site at Butterworth Heinemann

Return to Home Page   Back to Books I Have Written

Take note

If your publication will have more than one page, add the number of pages required – see page 65.

Basic steps

1 Select the text or picture, that you want to create a hyperlink from.

2 Click 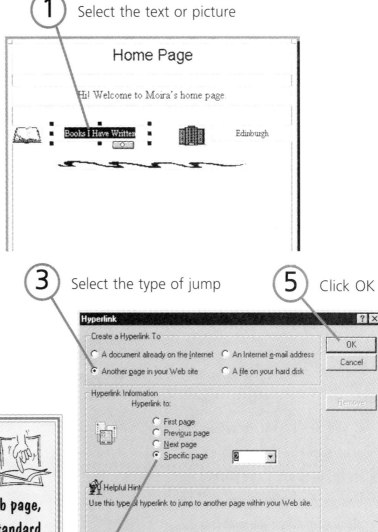 the **Hyperlink** tool on the Standard toolbar.

3 Select the option that describes where you want to jump to – **Another page in your Web site** in this case.

4 Specify where the hyperlink will take you.

5 Click **OK**.

❏ When you return to your Web page, the hyperlinked text will be underlined and in blue. Hyperlinked pictures are not visibly different.

Hyperlinks are 'hot spots' on a page that enable you to jump from one page to another, or one file to another. You can create hyperlinks from text or graphics. You can easily set up hyperlinks on the pages of your Web site.

(1) Select the text or picture

(3) Select the type of jump   (5) Click OK

(4) Define the hyperlink

Take note

When you are setting up a Web page, these new tools appear in the Standard toolbar. ☒ – insert hyperlink, and ☒ – preview Web site.

Links across the Internet

For the most part, the hyperlinks on this site will jump you from one page to another. You can, however, jump to another file, or Web site on the Internet. In this example, I set up a link to Butterworth Heinemann's home page, so you can find out about the other books that they publish.

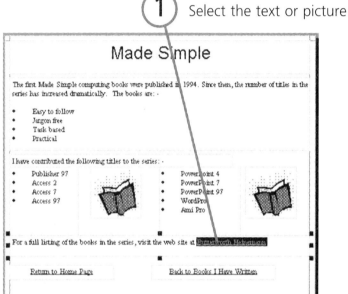

① Select the text or picture

③ Select the type of jump

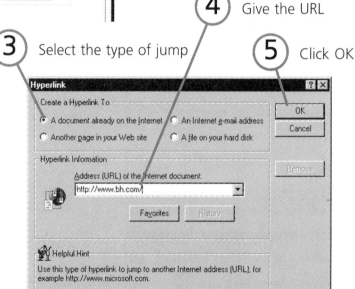

1 Select the text or picture to create a hyperlink from.

2 Click 🖳 the **Hyperlink** tool on the Standard toolbar.

3 Select the type of jump – **A document already on the Internet** in this case.

4 Specify where the hyperlink will take you – the URL of the page you want to jump to.

5 Click **OK**.

④ Give the URL

⑤ Click OK

Basic steps

1 Open the **File** menu.

2 Choose **Preview Web Site...**

Or

3 Click the **Preview Web Site** tool [icon].

❑ Your browser will be launched and the first page of your Web site will appear

4 When you've finished previewing your site, close your browser.

Take note

You can edit your publication in Publisher while previewing. Any changes you make are not reflected in the preview until you choose Preview Web Page... from the File menu again.

Previewing your Web site

You can check how your Web site is coming along at any time. You should certainly preview your Web site before you publish it, to check that the hyperlinks work as expected, and to make sure that the pages look okay on the screen. Your Web site publication file must be open.

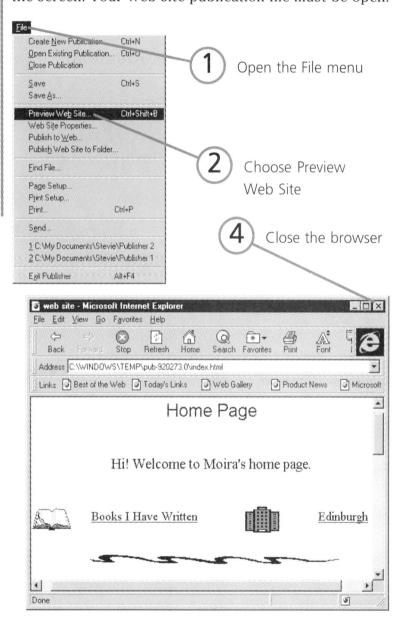

① Open the File menu

② Choose Preview Web Site

④ Close the browser

Colour schemes

In addition to using text and graphics to make your page look interesting, you could try adding an interesting background to your pages.

The simplest way to do this is to pick a complete colour scheme, but you can also define your background and text colours separately.

Basic steps

1 Open the **Format** menu.

2 Choose **Background and Text Colors...**

3 Select a colour scheme from the **Standard** tab.

Or

4 Go to the **Custom** tab and set up your own colour scheme.

5 Click **OK**.

❑ Preview your Web site to check that it looks okay.

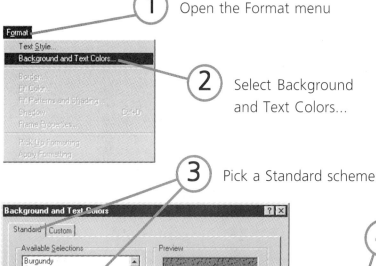

① Open the Format menu

② Select Background and Text Colors...

③ Pick a Standard scheme

④ Define your own scheme

⑤ Click OK

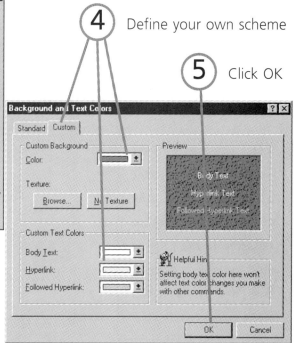

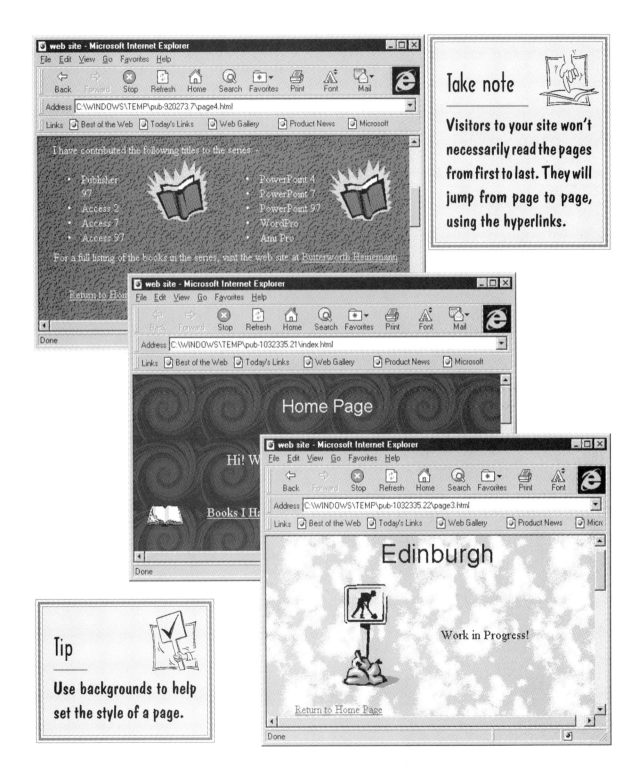

Take note

Visitors to your site won't necessarily read the pages from first to last. They will jump from page to page, using the hyperlinks.

Tip

Use backgrounds to help set the style of a page.

Design Checker

Before you go ahead and publish your Web site, you should use the Design Checker to help highlight any potential problems with it.

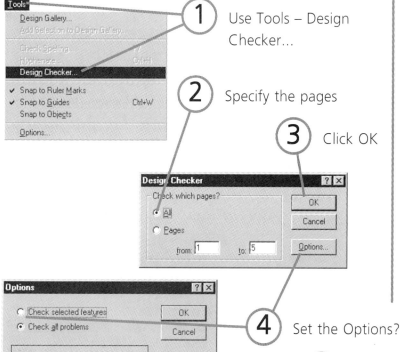

Use Tools – Design Checker...

Specify the pages

Click OK

Set the Options?

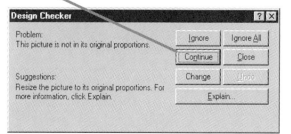

Deal with any problems

Check download time

Basic steps

1 Choose **Design Checker...** from the **Tools** menu.

2 Specify the pages you want to check.

3 Click **OK**.

4 If you want to select which features to check, click the **Options...** button and adjust as required.

5 Respond to any problems.

6 At the prompt, check that your pages will download quickly.

Preparing for publication

1 Open the **File** menu.

2 Choose **Publish Web Site to Folder...** this will generate the HTML and GIF files and save them.

3 Locate the folder into which you want to save your Web site.

4 Click **OK**.

5 If you have already saved a Web site into the folder that you have selected, a prompt will warn you – select **Yes** to replace the old Web site with the new, or **No** if you want to select a different folder.

Once you're happy with the way your pages look and work together, save the publication to a folder ready to publish on the Web. Publisher will automatically convert your pages to HTML files and GIF files as necessary.

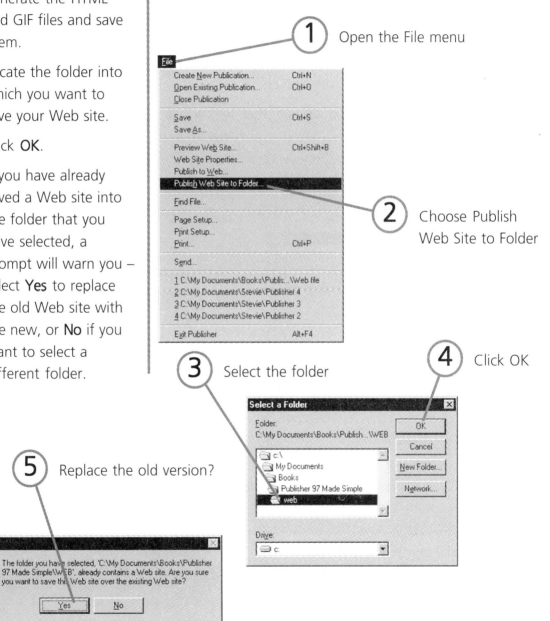

(1) Open the File menu

(2) Choose Publish Web Site to Folder

(3) Select the folder

(4) Click OK

(5) Replace the old version?

137

Publishing to the Web

Basic steps

1 Start **WS_FTP** and select, or create, a session to access your Web space.

2 Login using your normal User ID and Password.

3 Change the local folder to the one into which you saved your Web site (page 137).

4 Select the files you want to upload.

5 Select **Auto**.

To publish your Web site you must transfer the files in your Web folder from your own computer to a server that is provided by your service provider.

Your service provider's server will be switched on 24 hours a day so anyone who knows the URL of your Web site will be able to access it at any time. Most service providers will allocate some free space to you for your own Web pages – 10 Mb is fairly typical.

There are a number of ways to 'upload' files to a service providers' server – contact your service provider to find out how best to upload your files to their server. The instructions here illustrate how it is achieved using a piece of software called WS_FTP.

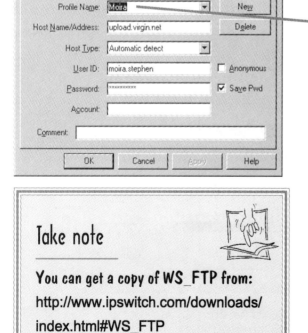

Run WS_FTP, selecting your Web space session

Login to your service provider

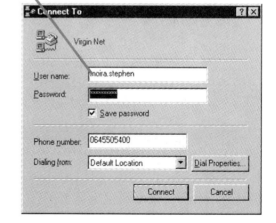

Take note

You can get a copy of WS_FTP from:
http://www.ipswitch.com/downloads/
index.html#WS_FTP

6 Click →.

7 Check that all your files appear on your service provider's computer.

8 Close the connection and exit WS_FTP.

9 Visit your Web site using your browser.

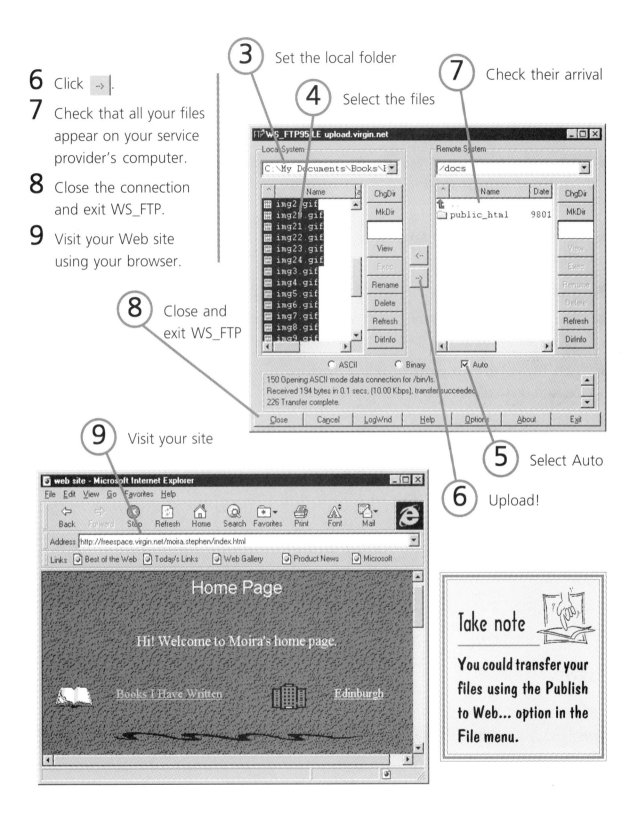

③ Set the local folder

④ Select the files

⑦ Check their arrival

⑧ Close and exit WS_FTP

⑨ Visit your site

⑤ Select Auto

⑥ Upload!

Take note

You could transfer your files using the Publish to Web... option in the File menu.

Summary

- **Get used to the jargon** – you'll find it everywhere.

- **Don't overdo the graphics** – your pages may take a long time to download.

- Too many graphics will result in your Web site taking up a lot of **storage space** – perhaps more than your service provider allows!

- Layout the pages using **text frames, tables** and **ClipArt**.

- **Hyperlinks** let you jump from one location to another.

- You can **preview your Web site** at any time to check how it's coming along.

- Add interest to your pages by giving them a **background colour**.

- Use the **Design Checker** to highlight any potential problems.

- When you **publish your Web site**, it is saved in a folder on your hard disk, as a set of Web-ready files.

- **To publish to the Web**, you must upload your Web site files to your service provider's computer.

Take note

The site set up here can be accessed on:

http://freespace.virgin.net/moira.stephen/index.html

Index

THE INTERNET for Windows 95 (Second edition), P.K.McBride, ISBN 0 7506 3846 X

Now in the second editions, this massively popular book has been expanded to 200 pages, and revised to cover all what's new and cool about the Internet. It explain the basics of using the Internet in clear, simple English. Don't be confused with all the hype and buzz about the Internet, buy this book and get quickly up to speed on the subject.

In 200 fact-filled visual pages this book will show you how to:

- set up hardware and software to get on-line
- find the best service provider for your needs
- send e-mail, read the news and down load files from around the world
- explore the World Wide Web via Windows 95

'*Anyone daunted by the technological jungle of the Internet and its associated jargon will appreciate the clear and concise content*' - Sound & Communication Systems International

SEARCHING THE INTERNET , P.K.McBride, ISBN 0 7506 3794 3

Searching the Internet Made Simple will show you how to:

- search the Internet for files and information
- download the software you need to get the best out of the Web
- encode and decode pictures, images and files from Newsgroups
- find people on the Internet

WINDOWS 95, P.K.McBride, ISBN 0 7506 2306 3

If you want to know how to:
- use Windows 95 on a new computer in the home or office
- upgrade to Windows 95 from Windows 3.1
- customise Windows 95 to suit your way of working
- manage your files and hardware efficiently and safely

then Windows 95 Made Simple is for you!

'..it manages to cover a surprisingly wide range of tasks one would want to know about at a simple unambitious level.' - The Daily Telegraph

OFFICE 97 for Windows, P. K. McBride, ISBN 0 7506 3798 6

This book shows you how to
- set up Office 97 to suit your way of working
- organise your time, tasks and contacts with Outlook
- copy and share data between Office applications
- add graphs and graphics to your documents
- bring the Internet on to your desktop

WORD 97 for Windows, Keith Brindley, ISBN 0 7506 3801 X

This book explains the basics of Word 97 for Windows in clear simple English, giving you just enough information to get you started. If all you want are the basics, and you don't want to be bothered with all the advanced stuff yet – then this is the book for you!

EXCEL 97 for Windows, Stephen Morris, ISBN 0 7506 3802 8

Powerful but user-friendly, and offering a high level of integration with the other programs in the Office suite, Excel has become established as the world's leading spreadsheet. This book will soon show you how to produce spreadsheets, charts, graphs, etc.

ACCESS 97 for Windows, Moira Stephen, ISBN 0 7506 3800 1

Do you need a database for business or personal use but are not sure how to set one up? This book will show you all you need to get started, and well on your way to building databases. If you:
- want to get the job done, quickly and efficiently
- need a self teaching approach
- want results fast

the Made Simple books are for you!

This book belongs to

....

Fairy stories

Compiled by Tig Thomas

Miles Kelly

First published in 2013 by Miles Kelly Publishing Ltd
Harding's Barn, Bardfield End Green, Thaxted, Essex, CM6 3PX, UK

Copyright © Miles Kelly Publishing Ltd 2013

This edition published 2019

4 6 8 10 9 7 5 3

Publishing Director *Belinda Gallagher*
Creative Director *Jo Cowan*
Editorial Director *Rosie Neave*
Senior Editor *Claire Philip*
Designers *Jo Cowan, Joe Jones, Michelle Foster, Venita Kidwai*
Image Manager *Liberty Newton*
Production *Elizabeth Collins, Jennifer Brunwin-Jones*
Reprographics *Stephan Davis, Callum Ratcliffe-Bingham*
Assets *Lorraine King*

ISBN 978-1-78617-880-0

Printed in China

British Library Cataloguing-in-Publication Data
A catalogue record for this book is available from the British Library

ACKNOWLEDGEMENTS
The publishers would like to thank the following artists
who have contributed to this book:
Beehive Illustration: Elena Selivanova
The Bright Agency: Zdenko Basic, Mélanie Florian,
Jasmine Foster, Morgan Huff (cover), Patricia Moffett, Katy Wright
Plum Pudding Illustration Agency: Christine Pym

Made with paper from a sustainable forest

www.mileskelly.net

CONTENTS

FAIRY HELPERS

MAGIC AND MISCHIEF

VISITORS TO FAIRYLAND

I WISH, I WISH

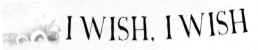

ABOUT THE AUTHORS

Learn more about some of the famous
authors behind these much-loved stories.

Louisa M Alcott
1832–1888

The second of four daughters, Louisa May
Alcott's most famous book, *Little Women*
(1868), was based on her own experiences. It
describes a few months in the lives of the four
March sisters while their father is away from
home as Army Chaplain in the U.S. Civil War.

Eva's Visit to Fairyland

William Elliot Griffis
1843–1928

Both a minister and an author, American
William Elliot Griffis spent several years
teaching in Japan. He wrote over fifty books,
including many collections of fairy stories.

The Touch of Iron • A Boy that Visited Fairyland

About the Authors

J M Barrie
1860–1937

James Matthew Barrie grew up in Scotland. After graduating from the University of Edinburgh in 1882 he worked as a journalist, and three years later moved to London where he became a novelist and playwright. He is best known as the creator of Peter Pan, the boy who refused to grow up. The first stories about Peter were published in *The Little White Bird* (1902).

Peter's Two Wishes

Joseph Jacobs
1854–1916

Born in Australia, Jacobs studied in England and Germany as a young man, researching Jewish history. Eventually he settled in America, and, inspired by the Brothers Grimm, went on to edit five collections of fairy tales.

Connla and the Fairy Maiden • Fairy Ointment

About the Authors

E Nesbit
1858–1924

Edith Nesbit used the initial 'E' rather than 'Edith' to disguise the fact that she was a woman. She wrote more than forty books for children, and created the idea of mixing real-life characters and settings with magical elements. Her best-known books include *The Railway Children*, *Five Children and It* and *The Treasure Seekers*.

A Midsummer Night's Dream • Melisande • Beautiful as the Day

Katharine Pyle
1863–1938

Born into a warm and creative Quaker household, Katharine Pyle worked all her life as a writer and illustrator, like her brother, Howard Pyle (1853–1911). She worked on over fifty books, mostly for children, and these include fairy tales and animal stories.

The Counterpane Fairy

About the Authors

Sophia Morrison
1859–1917

Born on the Isle of Man, Morrison worked to promote the region's literature and music. She was a renowned authority on Manx folklore and fairylore, and wrote, collected and edited stories to preserve the island's language and history.

Billy Beg, Tom Beg, and the Fairies

Kate Douglas Wiggin
1856–1923

Born in Philadelphia, USA, Kate started the first free kindergarten in San Francisco. With her sister, Nora Archibald Smith (1859–1934), she set up a training school for kindergarten teachers, raising money for the school by writing stories.

The Smith and the Fairies • Drak, the Fairy

ABOUT THE ARTISTS

Holly Clifton-Brown A freelance illustrator living in London, Holly's work combines traditional painting with contemporary techniques to create a unique and imaginative visual language. Her work has been published in books and magazines worldwide.
Cover

Zdenko Basic Award-winning Croatian artist Zdenko uses a mixture of photography and illustration in his pieces, and also works in costume and set design, puppetry and animation.
The Smith and the Fairies • The Laird and the Man of Peace
A Boy That Visited Fairyland • The Counterpane Fairy
Billy Beg, Tom Beg, and the Fairies • Iktomi and the Muskrat

Mélanie Florian French illustrator Mélanie has always had a passion for drawing and telling stories. Her favourite medium is watercolour, for the freshness, lightness and freedom it offers. Her work has been published all over the world.
Connla and the Fairy Maiden • Christmas Every Day
The Phantom Vessel

Jasmine Foster As a child, Jasmine was drawn to illustrations with a dreamlike quality, and she now strives to capture that same sense in her own work.
A French Puck • Murdoch's Rath • The Prince with the Nose
Under the Sun • Sweet-one-darling and the Dream-fairies
Mrs Bedonebyasyoudid and Mrs Doasyouwouldbedoneby
The Fairy Wife • Rosanella

About the Artists

Christine Pym Since studying illustration for children's publishing in Wales, Christine has illustrated books, greetings cards and advent calendars, all in watercolour and pencil crayon.
Melisande • Betty and the Wood Maiden • The Touch of Iron
The Fairy Fluffikins • Drak, the Fairy • Beautiful as the Day

Patricia Moffett After 15 years as a designer and art buyer, Patricia decided to rekindle her desire to be an illustrator. Her favourite subjects are classics, mythology, fantasy and horror – anything that involves figures in an atmospheric setting.
Eva's Visit to Fairyland • The Fairies and the Envious Neighbour
Peter's Two Wishes

Elena Selivanova A graduate of Moscow State University of Printing Arts, Elena has been working as an illustrator with major publishing houses for more than 20 years.
Farmer Mybrow and the Fairies • The Fairy Cure

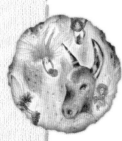

Katy Wright After growing up on a farm and studying illustration in Cornwall, UK, Katy packed up her belongings and moved to France. She can now be found sketching in her little studio in the heart of the beautiful city of Bordeaux.
A Midsummer Night's Dream

ENCHANTMENTS

A Midsummer Night's Dream

Retold by E Nesbit

*H*ermia and Lysander were lovers, but Hermia's father wished her to marry another man, named Demetrius.

Now, in Athens, where they lived, there was a wicked law, by which any girl who refused to marry according to her father's wishes, might be put to death. Hermia's father was so angry with her for refusing to do as he wished, that he actually brought

her before the duke of Athens to ask that she might be killed, if she still refused to obey him. The duke gave her four days to think about it, and, at the end of that time, if she still refused to marry Demetrius, she would have to die.

Lysander of course was nearly mad with grief, and the best thing to do seemed to him for Hermia to run away to his aunt's house at a place beyond the reach of the law, and there he would come to her and marry her. But before she started out, Hermia told her friend, Helena, what she was going to do.

Helena had been Demetrius' sweetheart long before his marriage with Hermia had been thought of, and being very silly, like all jealous people, she could not see that it was not poor Hermia's fault that Demetrius wished to marry her instead of his own lady, Helena. She knew that if she told Demetrius that Hermia was going, as she was, to the wood outside Athens, he would follow her, 'and I can follow him, and at least I shall see him,' she said to herself. So she went to him, and betrayed her friend's secret.

Now this wood where Lysander was to meet Hermia, and where the other two had decided to follow them, was full of fairies, as most woods are, if one only had the eyes to see them, and in this wood on this night were the king and queen of the fairies, Oberon and Titania. Now fairies are very wise people, but now and then they can be quite as foolish as mortal folk. Oberon and Titania, who might have been as happy as the days were long, had thrown away all their joy in a foolish quarrel. They never met without saying disagreeable things to each other, and scolded each other so dreadfully that all their little fairy followers, for fear, would creep into acorn cups and hide there.

So, instead of keeping one happy court and dancing all night through in the moonlight as is the usual fairy manner, the king with his attendants wandered through one part of the wood, while the

queen with hers kept state in another. And the cause
of all this trouble was a little Indian boy whom
Titania had taken to be one of her followers.
Oberon wanted the child to follow him and be one
of his fairy knights, but the queen would not give
him up.

On this night, in a mossy moonlit glade, the king
and queen of the fairies met.

"Ill met by moonlight, proud Titania," remarked
the king.

"What! Jealous, Oberon?" answered the queen.
"Why must you spoil everything with your
quarrelling? Come, fairies, let us leave him. I am not
friends with him now."

"It rests with you to make up the quarrel," said
the king. "Give me that little Indian boy, and I will
again be your humble servant and suitor."

"Please, set your mind at rest," said the queen,
coldly. "Your whole fairy kingdom buys not that
boy from me."

19

And she and her train rode off down the moonbeams.

"Well, go your ways," Oberon called after her, angrily. "But I will be even with you before you leave this wood."

Then Oberon called his favourite fairy, Puck. Puck was the spirit of mischief. He used to slip into the dairies and take the cream away, and get into the churn so that the butter would not come, and turn the beer sour, and lead people out of their way on dark nights and then laugh at them, and tumble people's stools from under them when they were going to sit down, and upset their hot ale over their chins when they were going to drink.

"Now," said Oberon to this little sprite, "fetch me the flower called Love-in-idleness. The juice of that little purple flower laid on the eyes of those who sleep will make them, when they wake, love the first thing they see. I will put some of the juice of that flower on my Titania's eyes, and when she wakes she

20

will love the very first thing she sees, were it lion, bear, or wolf, or bull, or meddling monkey, or a busy ape."

While Puck was gone, Demetrius passed through the glade. He was followed by poor Helena, and still she told him how she loved him and reminded him of all his promises, and still he told her that he did not and could not love her, and that his promises were nothing. Oberon was sorry for poor Helena, and when Puck returned with the flower, he bade him follow Demetrius and put some of the juice on his eyes, so that he might love Helena when he woke and looked on her, as much as she loved him.

So Puck set off, and wandering through the wood found, not Demetrius, but Lysander and Hermia, sleeping peacefully. And so it was on Lysander's eyes that Puck put the juice. Unfortunately, when Lysander woke, he saw not his own Hermia, but Helena, who was walking

through the wood looking for the cruel Demetrius.
Directly he saw her, he loved her, and left his own
lady, under the spell of the purple flower.

When Hermia woke she found Lysander gone,
and wandered about the wood trying to find him.
Puck went back and told Oberon what he had
done, and Oberon soon found out the mistake, and
set about looking for Demetrius. Having found
him, he put some of the juice on his eyes. The
first thing Demetrius saw when he woke was
also Helena. So now Demetrius and
Lysander were both following
her through the wood,

and it was Hermia's turn to follow her lover as Helena had done before. The end of it was that Hermia and Helena began to quarrel, and Demetrius and Lysander went off to fight. Oberon was very sorry to see his kind scheme turn out so

badly. So he said to Puck, "These two young men are going to fight. You must overhang the night with drooping fog, and lead them so astray, so that one will never find the other. When they are tired, they will fall asleep. Then drop this other herb on Lysander's eyes. It will give him his old sight and his old love. Then each man will have the lady who loves him, and they will all think that this has been only a midsummer night's dream."

So Puck did as he was told, and when the two had fallen asleep without meeting each other, Puck poured the juice on Lysander's eyes, and said:

"When thou wakest,
Thou takest
True delight
In the sight
Of thy former lady's eye:
Jack shall have Jill;
Nought shall go ill."

Meanwhile Oberon found Titania asleep on a bank where grew wild thyme, oxlips, and violets, and woodbine, musk-roses and eglantine. There Titania always slept a part of the night, wrapped in the enameled skin of a snake. Oberon stooped over her and laid the juice on her eyes, saying:

"What thou seest when thou wake,
Do it for thy true love take."

Now, it happened that when Titania woke the first thing she saw was a stupid clown, one of a party of players who had come out into the wood to rehearse their play. This clown had met with Puck, who had clapped an ass's head on his shoulders so that it looked as if it grew there. When Titania woke and saw this monster, she said, "What angel is this? Are you as wise as you are beautiful?"

"If I am wise enough to find my way out of this wood, that's enough for me," said the foolish clown.

ENCHANTMENTS

"Do not desire to go out of the wood," said Titania. The spell of the love-juice was on her, and to her the clown seemed the most beautiful creature on the earth. "I love you," she went on. "Come with me, and I will give you fairies to attend on you."

So she called four fairies, whose names were Peaseblossom, Cobweb, Moth, and Mustardseed.

"You must attend this gentleman," said the queen. "Feed him with apricots and dewberries, purple grapes, green figs, and mulberries. Steal honey-bags for him from the bumble-bees, and with the wings of painted butterflies fan the moonbeams from his sleeping eyes."

"I will," said one of the fairies, and all the others said, "I will."

"Now, sit down with me," said the queen to the clown, "and let me stroke your dear cheeks, and stick musk-roses in your smooth, sleek head, and kiss your fair large ears, my gentle joy."

"Where's Peaseblossom?" asked the clown with

27

the ass's head. He did not care much about the queen's affection, but he was very proud of having fairies to wait on him.

"Ready," said Peaseblossom.

"Scratch my head, Peaseblossom," said the clown. "Where's Cobweb?"

"Ready," said Cobweb.

"Kill me," said the clown, "the red bumble-bee on the top of the thistle yonder, and bring me the honey-bag. Where's Mustardseed?"

"Ready," said Mustardseed.

"Oh, I want nothing," said the clown. "Only just help Cobweb to scratch. I must go to the barber's, for methinks I am marvellous hairy about the face."

"Would you like anything to eat?" asked the fairy queen, kindly.

"I should like some good dry oats," said the clown – for his donkey's head made him desire donkey's food – "and some hay to follow."

"Shall some of my fairies fetch you new nuts

from the squirrel's house?" asked the queen.

"I'd rather have a handful or two of good dried peas," said the clown. "But please don't let any of your people disturb me – I am going to sleep."

Then said the beautiful queen, "And I will wind thee in my arms."

And so when Oberon came along he found his queen lavishing kisses and endearments on a clown with a donkey's head.

And before he released her from the enchantment, he persuaded her to give him the little Indian boy he so much desired to have. Then he took pity on her, and threw some juice of the disenchanting flower on her pretty eyes, and then in a moment she saw plainly the donkey-headed clown she had been loving, and knew how foolish she had been.

Oberon took off the ass's head from the clown, and left him to finish his sleep with his own silly head lying on the thyme and violets.

Thus all was made plain and straight again.

ENCHANTMENTS

Oberon and Titania loved each other more than ever. Demetrius thought of no one but Helena, and Helena had never had any thought of anyone but Demetrius.

As for Hermia and Lysander, they were as loving a couple as you could meet in a day's march, even through a fairy wood.

So the four mortal lovers went back to Athens and were married, and the fairy king and queen live happily together in that very wood at this very day.

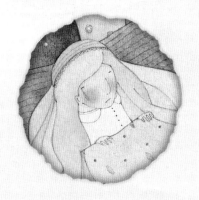

Melisande

By E Nesbit

When the Princess Melisande was born, her mother, the queen, wished to have a christening party, but the king put his foot down and said he would not have it.

"I've seen too much trouble come of christening parties," said he. "However carefully you keep your visiting-book, some fairy is sure to get left out, and you know what that leads to. We'll have no nonsense about it. We won't ask a single fairy, then none of them can be offended."

"Unless they all are," said the queen.

And that was exactly what happened. When the king and the queen and the baby got back from the christening the great throne room was crammed with fairies of all ages and of all degrees of beauty and ugliness – good fairies and bad fairies, flower fairies and moon fairies, fairies like spiders and fairies like butterflies – and as the queen opened the door they all cried, with one voice, "Why didn't you ask me to your christening party?"

"I'm very sorry," said the poor queen, but Malevola pushed forward and said, "Hold your tongue," most rudely.

Malevola is the oldest, as well as the most wicked, of the fairies. "Don't begin to make excuses," she said, shaking her finger at the queen. "You know well enough what happens if a fairy is left out of a christening party. We are all going to give our christening presents now. I shall begin. The princess shall be bald."

Melisande

The queen nearly fainted as Malevola drew back.
But the king stepped forward too.

"Oh no you don't!" said he, raising his voice.
"How can you all be so very unfairylike? Have none
of you ever been to school? Have none of you

studied the traditions of your own race?"

"How dare you?" cried a fairy in a bonnet. "It is my turn, and I say the princess shall be—"

The king actually put his hand over her mouth.

"Look here," he said, "I won't have it. A fairy who breaks the rules of fairy history goes out – you know she does – like the flame of a candle. And all tradition shows that only one bad fairy is ever forgotten at a christening party and the good ones are always invited. So either this is not a christening party, or else you were all invited except one, and, by her own showing, that was Malevola. Try it, if you don't believe me. Give your nasty gifts to my innocent child – but as sure as you do, out you go, like a candle flame. Now, then, will you risk it?"

No one answered, but one by one all the fairies said goodbye and thanked the queen for the delightful afternoon they had spent with her.

When the very last fairy was gone the queen ran to look at the baby. She tore off its lace cap and

burst into tears. For all the baby's downy golden hair came off with the cap, and the Princess Melisande was as bald as an egg.

"Don't cry, my love," said the king. "I have a wish lying by, which my fairy godmother gave me for a wedding present, but since then I've had nothing to wish for!"

"Thank you, dear," said the queen, smiling through her tears.

"I'll keep the wish till the baby grows up," the king went on. "And then I'll give it to her and if she likes to wish for hair, she can."

"Oh, won't you wish for it now?" said the queen.

"No, dearest. She may want something else more when she grows up. And besides, her hair may grow by itself."

But it never did. Princess Melisande grew up as beautiful as the sun and as good as gold, but never a hair grew on that little head of hers. The queen sewed her little caps of green silk, and the princess's

pink and white face looked out of these like a flower peeping out of its bud. And every day as she grew older she grew dearer, and as she grew dearer she grew better, and as she grew more good she grew more beautiful.

Now, when she was grown up the queen said to the king, "My love, our dear daughter is old enough to know now what she wants. I think it is time you let her have the wish."

So the king unlocked his gold safe with the seven diamond-handled keys that hung at his girdle, and took out the wish and gave it to his daughter.

Then the queen said, "Dearest, for my sake, wish what I tell you."

"Why, of course I will," said Melisande. The queen whispered in her ear, and Melisande nodded. Then she said, aloud, "I wish I had golden hair that was a yard long, and that it would grow an inch every day, and grow twice as fast every time it was cut, and—"

"Stop!" cried the king. But the wish went off, and the next moment the princess stood smiling at him through a shower of golden hair.

"Oh, how lovely," said the queen. "What a pity you interrupted her, dear. What's the matter?"

"You'll know soon enough," said the king. "Come, let's be happy while we may. Give me a kiss, little Melisande, and then go to nurse and ask her to teach you how to comb your hair."

"I know how," said Melisande, "I've often combed mother's."

"Your mother has beautiful hair," said the king, "but I fancy you will find your own a little less easy to manage."

And, indeed, it proved to be just as the king said. The princess's hair began by being a yard long, and it grew another inch every night. If you know anything at all about the simplest sums you will see that in about five weeks her hair was about two yards long. This is a very inconvenient length. It

ENCHANTMENTS

trails on the floor and sweeps up all the dust. And the princess's hair was growing an inch every night. When it was three yards long the princess could not bear it any longer – it was so heavy and so hot – so she cut it all off, and then for a few hours she was comfortable. But the hair went on growing, and now it grew twice as fast as before,

Melisande

so that in thirty-six days it was as long as ever. The poor princess cried with tiredness.

When she couldn't bear it anymore she cut her hair and was comfortable for a very little time. For the hair now grew four times as fast as at first, and in eighteen days it was as long as before, and she had to have it cut and so on, growing twice as fast after each cutting, till the princess would go to bed at night with her hair clipped short, and wake up in the morning with yards and yards and yards of golden hair flowing all about the room, so that she could not move without pulling her own hair, and nurse had to come and cut the hair off before she could get out of bed.

"I wish I was bald again," sighed poor Melisande. And still the hair grew and grew. Then the king said, "I shall write to my fairy godmother and see if something cannot be done."

So he wrote and sent the letter by a skylark, and
by return of bird came this answer:

> Why not advertise
> for a prince?
> Offer the usual reward.

So the king sent out his heralds all over the world
to proclaim that any respectable prince with proper
references should marry the Princess Melisande if
he could stop her hair growing.

Then from far and near came trains of princes
anxious to try their luck, and they brought all sorts
of nasty things with them in bottles and round
wooden boxes. The princess tried all the remedies,
but she did not like any of them, and she did not
like any of the princes, so in her heart she was rather
glad that none of them made the least difference to
her hair.

Melisande

The princess had to sleep in the throne room now, for no other room was big enough to hold her and her hair. When she woke in the morning the long high room would be quite full of her golden hair, packed tight and thick like wool in a barn. And every evening when her hair had been cut close to her head again, she would sit in her green silk gown at the window of the tallest tower and cry, and kiss the green caps she used to wear, and wish herself bald again. It was as she sat crying there on Midsummer Eve that she first saw Prince Florizel.

He was walking in the garden in the moonlight, and he looked up and she looked down, and for the first time Melisande, looking on a prince, wished that he might have the power to stop her hair from growing. As for the prince, he wished many things, and the first was granted him. For he said, "You are Melisande?"

"And you are Florizel?"

"There are many roses round your window," said

41

he to her, "and none down here."

She threw him one of three white roses she held in her hand.

Then he said, "If I can do what your father asks, will you marry me?"

"My father has promised that I shall," said Melisande, playing with the white roses in her hand.

"Dear princess," said Prince Florizel, "your father's promise is nothing to me. I want yours. Will you give it to me?"

"Yes," said she, and gave him the second rose.

"I want your hand."

"Yes," she said.

"And your heart with it."

"Yes," said the princess, and she threw down the third rose.

"Then," said he, "stay by your window and I will stay down here in the garden and watch. And when your hair has grown to the filling of your room, call to me and then do as I tell you."

"I will," said the princess.

So at dewy sunrise the prince, lying on the turf beside the sundial, heard her voice. "Florizel! Florizel! My hair has grown so long that it is pushing me out of the window."

"Get out on to the windowsill," said he, "and twist your hair three times round the great iron hook that is there."

And she did.

43

Then the prince climbed up the rose bush with his naked sword in his teeth, and he took the princess's hair in his hand about a yard from her head and said, "Jump!"

The princess jumped, and screamed, for there she was hanging from the hook by a yard and a half of her bright hair. The prince tightened his grasp of the hair and drew his sword across it.

Then he let her down gently by her hair till her feet were on the grass, and jumped down after her.

They stayed talking in the garden till all the shadows had crept under their proper trees and the sundial said it was breakfast time.

Then they went in to breakfast, and all the court crowded round to wonder and admire. For the princess's hair had not grown.

"How did you do it?" asked the king, shaking Florizel warmly by the hand.

"The simplest thing in the world," said Florizel, modestly. "You have always cut the hair off the

princess. I just cut the princess off the hair."

"You are a young man of sound judgment," said the king, embracing him.

The princess kissed her prince a hundred times, and the very next day they were married. Everyone remarked on the beauty of the bride, and it was noticed that her hair was quite short – only five feet five and a quarter inches long – just down to her pretty ankles.

Connla and the Fairy Maiden

By Joseph Jacobs

Connla of the Fiery Hair was son of Conn of the Hundred Fights. One day as he stood by the side of his father on the height of Usna, he saw a maiden clad in strange attire coming towards him.

"Whence comest thou, maiden?" said Connla.

"I come from the Plains of the Ever Living," she said, "there where there is neither death nor sin. There we keep holiday always, nor need we help

46

from any in our joy. And in all our pleasure we have no strife. And because we have our homes in the round green hills, men call us the Hill Folk."

The king and all with him wondered much to hear a voice when they saw no one. For save Connla alone, none saw the Fairy Maiden.

"To whom art thou talking, my son?" said Conn the king.

Then the maiden answered, "Connla speaks to a fair maid, whom neither death nor old age awaits. I love Connla, and now I call him away to the Plain of Pleasure, Moy Mell, where Boadag is king, nor has there been complaint or sorrow in that land since he has held the kingship. Oh, come with me, Connla of the Fiery Hair. A fairy crown awaits thee to grace thy comely face and royal form. Come, and never shall thy comeliness fade, nor thy youth, till the last awful day of judgment."

The king in fear at what the maiden said, which he heard though he could not see her, called aloud

to his druid, Coran by name.

"Oh, Coran of the many spells," he said, "and of the cunning magic, I call upon thy aid. A task is upon me too great for all my skill and wit, greater than any laid upon me since I seized the kingship. A maiden unseen has met us, and by her power would take from me my dear, my comely son. If thou help not, he will be taken from thy king by woman's wiles and witchery."

Then Coran the druid stood forth and chanted his spells towards the spot where the maiden's voice had been heard. And none heard her voice again, nor could Connla see her longer. Only as she vanished before the druid's mighty spell, she threw an apple to Connla.

For a whole month from that day Connla would take nothing, either to eat or to drink, save only from that apple. But as he ate it grew again and always kept whole. And all the while there grew within him a mighty yearning and longing after

the maiden he had seen.

But when the last day of the month of waiting
came, Connla stood once more by the side of his
father on the Plain of Arcomin, and again he saw
the maiden come towards him, and again she spoke
to him.

"'Tis a glorious place that Connla holds among
short-lived mortals awaiting the day of death. But
now the folk of life beg and bid thee come with me
to Moy Mell, the Plain of Pleasure, for they have
learnt to know thee, seeing thee in thy home among
thy dear ones."

When the king heard the maiden's voice he
called out to his men, "Summon swift my druid, for
I see the maiden has once more this day the power
of speech."

Then the maiden addressed the king. "Oh,
mighty Conn, fighter of a hundred fights, Coran
the druid's power is little loved. It has no honour in
the mighty land, peopled with so many of the

upright. When the Law will come, it will do away with the druid's many magic spells that come from the lips of the false black demon."

Then the king observed that since the fairy maiden came Connla his son spoke to none that spoke to him. So Conn of the hundred fights said to him, "Is it to thy mind what the unseen woman says, my son?"

"'Tis hard upon me," said Connla. "I love my own folk above all things, but yet a longing seizes me for the maiden."

When the maiden heard Connla's reply, she said to him, "The ocean is not so strong as the waves of thy longing. Come with me in my curragh – the gleaming, crystal canoe. Soon we can reach Boadag's realm. I see the bright sun has started to sink, yet far as it is, we can reach it before dark. There is, too, another land worthy of thy journey, a land joyous to all that seek it. Only wives and maidens dwell there. If thou wilt, we can seek it and

live there together in joy."

When the maiden ceased to speak, Connla of the Fiery Hair sprang into the the gleaming crystal canoe. And then they all, king and court, saw it glide away over the bright sea towards the setting sun. Away and away, till eye could see it no longer, and Connla and the fairy maiden went their way on the sea, and were no more seen.

Rosanella

By Comte de Caylus

*Inconstant, fickle, faithless – these are all words to describe
someone who cannot stay true to one love, but is always finding
a new person to fall in love with. But what happens when an
incurably fickle prince meets a princess no one can resist?*

Everybody knows that though the fairies live
hundreds of years they do sometimes die, and
especially as they pass one day in every week under
the form of some animal, when of course they are
liable to accident. It was in this way that death once
overtook the queen of the fairies, and it became

necessary to elect a new sovereign. After much discussion, it appeared that the choice lay between two fairies, one called Surcantine and the other Paridamie, and their claims were so equal that it was impossible to choose one over the other.

In the end, the fairy court decided that whichever of the two could show to the world the greatest wonder should be queen, but it was to be a special kind of wonder, no moving of mountains or any such common fairy tricks would do. Surcantine, therefore, decided that she would bring up a prince whom nothing could make faithful and constant to one love. While Paridamie decided to display to admiring mortals a princess so charming that no one could see her without falling in love with her. They were allowed to take their own time, and meanwhile the four oldest fairies were to attend to the affairs of the kingdom.

Now Paridamie had for a long time been very friendly with King Bardondon, who was a most

noble monarch, and whose court was the model of
what a court should be. His queen, Balanice, was
also charming – indeed it is rare to find a husband
and wife so perfectly of one mind
about everything.

They had one little
daughter, whom they had
named 'Rosanella', because
she had a pink rose
birthmark upon her throat.

On the night following the
assembly of fairies, Queen Balanice woke up with a
shriek, and when her maids of honour ran to see
what was the matter, they found she had had a
frightful dream.

"I thought," said she, "that my little daughter had
changed into a bouquet of roses, and that as I held it
in my hand a bird swooped down suddenly and
snatched it from me and carried it away."

The queen would not be comforted, and sent her

maids to see that all was well with the princess. So they ran, but they found the cradle empty. Though they sought high and low, not a trace of Rosanella could they find. The queen was beside herself with grief, and so, indeed, was the king, only being a man he did not say quite so much about his feelings.

He presently suggested to Balanice that they should spend a few days at one of their palaces in the country, and she agreed, since in her sorrow she no longer enjoyed the pleasures of town. One summer evening, as they sat together on a shady lawn shaped like a star, from which radiated twelve splendid avenues of trees, the queen looked round and saw a charming peasant girl approaching by each path, and that each girl carried something in a basket with the greatest care. As each girl drew near she laid her basket at Balanice's feet, saying, "Charming queen, may this be some slight comfort to you in your unhappiness!"

The queen hastily opened the baskets, and found

in each a lovely baby girl, about the same age as the
little princess for whom she sorrowed so deeply. At
first the sight of them renewed her grief, but
presently their charms so gained upon her that she
forgot her sadness in looking after the babies,
providing them with maids, cradle-rockers, and
ladies-in-waiting, and in sending hither and thither
for swings and dolls and tops.

Oddly enough, every baby had upon its throat a
tiny pink rose. The queen found it so difficult to
decide on suitable names for all of them, that until
she could settle the matter she chose a special colour
for each girl, pink for one, purple for another, so
that when they were all together they looked like
nothing so much as a nosegay of flowers. As they
grew older it became clear that though they were all
remarkably intelligent, they differed one from
another in character, so much so that they gradually
ceased to be known as 'Ruby,' or 'Primrose,' or
whatever might have been their colour, and the

queen instead would say, "Where is my Sweet?" or "my Kind," or "my Happy."

Of course, with all these charms they had lovers by the dozen. Not only in their own court, but princes from afar, who were constantly arriving, attracted by the reports which were spread abroad. But these lovely girls, the first maids of honour, were as sensible as they were beautiful, and favoured no one.

But let us return to Surcantine. She had fixed upon the son of a king who was cousin to Bardondon, to bring up as her fickle prince. She had before, at his christening, given him all the graces of mind and body that a prince could possibly require, but now she redoubled her efforts, and spared no pains in adding every imaginable charm and fascination. So that whether he happened to be cross or amiable, splendidly or simply attired, serious or frivolous, he was always perfectly irresistible! In truth, he was a charming young fellow, since the fairy had given him the best heart in the world as well as the best head, and had left nothing to be desired except faithfulness. For it cannot be denied that Prince Mirliflor was a desperate flirt, and as fickle as the wind.

By the time he arrived at his eighteenth birthday there was not a heart left for him to conquer in his father's kingdom – they were all his own, and he was tired of everyone! Things were in this state when he was invited to visit the court of his father's cousin, King Bardondon.

Imagine his feelings when he arrived and was presented at once to twelve of the loveliest creatures in the world, and they all liked him as much as he liked each one of them, so that things came to such a pass that he was never happy a single instant without them. For could he not whisper soft speeches to Sweet, and laugh with Joy, while he looked at Beauty? And in his more serious moments what could be pleasanter than to talk to

Thoughtful upon some shady lawn, while he held the hand of Loving in his own, and all the others lingered near?

For the first time in his life he really loved, though the object of his devotion was not one person, but twelve, to whom he was equally attached, and even Surcantine was deceived into thinking that this was indeed the height of inconstancy. But Paridamie said not a word.

One day the queen gave a large garden party, and just as the guests were all assembled, and Prince Mirliflor was as usual dividing his attentions between the twelve beauties, a humming of bees was heard. The Rose-maidens, fearing their stings, uttered little shrieks, and fled to a distance from the rest of the company. Immediately, to the horror of all who were looking on, the bees pursued them, and, growing suddenly to an enormous size, pounced each upon a maiden and carried her off into the air, and in an instant they were all lost to view. This amazing occurrence plunged the whole court into the deepest sadness, and Prince Mirliflor, after giving way to the most violent grief at first, fell gradually into a state of such deep dejection that it was feared if nothing could rouse him he would certainly die.

Surcantine came in all haste to see what she could do for her darling, but he rejected with scorn all the portraits of lovely princesses which she offered him for his collection. In short, it was evident that he was in a bad way, and the fairy was at her wits' end.

One day, as he wandered about absorbed in melancholy reflections, he heard sudden shouts and exclamations of amazement, and if he had taken the trouble to look up he could not have helped being as astonished as everyone else, for through the air a chariot of crystal was slowly approaching, which glittered in the sunshine.

Six lovely maidens with shining wings drew it by

ENCHANTMENTS

rose-coloured ribbons,
while others, equally beautiful, were holding long
garlands of roses crossed above it, so as to form a
canopy. In it sat the Fairy Paridamie, and by her side
a princess whose beauty dazzled all who saw her.

Rosanella

At the foot of the great
staircase they descended, and
proceeded to the queen's apartments, though
everyone had run together to see this marvel, till it
was difficult to make a way through the crowd, and
exclamations of wonder rose on all sides at the
loveliness of the strange princess. "Great queen,"
said Paridamie, "permit me to restore to you your
daughter Rosanella, whom I stole out of her cradle."

After the first transports of joy were over the
queen said to Paridamie, "But my twelve lovely
ones, are they lost to me for ever? Shall I never see
them again?"

But Paridamie only said, "Very soon you will
cease to miss them!" in a tone that evidently meant
'Don't ask me any more questions.' Then mounting

again into her chariot she swiftly disappeared.

The news of his beautiful cousin's arrival was soon carried to the prince, but he had hardly the heart to go and see her. However, it became absolutely necessary that he should pay his respects, and he had scarcely been five minutes in her presence before it seemed to him that she combined in her own charming person all the gifts and graces which had so attracted him in the twelve Rose-maidens whose loss he had so truly mourned.

And after all it is really more satisfactory to be in love with one person at a time. So it came to pass that before he knew where he was he was entreating his lovely cousin to marry him, and the moment the words had left his lips, Paridamie appeared, smiling and triumphant, in the chariot of the queen of the fairies, for by that time they had all heard of her success, and declared her to have earned the kingdom. She had to give a full account of how she had stolen Rosanella from her cradle, and divided

her character into twelve parts, that each might charm Prince Mirliflor, and when once more united might cure him of his inconstancy once and for all.

And as one more proof of the fascination of the whole Rosanella, I may tell you that even the defeated Surcantine sent her a wedding gift, and was present at the ceremony which took place as soon as the guests could arrive. Prince Mirliflor was faithful only to his adored Rosanella for the rest of his life. And indeed who would not have been in his place?

As for Rosanella, she loved him as much as all the twelve beauties put together, so they reigned in peace and happiness to the end of their long lives.

The Smith and the Fairies

By Kate Douglas Wiggin

It was a superstition in Celtic lands that fairies stole babies and left changelings (fairy babies) in their place. In this story the fairies are called by their Gaelic name of Daione Sith, *and the word for a changeling is* Sibhreach. *A* dirk *is a short knife.*

Years ago there lived in Crossbrig a smith of the name of MacEachern. This man had an only child, a boy of about thirteen or fourteen years of age, cheerful, strong and healthy. All of a sudden he fell ill, took to his bed and moped whole days away.

The Smith and the Fairies

No one could tell what was the matter with him,
and the boy himself could not, or would not, tell
how he felt. He was wasting away fast – getting
thin, old, and yellow – and his father and all his
friends were afraid that he would die.

After the boy had been lying in this condition for
a long time, getting neither better nor worse (but
with an extraordinary appetite) an old man, well
known for his knowledge of out-of-the-way things,
walked into the smith's workshop. The smith told
him the occurrence which had clouded his life.

The old man looked grave as he listened, and
after sitting a long time pondering over all he had
heard, gave his opinion, "It is not your son you have
got. The boy has been carried away by the Daione
Sith, and they have left a Sibhreach in his place."

"Alas! And what then am I to do?" said the
smith. "How am I ever to see my own son again?"

"I will tell you how," answered the old man. "But,
first, to make sure that it is not your own son you

67

have got, take as many empty eggshells as you can get, go into his room, spread them out carefully before his sight, then proceed to draw water with them, carrying them two and two in your hands as if they were a great weight, and arrange them when full, around the fire."

The smith proceeded to carry out all his instructions. He had not been long at work before there arose from the bed a loud shout of laughter, and the voice of the seemingly sick boy exclaimed, "I am eight hundred years of age, and I have never seen the like of that before." The smith returned and told the old man.

"Well, now," said the old man to him, "did I not tell you that it was not your son you had – your son is in Borracheill in a digh there (that is, a round green hill frequented by fairies). Get rid as soon as possible of this intruder, and I think I may promise you your son. You must light a very large and bright fire before the bed on which this stranger is lying.

The Smith and the Fairies

He will ask you, 'What is the use of such a fire as that?' Answer him at once, 'You will see that presently!' and then seize him, and throw him into the middle of it. If it is your own son you have got, he will call out to you to save him, but if not, the thing will fly through the roof."

The smith again followed the old man's advice. He kindled a large fire, answered the question put to him as he had been directed to do, and seizing the child flung him in without hesitation. The Sibhreach gave an awful yell, and sprang through the roof, where a hole had been left to let the smoke out.

The old man told the smith that on a certain night the green round hill, where the fairies kept the boy, would be open. On that date the smith, having provided himself with a Bible and a dirk, was to proceed to the hill. He would hear singing and dancing, and much merriment going on, but he was to advance boldly – the Bible he carried would be a safeguard to him against danger from the fairies.

ENCHANTMENTS

On entering the hill he was to stick the dirk in the threshold, to prevent the hill from closing upon him. "And then," said the old man, "on entering you will see a spacious apartment before you, and there, standing far within, working at a forge, you will also see your son. When you are questioned, say you come to seek him, and will not go without him."

Not long after this, the time came round, and the smith sallied forth, prepared as instructed. Sure enough as he approached the hill, there was a light where light was seldom seen before. Soon after, a sound of piping, dancing, and joyous merriment reached the anxious father on the night wind.

Overcoming every impulse of fear, the smith approached the threshold steadily, stuck the dirk into it as directed, and entered. Protected by the Bible he carried on his breast, the fairies could not touch him, but they asked him, with a good deal of displeasure, what he wanted there. He answered, "I want my son, whom I see down there, and I will not go without him."

The fairies, incensed, seized the smith and his son, and throwing them out of the hill, flung the dirk after them, and in an instant all was dark.

For a year and a day the boy never did a turn of work, and hardly ever spoke a word. At last one day, sitting by his father and watching him finishing a sword, he suddenly exclaimed, "That is not the way to do it." And taking the tools from his father's hands he set to work himself in his place, and soon fashioned a sword, the like of which was never seen

in the country before.

From that day the young man wrought
constantly with his father, and became the
inventor of a peculiarly fine and well-
tempered weapon, the making of which kept
the two smiths, father and son, in constant
employment, spread their fame far and wide,
and gave them the means to live content
with all the world and very happily with
each other.

The Prince
with the Nose

By Dinah Maria Mulock Craik

*T*here was once a king who was passionately in love with a beautiful princess, but she could not marry because a magician had enchanted her. The king went to a good fairy to inquire what he should do. Said the fairy, after receiving him graciously, "Sir, I will tell you a secret. The princess will be obliged to marry any person nimble enough to walk upon her cat's tail."

'That will not be very difficult,' thought the king to himself, and departed, resolving to trample the cat's tail to pieces rather than not succeed in walking upon it. He went immediately to the palace of his fair mistress and the cat. The animal came in front of him, and the king lifted up his foot, thinking nothing would be so easy as to tread on the tail, but he found himself mistaken. Minon – that was the creature's name – twisted itself round so sharply that the king only hurt his own foot by stamping on the floor.

For eight days he pursued the cat everywhere – up and down the palace from morning till night. But with no success – the tail seemed made of quicksilver, so very lively was it. At last the king had the good fortune to catch Minon sleeping, and – *tramp, tramp* – he trod on the tail with all his force.

Minon woke up, and immediately changed from a cat into a large, fierce-looking man, who regarded the king with flashing eyes.

The Prince with the Nose

"You have broken the enchantment in which I held the princess, but I will be revenged. You shall have a son with a nose as long as this," – he made in the air a curve of half a foot – "yet he shall believe it is just like all other noses, and shall be always unfortunate till he has found out it is not. And if you ever tell anybody of this threat, you shall die on the spot." So saying, the magician disappeared.

The king, who was at first terrified, soon began to laugh at this adventure. 'My son might have a worse misfortune than too long a nose,' thought he. 'I will find the princess, and marry her at once.'

He did so, but he only lived a few months after, and died before his little son was born, so that nobody knew anything about the secret of the nose.

The little prince was so much wished for that when he came into the world they agreed to call him Prince Wish. He had beautiful blue eyes, and a sweet little mouth, but his nose was so big that it covered half his face. The queen's ladies tried to

satisfy her by telling her that the nose would grow smaller as the prince grew bigger, and that if it did not, a large nose was indispensable to a hero. The queen listened eagerly to this comfort. She grew so used to the prince's nose that it did not seem to her any larger than ordinary noses of the court, where, in process of time, everybody with a long nose was very much admired, and the unfortunate people who had only snubs were taken little notice of.

Great care was observed in the education of the prince, and as soon as he could speak they told him all sorts of amusing tales, in which all the bad people had short noses, and all the good people had long ones. His tutor taught him history, and whenever any great king was referred to, the tutor always took care to mention that he had a long nose. The royal apartments were filled with pictures and portraits having this peculiarity, and Prince Wish began to regard the length of his nose as his greatest perfection.

ENCHANTMENTS

When he was twenty years old his mother and his people wished him to marry. They procured for him the portraits of many princesses, but the one he preferred was Princess Darling, daughter of a powerful monarch and heiress to several kingdoms. Alas! With all her beauty, this princess had one great misfortune, a little turned-up nose, which, everyone else said, made her only the more bewitching. But here, in the kingdom of Prince Wish, the courtiers were thrown by it into the utmost perplexity. They were in the habit of laughing at all small noses, but how dared they make fun of the nose of Princess Darling?

They would have found themselves in constant difficulties, had not one clever person struck upon a bright idea. He said that though it was necessary for a man to have a long nose, women were very different creatures, and that a learned man had discovered in an old manuscript that the celebrated Cleopatra, queen of Egypt and the beauty of the ancient world, also had a turned-up nose. At this information Prince Wish was so delighted that he immediately sent off ambassadors to ask for Princess Darling's hand in marriage.

She accepted his offer at once, and returned with the ambassadors. He made all haste to meet and welcome her, but when she was only three leagues distant from his capital, before he had time even to kiss her hand, the magician who had once assumed the shape of his mother's cat, Minon, appeared in the air and carried her off before the prince's very eyes.

Prince Wish, almost beside himself with grief, declared that nothing should induce him to return to his throne and kingdom till he had found Princess Darling. He mounted a good horse, laid the reins on the animal's neck, and let him take him wherever he would.

The horse entered a wide, extended plain, and trotted on steadily the whole day without finding a single house. Master and beast began almost to

faint with hunger, and Prince Wish might have wished himself safe at home again, had he not discovered, just as night was falling, a dark cavern. Outside the cavern was a bright little lantern, and sitting in its light was a tiny woman – she looked as though she could easily have been more than a hundred years old.

She put on her spectacles the better to look at the stranger, and he noticed that her nose was so small that the spectacles would hardly stay on. Then the prince and the fairy – for it was a fairy – burst into a mutual fit of laughter.

"What a funny nose!" cried the one.

"Not so funny as yours, madam," returned the other. "But pray let us leave

our noses alone, and be good enough to give me
something to eat, for I am dying with hunger, and
so is my poor horse."

"With all my heart," answered the fairy.
"Although your nose is ridiculously long, you are no
less the son of one of my best friends. I loved your
father like a brother. He had a very handsome nose."

"What is wanting to my nose?" asked Wish,
rather savagely.

"Oh! Nothing at all. On the contrary, there is a
great deal too much of it, but never mind, one may
be a very honest man, and yet have too big a nose. I
will give you some supper directly, and while you
eat it I will tell you my history in six words, for I
hate much talking. A long tongue is as unbearable
as a long nose, and I remember when I was young
how much I used to be admired because I was not
a talker, indeed, my mother, for poor as you see
me now, I am the daughter of a great king,
who always—"

'Hang the king your father!' Prince Wish was about to exclaim, but he stopped himself, and only observed that however the pleasure of her conversation might make him forget his hunger, it could not have the same effect upon his horse, who was really starving.

The fairy, pleased at his civility, called her servants and bade them supply him with all he needed. "And," added she, "I must say you are very polite and good-tempered, in spite of your nose."

'What has the old woman to do with my nose?' thought the prince. 'If I were not so very hungry I would soon show her what she is – a regular old gossip and chatterbox. She fancies she talks little, indeed! One must be very foolish not to know one's own defects. This comes of being born a fairy. Flatterers have spoiled her, and persuaded her that she talks little.'

While the prince thus meditated, the servants were laying the table, the fairy asking them a

hundred unnecessary questions, simply for the pleasure of hearing herself talk. 'Well,' thought Wish, 'I am delighted that I came hither, if only to learn how wise I have been in never listening to flatterers, who hide from us our faults, or make us believe they are perfections. But they could never deceive me. I know all my own weak points, I trust.' And truly he believed he did.

So he went on eating contentedly, nor stopped till the old fairy began to address him.

"Prince," said she, "will you be kind enough to turn a little? Your nose casts such a shadow that I cannot see what is on my plate. And, as I was saying, your father admired me and always made me welcome at court. What is the court etiquette there now? Do the ladies still go to assemblies, balls, promenades? I beg your pardon for laughing, but how very long your nose is."

"I wish you would cease to speak of my nose," said the prince, becoming annoyed. "It is what it is,

and I do not desire it any shorter."

"Oh! I see that I have vexed you," returned the fairy. "Nevertheless, I am one of your best friends, and so I shall take the liberty of always—"

She would doubtless have gone on talking till midnight, but the prince, unable to bear it any longer, here interrupted her, thanked her for her hospitality, bade her a hasty adieu, and rode away.

He travelled for a long time, half over the world, but he heard no news of Princess Darling. However, in each place he went to, he heard one remarkable fact – the great length of his own nose. The little boys in the streets jeered at him, the peasants stared at him, and the more polite ladies and gentlemen whom he met in society used to try in vain to keep from laughing, and to get out of his way as soon as they could. So the poor prince became gradually quite forlorn and solitary. He thought all the world was mad, but still he never thought of there being anything queer about his own nose.

The Prince with the Nose

At last the old fairy, who, though she was a
chatterbox, was very good-natured, saw that he was
almost breaking his heart. She felt sorry for him,
and wished to help, for she knew the enchantment
which hid from him the Princess Darling could not
be broken till he discovered his own defect. So she
went in search of the princess, and being more
powerful than the magician, she took her away
from him, and shut her up in a palace of crystal,
which she placed on the road which Prince Wish
had to pass.

He was riding along, very melancholy, when he
saw the palace, and at its entrance was a room made
of glass, in which sat his beloved princess, smiling
and beautiful as ever. He leaped from his horse, and
ran towards her. She held out her hand for him to
kiss, but he could not get at it for the glass.
Transported with eagerness and delight, he dashed
his sword through the crystal, and succeeded in
breaking a small opening, to which she put up her

beautiful rosy mouth. But it was in vain, Prince Wish could not approach it. He twisted his neck about, and turned his head on all sides, till at length, putting up his hand to his face, he discovered the impediment.

"It must be confessed," exclaimed he, "that my nose is too long."

That moment the glass walls all split asunder, and the old fairy appeared, leading Princess Darling.

"Admit, prince," said she, "that you are very much obliged to me, for now the enchantment is ended. You may marry the object of your choice. But," added she, smiling, "I fear I might have talked to you forever on the subject of your nose, and you would not have believed me in its remarkable

length, until it became an obstacle to your own inclinations. Now behold it!" and she held up a crystal mirror. And will you be satisfied to be no different from other people?"

"Perfectly," said Prince Wish, who found his nose had shrunk to an ordinary length. And, taking the Princess Darling by the hand, he kissed her, courteously, affectionately and satisfactorily. Then they departed to their own country, and lived very happy all their days.

CHILDREN
AND FAIRIES

Sweet-one-darling and the Dream-fairies

By Eugene Field

A wonderful thing happened one night. Sweet-one-darling was lying in her cradle, and she was trying to make up her mind whether she should go to sleep or keep awake. Sweet-one-darling was ready for sleep. She had on her nightgown and nightcap, and her mother had kissed her goodnight. But the day had been so pleasant that Sweet-one-darling was unwilling to give it up.

Sweet-one-darling and the Dream-fairies

A cricket was chirping, and some folk believe that the cricket is in league with the Dream-fairies. They say that what sounds to us like a faint chirping is actually the call of the cricket to the Dream-fairies to tell those creatures that it is time for them to come with their dreams.

Then, all of a sudden, there was a sound as of the rustle of silken wings, and the next moment two of the sweetest fairies you ever saw were standing upon the windowsill, just over the honeysuckle.

They had come from Somewhere, and it was evident that they were searching for somebody, for they peered cautiously and eagerly into the room. One was dressed in a bright yellow suit of butterfly silk and the other wore a suit of dark-grey mothzine, which (as perhaps you know) is a dainty fabric made of the fine strands which grey moths spin. Both of these fairies together would not have weighed much more than the one-sixteenth part of four dewdrops.

"Sweet-one-darling! Oh, Sweet-one-darling!" they cried softly. "Where are you?"

Sweet-one-darling pretended that she did not hear, and she cuddled down close in her cradle and laughed, all to herself. The mischievous little thing knew well enough whom they were calling but she meant to fool them and hide from them awhile – that is why she did not answer. But nobody can hide from the Dream-fairies, and least of all could Sweet-one-darling hide from them, for presently her

laughter betrayed her and the two Dream-fairies perched on her cradle – one at each side – and looked smilingly down upon her.

"Hello!" said Sweet-one-darling.

This was the first time I had ever heard her speak, and I did not know till then that even wee little babies talk with fairies, particularly Dream-fairies.

"Hello, Sweet-one-darling!" said Gleam-of-the-dark, for that was the name of the Dream-fairy in the dark-grey mothzine.

"And hello from me, too!" cried Frisk-and-glitter, the other visitor – the one in the butterfly-silk suit.

"You have come earlier than usual," suggested Sweet-one-darling.

"No, indeed," answered Frisk-and-glitter, "But the day has been so happy that it has passed quickly. For that reason you should be glad to see me, for I bring dreams of the day – the beautiful golden day, with its sunlight, its grace of warmth, and its mirth and play."

"And I," said Gleam-of-the-dark, "I bring dreams, too. But my dreams are of the night, and they are full of the gentle, soothing music of the winds, of the whisper of pines, and of the chirps of crickets! You shall see the things of Fairyland and of Dreamland, and of all the mysterious countries that compose the vast world of Somewhere, away out beyond the silvery mist of night."

"Oh!" cried Sweet-one-darling. "I should never be able to make a choice between you two. I would love to have the play of the daytime brought back to me, and I am quite as sure that I want to see all the pretty sights that are unfolded by the dreams which Gleam-of-the-dark brings."

"You have no need to feel troubled," said Frisk-and-glitter, "for you are not expected to make any choice between us. We have our own way of solving the question, as you shall presently understand."

Then the Dream-fairies explained that whenever they came of an evening to bring their dreams to a

94

little child they climbed onto the child's eyelids and tried to rock them down. Gleam-of-the-dark would stand and rock upon one eyelid and Frisk-and-glitter would stand and rock upon the other. If Gleam-of-the-dark's eyelid closed first, the child would dream the dreams Gleam-of-the-dark brought it. If Frisk-and-glitter's eyelid closed first, why, then, of course, the child dreamt the dreams Frisk-and-glitter brought.

"But suppose," suggested Sweet-one-darling, "suppose both eyelids close at the same instant? Which one of you fairies has his own way then?"

"Ah, in that event," said they, "neither of us wins, and, since neither wins, the sleeper does not dream at all, but awakes next morning from a sound, dreamless, refreshing sleep."

Sweet-one-darling was not sure that she fancied this alternative, but of course she could not help herself. So she let the two little Dream-fairies flutter across her shoulders and clamber up her cheeks to

their proper places upon her eyelids. Gracious! How heavy they seemed when they stood on her eyelids! As I told you before, their actual combined weight hardly exceeded the sixteenth part of four dewdrops, yet when they are perched on a little child's eyelids (tired eyelids at that) it really seems sometimes as if they weighed a tonne! It was just all she could do to keep her eyelids open, yet Sweet-one-darling was determined to be strictly fair. She loved both the Dream-fairies equally well, and she would not for all the world have shown either one any favouritism.

Well, there the two Dream-fairies stood on Sweet-one-darling's eyelids, each one trying to rock his particular eyelid down, and each one sung his little lullaby in the pipingest voice imaginable. This was very soothing, as you would suppose. It was the most exciting contest (for an amicable one) I ever saw. As for Sweet-one-darling, she seemed to be lost presently in the magic of the Dream-fairies, and

although she has never said a word
about it to me I am quite sure
that, while her dear eyelids
drooped and drooped and
drooped to the rocking and
singing of the Dream-fairies,
she enjoyed a confusion of
all those precious things
promised by her two
fairy visitors.

Yes, I am sure that from
under her drooping eyelids she beheld
the scenes of the day mingled with peeps of
fairyland. And when at last she was fast asleep I
could not say for certain which of her eyelids had
closed first, so simultaneous was the downfall of her
long dark lashes upon her flushed cheeks. I meant
to have asked the Dream-fairies about it, but before
I could do so they whisked out of the window and
away with their dreams to a very sleepy little boy

who was waiting for them somewhere in the neighbourhood. So you see I am unable to tell you which of the Dream-fairies won. Maybe neither did, maybe Sweet-one-darling's sleep that night was dreamless. I have questioned her about it and she will not answer me.

This is all the wonderful tale I had to tell. Maybe it will not seem so wonderful to you, for perhaps you, too, have felt the Dream-fairies rocking your eyelids down with gentle lullaby music. Perhaps you, too, know all the precious dreams they bring. In that case you will bear witness that my tale, even though it be not wonderful, is strictly true.

Betty and the
Wood Maiden

By A H Wratislaw

*In this story, Betty spins rough flax into thread. She uses a spindle
(stick) to spin the thread, but she is too poor to own a distaff (the tool
which holds the raw fibre before it is spun). Her mother then reels
the thread off the spindle into skeins (coils) ready for weaving.*

*B*etty was a little girl. Her mother was a widow,
and had no more of her property left than a
dilapidated cottage and two she-goats, but Betty
was, nevertheless, always cheerful. From spring to
autumn she pastured the goats in the birch wood.

Whenever she went from home, her mother always gave her in a basket a slice of bread and a spindle, with the order, "Let it be full."

As she had no distaff, she used to twine the flax round her head. Betty took the basket and skipped off singing merrily after the goats to the birch wood. When she got there, the goats went after pasture, and Betty sat under a tree, drew the fibres from her head with her left hand, and let down the spindle with her right so that it just hummed over the ground, and then she would sing till the wood echoed. When the sun indicated midday, she put aside her spindle, called the goats, and after giving them each a morsel of bread that they mightn't stray from her, bounded into the wood for a few strawberries or any other woodland fruit that might happen to be just then in season, that she might have dessert to her bread.

When she had finished her meal, she sprang up, danced and sang. After her dance, she spun again

industriously, and in the evening, when she drove
the goats home, her mother never had to scold her
for bringing back her spindle empty.

Once, when according to custom, exactly at
midday, after her scanty dinner, she was getting ready
for a dance, all of a sudden – where she came, there
she came – a very beautiful maiden stood before her.
She had on a white dress as fine as gossamer, golden-
coloured hair flowed from her head to her waist, and
on her head she wore a garland of woodland flowers.
Betty was struck dumb with astonishment. The
maiden smiled at her, and said in an attractive voice,
"Betty, are you fond of dancing?"

When the maiden spoke so prettily to her,
Betty's terror quitted her, and she answered, "Oh,
I should like to dance all day long!"

"Come, then, let's dance together. I'll teach
you!" So spoke the maiden, tucked her dress up on
one side, took Betty by the waist, and began to
dance with her. As they circled, such delightful

music sounded over their heads, that Betty's heart
skipped within her. It was a company of choice
musicians that had come together
at the beck of the beautiful
maiden – nightingales, larks,
linnets, goldfinches,
greenfinches, thrushes,
blackbirds, and a very
skilful mockingbird.

Betty's cheek flamed,
her eyes glittered, she
forgot her task and her
goats, and only gazed at her
partner, who twirled
before and round her
with the most charming movements, and so lightly
that the grass didn't even bend beneath her delicate
foot. They danced from noon till eve, and Betty's
feet were neither wearied nor painful. Then the
beautiful maiden stopped, the music ceased, and as

she came so she disappeared. Betty looked about
her. The sun was setting behind the wood. She
suddenly remembered the unspun flax, and saw that
her spindle, which was lying on the grass, was by no
means full. She called the goats, and drove them
home. The goats, hearing no merry song behind
them, looked round to see whether their own
shepherdess was really following them. Her mother,
too, wondered, and asked her daughter whether she
was ill, as she didn't sing.

"No, mother dear, I'm not ill, but my throat is
dry from singing, and therefore I don't sing," said
Betty in excuse, and went to put away the spindle
and the unspun flax.

Knowing that her mother was not in the habit of
reeling up the yarn at once, she intended to make
up the next day what she had neglected to do the
first day, and therefore did not say a word to her
mother about the beautiful maiden.

The next day Betty again drove the goats as usual

to the birch wood, and sang to herself again merrily. On arriving at the birch wood the goats began to pasture, and she sat under the tree and began to spin industriously, The sun indicated midday. Betty went off for strawberries, and after returning began to eat her dinner and chatter with the goats. "Ah, my little goats, I mustn't dance today," sighed she.

"And why mustn't you?" spoke a pleasing voice, and the beautiful maiden stood beside her, as if she had dropped from the clouds.

Betty answered modestly, "Excuse me, beautiful lady, I can't dance with you, because I should again fail to perform my task of spinning, and my mother would scold me. Today, before the sun sets, I must make up what I left undone yesterday."

"Only come and dance, and before the sun sets help will be found for you," said the maiden. She tucked up her dress, took Betty round the waist, the musicians sitting on the birch branches struck up, and the two dancers began to whirl.

At last the dancers stopped, the music ceased, the sun was on the verge of setting. Betty clapped her hand on the top of her head, where the unspun flax was twined, and began to cry. The beautiful maiden put her hand on Betty's head, took off the flax, twined it round the stem of a slender birch, seized the spindle, and began to spin. The spindle grew fuller before her eyes, and before the sun set behind the wood all the yarn was spun, as well as that which Betty had not finished the day before.

While giving the full spool into the girl's hand the beautiful maiden said, "Reel, and grumble not – remember my words – Reel, and grumble not!" After these words she vanished, as if the ground had sunk in beneath her. Betty was content, and thought on her way home, 'If she is so good and kind as to fill the spindle, I will dance with her again if she comes again.' But her mother gave her no cheerful welcome. Wishing in the course of the day to reel the yarn, she saw that the spindle was not full, and was therefore out of humour.

"What were you doing yesterday that you didn't finish your task?" asked her mother reprovingly.

"Pardon, mother – I danced a little too long," said Betty humbly, and, showing her mother the spindle, added, "Today it is more than full to make up for it." Her mother said no more, but went to milk the goats, and Betty put the spindle away. She wished to tell her mother of her adventure, but bethought herself again, 'No, not unless she comes again, and then I will ask her what kind of person she is, and will tell my mother.'

The third morning, as usual, she drove the goats to the birch wood. The goats began to pasture. Betty sat under the tree, and began to sing and spin. The sun indicated midday. Betty laid her spindle on the grass, gave each of the goats a morsel of bread, collected strawberries, ate her dinner, and while giving the crumbs to the birds, said, "My little goats, I will dance to you today!" She jumped up, folded

her hands, and was just going to see if she could manage to dance as prettily as the beautiful maiden, when all at once she herself stood before her.

"Let's go together, together!" said she to Betty, seized her round the waist, and at the same moment the music struck up over their heads, and the maidens circled round with flying step. Betty forgot her spindle and her goats, saw nothing but the beautiful maiden, whose body bent in every direction like a willow-wand, and thought of nothing but the delightful music, in tune with which her feet bounded of their own accord. They danced from midday till evening. Then the maiden stopped, and the music ceased.

Betty looked round. The sun was behind the wood. With tears she clasped her hands on the top of her head, and turning in search of the half-empty spindle, lamented about what her mother would say to her.

"Give me your basket," said the beautiful maiden.

Betty and the Wood Maiden

"I will make up to you for what you have left undone today."

Betty handed her the basket, and the maiden disappeared for a moment, and afterwards handed Betty the basket again, saying, "Not now – look at it at home," and was gone, as if the wind had blown her away.

Betty was afraid to peep into the basket immediately, but halfway home she couldn't restrain herself. The basket was as light as if there was just nothing in it. She couldn't help looking to see whether the maiden hadn't tricked her. And how frightened she was when she saw that the basket was full – of birch leaves! In anger she threw out two handfuls of leaves, and she was going to shake the entire basket out, but then she bethought herself, 'I will use them as litter for the goats,' and left some leaves in the basket. She was almost afraid to go home.

Her mother was waiting for her on the threshold,

full of anxiety. "For heaven's sake, girl! What sort of spool did you bring me home yesterday?" were her first words.

"Why?" asked Betty anxiously.

"When you went out in the morning, I went to reel. I reeled and reeled, and the spool still remained full. One skein, two, three skeins, the spool still full.

"'What evil spirit has spun it?' said I in a temper, and that instant the yarn vanished from the spindle, as if it were spirited away. Tell me what the meaning of this is!"

Then Betty confessed, and began to tell about the beautiful maiden.

"That was a wood-fairy!" cried her mother in astonishment. "About midday and midnight the wood-ladies hold their dances. Lucky that you are not a boy, or you wouldn't have come out of her arms alive. She would have danced with you as long as there was breath in your body, or have tickled you to death. But they have compassion on girls, and

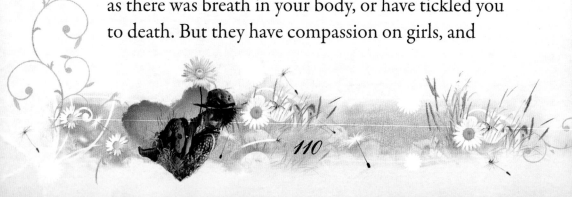

110

often give them rich presents. It's a shame that you didn't tell me about your meeting her. If I hadn't spoken in a temper, I might have had a whole room full of yarn."

Then Betty bethought herself of the basket, and it occurred to her that perhaps, after all, there might have been something under those leaves. She took out the spindle and unspun flax from the top, and looked once more, and, "See, mother!" she cried out. Her mother looked and clapped her hands. The birch leaves were turned into gold!

"She ordered me, 'Don't look now, but at home!' but I did not obey."

"Lucky that you didn't empty out the whole basket," said her mother. The next morning she went herself to look at the place where Betty had

thrown out the two handfuls of leaves, but on the road there lay nothing but fresh birch leaves. But the riches that Betty had brought home were large enough. Her mother bought a small estate, and they had many cattle. Betty had handsome clothes, and was not obliged to pasture goats. But whatever she had, however cheerful and happy she was, nothing ever gave her so great delight as the dance with the wood-lady. She often went to the birch wood. She hoped for the good fortune of seeing the beautiful maiden – but she never set eyes on her again.

Eva's Visit to Fairyland

By Louisa M Alcott

Down among the grass and fragrant clover lay little Eva by the brook-side, watching the bright waves, as they went singing by under the drooping flowers that grew on its banks. As she was wondering where the waters went, she heard a faint, low sound, as of far-off music. She thought it was the wind, but not a leaf was stirring, and soon through the rippling water came a strange little boat.

CHILDREN AND FAIRIES

It was a lily of the valley, whose tall stem formed
the mast, while the broad leaves that rose from the
roots, and drooped again till they reached the water,
were filled with fairies, who danced to the music of
the silver lily-bells above that rang a merry peal, and
filled the air with their fragrant breath.

Eva's Visit to Fairyland

On came the fairy boat till it reached a moss-grown rock, and here it stopped, while the fairies rested beneath the violet leaves, and sang with the dancing waves.

Eva looked with wonder and threw crimson fruit for the little folks to feast upon.

They looked kindly on the child, and, after whispering long among themselves, two little bright-eyed elves flew over the shining water, and, lighting on the clover blossoms, said gently, "Little maiden, many thanks for your kindness, our queen bids us ask if you will go with us to Fairyland, and learn what we can teach you."

"I would go with you, dear fairies," said Eva, "but I cannot sail in your little boat. See! I can hold you in my hand, and could not live among you without harming your tiny kingdom, I am so large."

The elves laughed, saying, "You are a good child to fear doing harm to those weaker than yourself. Look in the water and see what we have done."

CHILDREN AND FAIRIES

Eva looked into the brook, and saw a tiny child standing between the elves. "Now I can go with you," said she, "but I can no longer step from the bank to yonder stone, for the brook seems now like a great river, and you have not given me wings like yours."

But the fairies took each a hand, and flew lightly over the stream. The queen and her subjects came to meet her. "Now must we go home," said the queen, "and you shall go with us, little one."

Then there was a great bustle, as they flew about on shining wings, some laying cushions of violet leaves in the boat, others folding the queen's veil and mantle more closely round her, lest the falling dews should chill her.

The cool waves' gentle splashing against the boat, and the sweet chime of the lily-bells, lulled little Eva to sleep, and when she woke it was in Fairyland. A faint, rosy light, as of the setting sun, shone on the white pillars of the queen's palace as they passed in. They led Eva to a bed of pure white leaves, above

Eva's Visit to Fairyland

which drooped the fragrant petals of a crimson rose.

With the sun rose the fairies, and, with Eva, hastened away to the fountain, whose cool waters were soon filled with little forms, as the elves floated in the blue waves among the fair white lilies, or sat on the green moss, smoothing their bright locks, and wearing fresh garlands of dewy flowers. Then they flew away to the gardens, and soon, high up among the treetops, or under the broad leaves, sat the elves in little groups, taking their breakfast of fruit and pure fresh dew, while the bright-winged birds came fearlessly among them, pecking the same ripe berries, and dipping their little beaks in the same flower cups.

"Now, little Eva," said they, "you will see that Fairies are not idle, wilful spirits, as mortals believe. Come, we will show you what we do."

They led her to a lovely room, through whose walls of deep green leaves the light stole softly in. Here lay many wounded insects, and creatures,

117

and pale, drooping flowers grew beside urns of healing herbs, from whose fresh leaves came a faint, sweet perfume.

Eva wondered, but silently followed her guide, little Rose-Leaf, who went to the insects – first to a tiny fly who lay in a flower-leaf cradle.

"Do you suffer much, dear Gauzy-Wing?" asked the Fairy. "I will bind up your poor little leg." So she folded the cool leaves tenderly about the poor fly, bathed his wings, and brought him refreshing drink, while he hummed his thanks, and forgot his pain.

They passed on, and Eva saw beside each bed a fairy, who with gentle hands and loving words soothed the suffering insects.

Then Rose-Leaf led Eva away, saying, "Come now to the Flower Palace, and see the Fairy Court."

Beneath green arches, bright with birds and flowers, went Eva into a lofty hall. The roof of pure white lilies rested on pillars of green clustering vines, while many-coloured blossoms threw their

bright shadows on the walls, as they danced below in the deep green moss.

Suddenly the music grew louder and sweeter, and the fairies knelt, and bowed their heads, as on through the crowd of loving subjects came the queen, while the air was filled with gay voices singing to welcome her.

She placed the child beside her, saying, "Little Eva, you shall see now how the flowers on your great earth bloom so brightly. A band of loving little gardeners go daily forth from Fairyland, to tend and watch them. Now, Eglantine, what have you to tell us of your rosy namesakes on the earth?"

From a group of elves, whose rose-wreathed wands showed the flower they loved, came one bearing a tiny urn, and, answering the queen, she said, "Over hill and valley they are blooming fresh and fair as summer sun and dew can make them and this, the loveliest of their sisters, have I brought to place among the fairy flowers that never pass away."

Eglantine then laid the urn before the queen, and placed the fragrant rose on the dewy moss beside the throne, while a murmur of approval went around the hall, and each wand in turn waved to the little fairy who could bring so fair a gift to their good queen.

Said little Rose-Leaf to Eva, "Come now and see where we are taught to read the tales written on flower-leaves, and the sweet language of the birds, and all that can make a fairy heart wiser and better."

Then into a cheerful place they went, with many groups of flowers, and among the leaves sat child elves, and learned from their flower-books all that fairy hands had written there. Some studied when to spread tender buds to the sunlight, and when to shelter them from rain, how to guard the seeds, and when to lay them in the warm earth or send them on the summer wind to far off hills and valleys. Others learned to heal wounded insects, who, were it not for fairy hands, would die before half their

Eva's Visit to Fairyland

happy summer life had gone. Eva nodded to the little ones, as they peeped from among the leaves, and then she listened to the fairy lessons. Several tiny elves sat on leaves while the teacher sat among the petals of a flower beside them, and asked questions that none but fairies would care to know.

"Twinkle, if there lay nine seeds within a flower cup and the wind bore five away, how many would the blossom have?"

"Four," replied the little one.

"Rosebud, if a cowslip opens three leaves in one day and four the next, how many rosy leaves will there be when the whole flower has bloomed?"

"Seven," sang the gay little elf.

"Harebell, if a silkworm spins one yard of fairy cloth in an hour, how many will it spin in a day?"

"Twelve," said the fairy child.

"Primrose, where lies Violet Island?"

"In the Lake of Ripples."

"Lilla, what are the bounds of Rose Land?"

"On the north by Ferndale, south by Sunny Wave River, east by the hill of Morning Clouds, and west by the Evening Star."

"Now, little ones," said the teacher, "you may go to your painting."

Then Eva saw how, on large, white leaves, the

Eva's Visit to Fairyland

fairies learned to imitate the lovely colours, and with tiny brushes to brighten the blush on the anemone's cheek, to deepen the blue of the violet's eye, and add new light to the golden cowslip.

"You have stayed long enough," said the elves at length, "we have many things to show you. Come now and see what is our dearest work."

So Eva said farewell to the child elves, and hastened with little Rose-Leaf to the gates. Here she saw many bands of fairies, folded in dark mantles that mortals might not know them, who, with the child among them, flew away over hill and valley. Some went to the cottages amid the hills, some to the seaside to watch above the humble fisher folks, but little Rose-Leaf and many others went into the noisy city.

Eva wondered within herself what good the tiny elves could do in this great place, but she soon learned, for the fairy band went among the poor and friendless, bringing pleasant dreams to the sick

and old, sweet, tender thoughts of love and gentleness to the young, strength to the weak, and patient cheerfulness to the poor and lonely.

Thus to all who needed help or comfort went the faithful fairies, and when at length they turned towards Fairyland, many were the grateful, happy hearts they left behind.

All Fairyland was dressed in flowers, and the soft wind went singing by, laden with their fragrant breath. Sweet music sounded through the air, and troops of elves in their gayest robes hastened to the palace where the feast was spread.

Soon the hall was filled with smiling faces and fair forms, and little Eva, as she stood beside the queen, thought she had never seen a sight so lovely.

The many-coloured shadows of the fairest flowers played on the pure white walls, and fountains sparkled in the sunlight, making music as the cool waves rose and fell, while to and fro, with waving wings and joyous voices, went the smiling

elves, bearing fruit and honey, or fragrant garlands for each other's hair.

Long they feasted, gaily they sang, and Eva, dancing merrily among them, longed to be an elf that she might dwell forever in so fair a home.

At length the music ceased, and the queen said, as she laid her hand on little Eva's shining hair, "Dear child, tomorrow we must bear you home, therefore we will guide you to the brook-side, and there say farewell till you come again to visit us. Nay, do not weep, dear Rose-Leaf, you shall watch over little Eva's flowers, and when she looks at them she will think of you. Come now and lead her to the fairy garden, and show her what we think our fairest sight."

With Rose-Leaf by her side, they led her through the palace, and along green, winding paths, till Eva saw what seemed a wall of flowers before her, while the air was filled with the most fragrant odours, and the low, sweet music as of singing blossoms.

"Where have you brought me, and what mean these lovely sounds?" asked Eva.

"Look here, and you shall see," said Rose-Leaf, as she bent aside the vines, "but listen silently or you cannot hear."

Then Eva, looking through the drooping vines, beheld a garden filled with the loveliest flowers. Fair as were all the blossoms she had seen in Fairyland, none were so beautiful as these. The rose glowed with a deeper crimson, the lily's soft leaves were more purely white, the crocus and humble cowslip shone like sunlight, and the violet was blue as the sky that smiled above it.

"How beautiful they are," whispered Eva, "but, dear Rose-Leaf, why do you keep them here, and why call you this your fairest sight?"

"Look again, and I will tell you," said the fairy.

Eva looked, and saw from every flower a tiny form come forth to welcome the elves, who all, save Rose-Leaf, had flown above the wall, and were now

scattering dew upon the flowers' bright leaves and talking gaily with the spirits, who gathered around them, and seemed full of joy that they had come. The child saw that each one wore the colours of the flower that was its home. Delicate and graceful were the little forms, bright the silken hair that fell about each lovely face, and Eva heard the low, sweet murmur of their silvery voices and the rustle of their wings. She gazed in silent wonder, forgetting she knew not who they were, till the fairy said, "These are the spirits of the flowers, and this the fairy home where they come to bloom in fadeless beauty here, when their earthly life is past. Come now, for you have seen enough. We must be away."

On a rosy morning cloud, went Eva through the sunny sky. The fresh wind bore them gently on, and soon they stood again beside the brook, whose waves danced brightly as if to welcome them.

"Now, we say farewell," said the queen, as they gathered nearer to the child.

They clung about her
tenderly, and little Rose-Leaf
placed a flower crown on her
head, whispering softly, "When
you would come to us again,
stand by the brook-side
and wave this in the air,
and we will gladly take
you to our home again.
Farewell, dear Eva.
Think of your little
Rose-Leaf when
among the flowers."

For a long time
Eva watched their
shining wings, and
listened to the music of their
voices as they flew singing home, and when at
length the last little form had vanished among the
clouds, she saw that all around her where the elves

Eva's Visit to Fairyland

had been, the fairest flowers had
sprung up, and the lonely brook-side
was a blooming garden.

Thus she stood among the waving
blossoms, with the fairy garland in
her hair, and happy feelings in her
heart, better and wiser for her
visit to Fairyland.

The Counterpane Fairy

By Katharine Pyle

*T*eddy was all alone, for his mother had been up with him so much the night before that at four o'clock in the afternoon she said that she was going to lie down.

She set a glass of milk on his bedside table, and left the door ajar so that he could call the cook if he wanted anything, and then she had gone to bed.

The little boy usually quite liked being ill, for

then he was read aloud to and had lemonade, but this had been a real illness, and though he was better now, he was still only allowed milk and gruel. He was feeling rather lonely, too, though the fire crackled cheerfully, and he could hear Hannah singing to herself in the kitchen below.

He lay staring out of the window at the grey clouds sweeping across the sky. He grew lonelier and lonelier and a big tear trickled down his cheek and dripped off his chin.

"Oh dear, oh dear!" said a little voice just behind the hill his knees made as he sat with them drawn up in bed, "What a hill to climb!"

Teddy stopped crying and gazed wonderingly at where the voice came from, and over the top of his knees appeared a brown peaked hood, a tiny withered face, a brown cloak, and last of all two small feet in buckled shoes. It was a little old woman, so weazened and brown that she looked more like a dried leaf than anything else.

CHILDREN AND FAIRIES

She seated herself on Teddy's knees and gazed at him solemnly, and she was so light that he felt her weight no more than if she had been a feather.

Teddy stared at her for a while, and then he asked, "Who are you?"

"I'm the Counterpane Fairy," said the little

figure, in a thin little voice. "I came to you, because you were lonely and sick, and I thought maybe you would like me to show you a story."

"Do you mean tell me a story?" asked Teddy.

"No," said the fairy, "I mean show you a story. It's a game I invented after I joined the Counterpane Fairies. Choose any one of the squares of the counterpane and I will show you how to play it. That's all you have to do – choose a square."

Teddy looked the counterpane over carefully. "I think I'll choose that yellow square," he said, "because it looks so nice and bright."

"Very well," said the Counterpane Fairy. "Look straight at it and don't turn away until I count seven times seven and then you shall see the story of it."

Teddy fixed his eyes on the square and the fairy began to count. "One – two – three – four," she counted, Teddy heard her voice, thin and clear as the hissing of the logs on the hearth. "Don't look away from the square," she cried. "Five – six –

seven," it seemed to Teddy that the yellow silk square was turning to a mist before his eyes and wrapping everything about him in a golden glow. "Thirteen – fourteen," the fairy counted on and on. "Forty-six – forty-seven – forty-eight – *forty nine*!"

At the words 'forty-nine', the Counterpane Fairy clapped her hands and Teddy looked about him. He was no longer in a golden mist. He was standing in a wonderful enchanted garden. The sky was like the golden sky at sunset, and the grass was so thickly set with tiny yellow flowers that it looked like a golden carpet. From this garden stretched a long flight of glass steps. They reached up and up and up to a great golden castle with shining domes and turrets.

"Listen!" said the Counterpane Fairy. "In that golden castle there lies an enchanted princess. For more than a hundred years she has been lying there waiting for the hero who is to come and rescue her, and you are the hero who can do it if you will."

With that the fairy led him to a little pool close

by, and bade him look in the water. When Teddy looked, he saw himself standing there in the golden garden, and he did not appear as he ever had before. He was tall and strong and beautiful, like a hero.

"Yes," said Teddy, "I will do it." Without further pause, he ran to the glass steps and began to climb.

Up and up and up he went. Once he turned and waved his hand to the Counterpane Fairy in the golden garden below. She waved her hand, and he heard her voice faint and clear, "Goodbye! Be brave and strong, and beware of what is little and grey."

Then Teddy turned towards the castle, and in a moment he was standing before the shining gates.

He raised his hand and struck bravely upon the door. There was no answer. Again he struck upon it, and his blow rang through the hall inside. Then he opened the door and went in.

The hall was five-sided, and all of pure gold, as clear and shining as glass. Upon three sides of it were three arched doors – one was of emerald, one

135

was of ruby, and one was of diamond. They were arched, and tall, and wide – fit for a hero to go through. The question was, behind which one lay the enchanted princess?

While Teddy stood there looking at them and wondering, he heard a little thin voice, that seemed to be singing to itself, and this is what it sang:

> *"In and out and out and in,*
> *Quick as a flash I weave and spin.*
> *Some may mistake and some forget,*
> *But I'll have my spider web finished yet."*

When Teddy heard the song, he knew that someone must be awake in the enchanted castle, so he began looking about him.

On the fourth side of the wall there hung a curtain of silvery-grey spider web, and the voice seemed to come from it. The hero went towards it, but he saw nothing, for the spider that was spinning

"In and out and out and in,

Quick as a flash I weave and spin.

Some may mistake and some forget,

But I'll have my spider web finished yet."

it moved so fast that no eyes could follow it. Presently it paused up in the corner of the web, and then Teddy saw it. It looked very little to have spun all that curtain of silvery web.

"Mistress Spinner!" cried Teddy. "Can you tell me where to find the enchanted princess who lies asleep waiting for me to rescue her?"

The spider sat quite still for a while, and then it said in a voice as thin as a hair:

"You must go through the emerald door,
You must go through the emerald door.
What so fit as the emerald door,
For the hero who would do great deeds?"

Teddy did not so much as stay to thank the little grey spinner, he was in such a hurry to find the princess, but turning he sprang to the emerald door, flung it open, and stepped outside.

He found himself standing on the glass steps,

and as his foot touched the topmost one the whole flight closed up like an umbrella, and in a moment Teddy was sliding down the smooth glass pane, faster and faster and faster until he could hardly catch his breath.

The next thing he knew he was standing in the golden garden, and there was the Counterpane Fairy beside him looking at him sadly. "You should have known better than to try the emerald door," she said, "and now shall we break the story?"

"Oh, no, no!" cried Teddy, and he was still the hero. "Let me try once more, for it may be I can yet save the princess."

The Counterpane Fairy smiled. "Very well," she said. "Try again. But remember what I told you: beware of what is little and grey, and take this with you – it may be of use." She picked up a blade of grass from the ground and handed it to him.

The hero took it, and in his hands it changed to a sword that shone so brightly that it dazzled his eyes.

CHILDREN AND FAIRIES

Then he turned, and there was the long flight of
glass steps leading up to the golden castle just as
before, so thrusting the sword into his belt, he ran
nimbly up and up. When he reached the topmost
step he waved farewell to the Counterpane Fairy
below. She waved her hand to him. "Remember,"
she called, "beware of what is little and grey."

He opened the door and went into the five-sided
golden hall, and there were the three doors just as
before, and the spider spinning on the fourth side:

"Now the brave hero is wiser indeed,
He may have failed once, but he still may succeed.
Dull are the emeralds, diamonds are bright,
So is his wisdom that shines as the light."

"The diamond door!" cried Teddy. "Yes, that is
the door that I should have tried. How could I have
thought the emerald door was it?" And opening the
diamond door he stepped through it.

140

The Counterpane Fairy

He hardly had time to see that he was standing at the top of the glass steps, before – *brrrr!* – they had shut up again into a smooth glass hill, and there he was spinning down them so fast that the wind whistled past his ears.

In less time than it takes to tell, he was back again for the third time in the golden garden, with the Counterpane Fairy standing before him, and he was ashamed to raise his eyes.

"So!" said the Counterpane Fairy. "Did you know no better than to open the diamond door?"

"No," said Teddy, "I knew no better."

"Then," said the fairy, "if you can pay no better heed to my warnings than that, the princess must wait for another hero, for you are not the one."

"Let me try but once more," cried Teddy, "for this time I shall surely find her."

"Then you may try once more and for the last time," said the fairy, "but beware of what is little and grey." Stooping she picked from the grass beside

her a fallen acorn cup and handed it to him. "Take this with you," she said, "for it may serve you well."

As he took it from her, it was changed in his hand to a goblet of gold set round with precious stones. Turning he ran for the third time up the flight of glass steps. All the time he ran he was wondering what the fairy meant about her warning. She had said, 'Beware of what is little and grey.' What had he seen that was little and grey?

When he reached the golden hall the spider was spinning fast, but presently it stopped up in the corner of the web. As the hero looked at it he saw that it was little and grey. Then it began to sing to him in its tiny thin voice:

"Great hero, wiser than ever before,
Try the red door, try the red door.
Open the door that is ruby, and then
You never need search for the princess again."

142

The Counterpane Fairy

"No, I will not open the ruby door," cried Teddy. "I have followed your instructions twice and both times you have you sent me back to the golden garden, and now you shall fool me no more."

As he said this he saw that a corner of the web was unfinished, and underneath was something that looked like a little yellow door. Suddenly he knew that this was the door he must go through. He pulled at the curtain of web but it was as strong as steel. Quickly he snatched from his belt the magic sword, and with one blow the curtain was cut in two, and fell at his feet.

He heard the spider calling to him but paid no heed, for he had opened the door and stooped his head and entered.

Beyond was a great gold courtyard with a fountain splashing into a golden basin in the middle. But what he saw first was the princess, who lay stretched out as if asleep upon a couch all covered with cloth of gold.

He knew she was a princess, because she was so beautiful and because she wore a delicate crown.

He stood looking at her without stirring, and at last he whispered, "Princess! Princess! I have come to save you."

Still she did not stir. He bent and touched her, but she lay there in her enchanted sleep, and her eyes did not open. Then Teddy looked about him, and seeing the fountain he drew the magic cup from his bosom and, filling it, sprinkled the hands and

face of the princess with the water.

Then her eyes opened and she raised herself upon her elbow and smiled. "Have you come at last?" she cried.

"Yes," answered Teddy, "I have come."

The princess looked about her. "But what became of the spider?" she said. Then Teddy, too, looked about, and there was the spider running across the floor towards where the princess lay. Quickly he sprang from her side and set his foot upon it. There was a thin squeak and then – there was nothing left of the little grey spinner but a tiny grey smudge on the floor.

Instantly the golden castle was shaken from top to bottom, and there was a sound of many voices shouting outside. The princess rose to her feet and caught the hero by the hand. "You have broken the enchantment," she cried, "and now you shall be the king of the golden castle and reign with me."

"Oh, but I can't," said Teddy, "because, because–"

But the princess drew him out with her through the hall, and there they were at the head of the flight of glass steps. A great host of soldiers and courtiers were running up it. They were dressed in cloth of gold, and they shouted at the sight of Teddy, "Hail to the hero! Hail to the hero!"

"And all this is yours," said the beautiful princess, turning towards him with—

"So that is the story of the yellow square," said the Counterpane Fairy.

Teddy looked about him. The golden castle had vanished, and the stairs, and the shouting courtiers. He was lying in bed with the coverlet over his knees and Hannah was still singing in the kitchen below.

"Did you like it?" asked the fairy.

Teddy heaved a deep sigh. "Oh! Wasn't it beautiful?" he said. Then he lay for a while thinking and smiling. "Wasn't the princess lovely?" he whispered half to himself.

The Counterpane Fairy got up slowly and stiffly,

and picked up the staff that she had laid down beside her. "Well, I must be journeying on," she said.

"Oh, no, no!" cried Teddy. "Please don't go yet."

"Yes, I must," said the Counterpane Fairy. "I hear your mother coming."

"But will you come back again?" cried Teddy.

The Counterpane Fairy made no answer. She was walking down the other side of the bed-quilt hill, and Teddy heard her voice, little and thin, dying away in the distance, "Oh dear, dear, dear! What a hill to go down! What a hill! Oh dear, dear, dear!"

Then the door opened and his mother came in. She was looking rested, and she smiled at him lovingly, but the little brown Counterpane Fairy was gone.

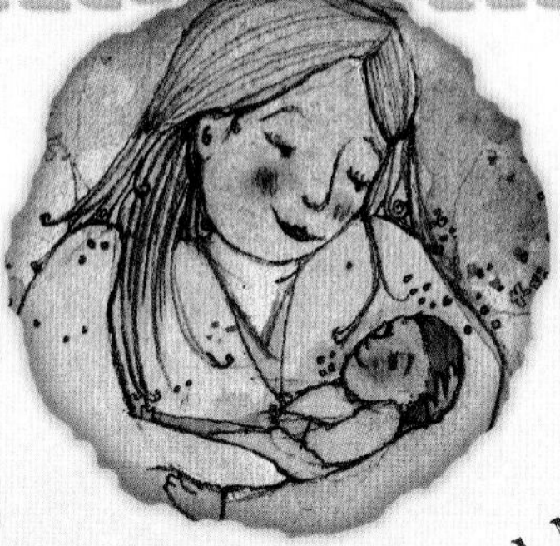

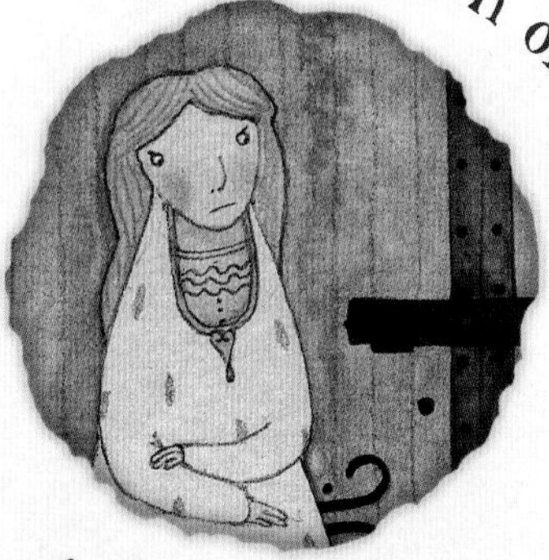

FAIRY HELPERS

Mrs Bedonebyasyoudid and Mrs Doasyouwouldbedoneby

From *The Water Babies* by Charles Kingsley

Tom is a chimney-sweep's boy who has run away from his cruel master. When he tried to wash away his soot in a stream, he fell in and became a water baby. He has been swimming around on his own for some time.

And now a wonderful thing happened to Tom – he came upon a water baby.

A real live water baby, sitting on the white sand, very busy about a little point of rock. And when it saw Tom it looked up for a moment, and then cried, "Why, you are not one of us. You are a new baby!

150

Mrs Bedonebyasyoudid and
Mrs Doasyouwouldbedoneby

Oh, how delightful!"

Tom looked at the baby again, and then he said, "Well, this is wonderful! I have seen things just like you again and again, but I thought you were shells, or sea creatures. I never took you for water babies like myself."

"Now," said the baby, "come and help me, or I shall not have finished before my brothers and sisters come, and it is time to go home."

"What shall I help you at?"

"At this poor dear little rock. A great clumsy boulder came rolling by in the last storm, and knocked all its head off, and rubbed off all its flowers. And now I must plant it again with seaweeds, coral and anemones, and I will make it the prettiest rock garden on all the shore."

So they worked away at the rock, and planted it, and smoothed the sand down round it, and capital fun they had till the tide began to turn. And then Tom heard all the other babies coming, laughing

151

and singing and shouting and romping, and the
noise they made was just like the noise of the ripple.
And in they came, dozens and dozens of them,
some bigger than Tom and some smaller, all in the
neatest little white bathing dresses, and when they
found that he was a new baby, they hugged him and
kissed him, and then put him in the middle and
danced round him on the sand, and there was no
one ever so happy as poor little Tom.

"Now then," they cried all at once, "we must come
away home, we must come away home, or the tide
will leave us dry. We have mended all the broken
seaweed, and put all the rock-pools in order, and
planted all the shells again in the sand, and nobody
will see where the ugly storm swept in last week."

And this is the reason why the rock-pools are
always so neat and clean – because the water
babies come inshore after every storm to sweep
them out, and comb them down, and put them all
to rights again.

FAIRY HELPERS

Only where men are wasteful and dirty, and let sewers run into the sea instead of putting the stuff upon the fields like thrifty reasonable souls, or throw herrings' heads and dead dog-fish, or any other refuse, into the water, or in any way make a mess upon the clean shore – only there the water babies will not come, sometimes not for hundreds of years (for they cannot abide anything smelly or foul). Instead they leave the sea anemones and the crabs to clear away everything, and after a time the good tidy sea covers up all the dirt in soft mud and clean sand.

And where is the home of the water babies? In St Brandan's fairy isle.

Did you never hear of the blessed St Brandan, who far away, before the setting sun, saw a blue fairy sea, and golden fairy islands, and he said, "Those are the islands of the blest." Then he and his friends got into a boat, and sailed away and away to the westward, and were never heard of again.

Mrs Bedonebyasyoudid and Mrs Doasyouwouldbedoneby

And when St Brandan and the hermits came to that fairy isle they found it overgrown with cedars and full of beautiful birds, and he sat down under the cedars and preached to all the birds in the air. And they liked his sermons so well that they told the fishes in the sea, and they came, and St Brandan preached to them. And the fishes told the water babies, who live in the caves under the isle, and they came up by hundreds.

He taught the water babies for a great many hundred years, until his eyes grew too dim to see, and his beard grew so long that he dared not walk for fear of treading on it, and then he might have tumbled down. And at last he and the five hermits fell fast asleep under the shade of the cedars, and there they sleep unto this day. So then the fairies took to the water babies, and taught them their lessons themselves.

And on still clear summer evenings, when the sun sinks down into the sea, among the golden cloud-capes and cloud-islands, and locks and friths of azure sky, the sailors fancy that they see, away to westward, St Brandan's fairy isle.

Now when Tom got there, he found that the isle stood all on pillars, and that its roots were full of caves all curtained and draped with seaweeds, purple and crimson, green and brown, and strewn with soft white sand, on which the water babies sleep every night. But, to keep the place clean and sweet, the crabs picked up all the scraps off the floor and ate them like so many monkeys, while the rocks were covered with ten thousand sea anemones, and corals, who scavenged the water all day long, and kept it nice and pure.

But I wish Tom had given up all his naughty tricks, and left off tormenting dumb animals now that he had plenty of playfellows to amuse him. Instead of that, I am sorry to say, he would meddle with the creatures, all but the water-snakes, for they would stand no nonsense.

Mrs Bedonebyasyoudid and Mrs Doasyouwouldbedoneby

So he frightened the crabs, to make them hide in the sand and peep out at him with the tips of their eyes, and put stones into the anemones' mouths, to make them fancy that their dinner was coming.

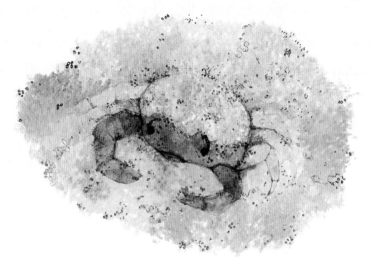

The other children warned him, and said, "Take care what you are at. Mrs Bedonebyasyoudid is coming." But Tom never listened to them, being quite riotous with high spirits and good luck, till, one Friday morning early, Mrs Bedonebyasyoudid came indeed.

157

FAIRY HELPERS

A very tremendous lady she was, and when the children saw her they all stood in a row, very upright indeed, and smoothed down their bathing dresses, and put their hands behind their backs – it was just as if they were all going to be examined by the inspector.

And she had on a black bonnet, and a black shawl, and a pair of large green spectacles, and a great hooked nose, hooked so much that the bridge of it stood quite up above her eyebrows, and under her arm she carried a great birch-rod. Indeed, she was so ugly that Tom was tempted to make faces at her – but did not, for he did not admire the look of the birch-rod under her arm.

And she looked at the children one by one, and seemed very much pleased with them, though she never asked them one question about how they were behaving, and then began giving them all sorts of nice sea-things – sea-cakes, sea-apples, sea-oranges, sea-bullseyes, sea-toffee, and to the very

Mrs Bedonebyasyoudid and
Mrs Doasyouwouldbedoneby

best of all she gave sea-ices, made out of sea-cows'
cream, which never melt under water.

And, if you don't quite believe me, then just
think – what is more cheap and plentiful than sea-
rock? Then why should there not be sea-toffee as
well? And every one can find sea-lemons (ready
quartered too) if they will look for them at low tide,
and sea-grapes too sometimes, hanging in bunches.
Now little Tom watched all these sweet things given
away, till his mouth watered, and his eyes grew as
round as an owl's. For he hoped that his turn would
come at last, and so it did. For the lady called him
up, and held out her fingers with something in
them, and popped it into his mouth – and, lo and
behold, it was a nasty cold hard pebble.

"You are a very cruel woman," said he, and began
to whimper.

"And you are a very cruel boy, who puts pebbles
into the sea anemones' mouths, to take them in, and
make them fancy that they had caught a good

dinner! As you did to them, so I must do to you."

"Who told you that?" said Tom.

"You did yourself, this very minute."

Tom had never opened his lips, so he was very much taken aback indeed.

"Yes, everyone tells me exactly what they have done wrong, and that without knowing it themselves. So there is no use trying to hide anything from me. Now go, and be a good boy, and I will put no more pebbles in your mouth, if you put none in other creatures."

"I did not know there was any harm in it," said Tom.

"Then you know now."

"Well, you are a little hard on a poor lad," said Tom, reproachfully.

"Not at all – I am the best friend you ever had in all your life. But I will tell you, I cannot help punishing people when they do wrong. I like it no more than they do. I am often very, very sorry for them, poor things, but I cannot help it. If I tried not to do it, I should do it all the same. For I work by machinery, just like an engine, and am full of wheels and springs inside, and am wound up very carefully, so that I cannot help going."

"Was it long ago since they wound you up?" asked Tom. For he thought, the cunning little fellow, 'She will run down some day, or they may forget to wind her up.'

"I was wound up once and for all, so long ago, that I forget all about it."

"You must have been made a long time!" exclaimed Tom.

"I never was made, my child, and I shall go forever and ever, for I am as old as Eternity, and yet as young as Time."

And there came over the lady's face a very curious expression – very solemn, and very sad, and yet very, very sweet. And she looked up and away, as if she were gazing through the sea, and through the sky, at something far, far off, and as she did so, there came such a quiet, tender, patient, hopeful smile over her face that Tom thought for the moment that she did not look ugly at all.

And Tom smiled in her face, she looked so pleasant for the moment. And the strange fairy smiled too, and said, "Yes. You thought me very ugly just now, did you not?"

Tom hung down his head, and got very red about the ears.

"And I am very ugly. I am the ugliest fairy in the world, and I shall be, till people behave themselves as they ought to do. And then I shall grow as

Mrs Bedonebyasyoudid and Mrs Doasyouwouldbedoneby

handsome as my sister – the loveliest fairy in the world. Her name is Mrs Doasyouwouldbedoneby. So she begins where I end, and I begin where she ends, and those who will not listen to her must listen to me, as you will see."

Poor old Mrs Bedonebyasyoudid! She has a great deal of hard work before her, and had better have been born a washerwoman, and stood over a tub all day. But, you see, people cannot always choose their own profession.

Tom determined to be a very good boy all Saturday, and he was, for he never frightened one crab, nor tickled any live corals, nor put stones into the sea anemones' mouths, to make them fancy they had got a dinner. And when Sunday morning came, sure enough, Mrs Doasyouwouldbedoneby came too. Whereat all the little children began dancing and clapping their hands and Tom danced too with all his might.

And as for the pretty lady, I cannot tell you what

the colour of her hair was, or of her eyes. No more could Tom, for, when anyone looks at her, all they can think of is that she has the sweetest, kindest, tenderest, funniest, merriest face they ever saw, or want to see. But Tom saw that she was a very tall woman, as tall as her sister. But instead of being gnarly and horny, and scaly, and prickly, like her, she was the most nice, soft, fat, smooth, cuddly creature who ever nursed a baby, and she understood babies thoroughly, for she had plenty of her own, whole rows and regiments of them, and has to this day.

And all her delight was, whenever she had a spare moment, to play with babies, in which she showed herself a woman of sense, for babies are the best company, and the pleasantest playfellows in the world, at least, so all the wise people in the world think. And therefore when the children saw her, they naturally all caught hold of her, and pulled her till she sat down on a stone, and climbed into her lap, and clung round her neck, and caught hold of

Mrs Bedonebyasyoudid and Mrs Doasyouwouldbedoneby

her hands. And then they all put their thumbs into their mouths, and began cuddling and purring like so many kittens, as they ought to have done. While those who could get nowhere else sat down on the sand, and cuddled her feet – for no one, you know, wears shoes in the water. And Tom stood staring, for he could not understand what it was all about.

"And who are you, you little darling?" she said.

"Oh, that is the new baby!" they all cried, pulling their thumbs out of their mouths, "And he never had any mother," and they all put their thumbs back again, for they did not wish to lose any time.

"Then I will be his mother, and he shall have the very best place, so get out, all of you, this moment."

And she took up two great armfuls of babies – nine hundred under one arm, and thirteen hundred under the other – and threw them away, right and left, into the water. But they did not even take their thumbs out of their mouths, but came paddling and wriggling back to her like so many tadpoles.

FAIRY HELPERS

But she took Tom in her arms, and laid him in the softest place of all, and kissed him, and patted him, and talked to him, tenderly and low, such

Mrs Bedonebyasyoudid and
Mrs Doasyouwouldbedoneby

things as he had never heard before in his life, and
Tom looked up into her eyes, and loved her, and
loved, till he fell fast asleep from pure love.

And when he woke she was telling the children a
story. And what story did she tell them? One story
she told them, which begins every Christmas Eve,
and yet never ends at all forever and ever. And, as
she went on, the children took their thumbs out of
their mouths and listened quite seriously, but not
sadly at all, for she never told them anything sad,
and Tom listened too, and never grew tired of
listening. And he listened so long that he fell fast
asleep again, and, when he woke, the lady was
nursing him still.

"Don't go away," said little Tom. "This is so nice.
I never had any one to cuddle me before."

"Now," said the fairy to Tom, "will you be a good
boy for my sake, and torment no more sea beasts till
I come back?"

"And you will cuddle me again?" said poor Tom.

167

"Of course I will, you little duck. I should like to take you with me and cuddle you all the way, only I must not," and away she went.

So Tom really tried to be a good boy, and tormented no sea beasts after that as long as he lived, and he is quite alive, I assure you, still.

The Touch of Iron

By William Elliot Griffis

Some people believe the fairies were the original inhabitants of ancient lands before humans came and drove them to hide in caves and wild places. Another common belief is that fairies cannot stand the touch of cold iron. This story uses these two ideas to tell its tale. Cymry is the Welsh word for the inhabitants of Wales.

Ages ago, before the Cymry travelled across the sea, a race of fairies already lived in the Land of Honey, as Great Britain was then called. These ancient fairies, who lived in caves, did not know how to build houses or to plough the ground.

FAIRY HELPERS

They had no idea that they could get their food out of the earth. As for making bread, pies and goodies, they never heard of such a thing. They did not know how to use fire for melting copper, nor did they know how to get iron from ore to make strong knives and spears, arrow heads and swords, and armour and helmets.

All they could do was mould clay to make things to cook with. When they baked this soft stuff in the fire, they found they had pots, pans and dishes as hard as stone, though these were easily broken.

To hunt the deer, or fight the wolves and bears, they fashioned clubs of wood. For javelins and arrows, they took hard stone like flint and chipped it to points and sharpened it with edges. This was the time which we now call the Stone Age, and when the fairies went to war, their weapons were wholly of wood or stone.

They had not yet learned to weave the wool of the sheep into warm clothing, but they wore the

The Touch of Iron

skins of animals. Each one of the caves in which they lived was a boarding house for dogs and pigs, as well as people.

When a young man of one fairy tribe wanted a wife, he sallied out secretly into another neighbourhood. There he lay in wait for a girl to come along. He then ran away with her, and back to his own daddy's cave.

When the Cymry came into the land, they had iron tools and better weapons of war. Then there were many and long battles and the fairies were beaten many times.

So the fairies hated everything that was made of iron. Anyone of them, girls or boys, who had picked up iron ornaments, and were found wearing or using iron tools, or buying anything of iron from the cave people's enemies, was looked upon as a rascal, or a villain, or even as a traitor and was driven out of the tribe.

However, some of the daughters of the fairies

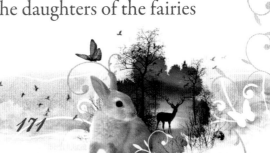

were so pretty and had such rosy cheeks, and lovely
figures, and beautiful, long hair, that quite often the
Cymric youth fell in love with them.

Many of the fairy daughters were captured and
became wives of the Cymry and mothers of
children. Over time, their descendants helped to
make the bright, witty, song-loving Welsh people.

Now the fairies usually like things that are old,
and they are very slow to alter the ancient customs
to which they have been used, for, in the fairy
world, there is no measure of time, nor any clocks,
watches, or bells to strike the hours, and no
calendars to mark the passing of the days.

The fairies cannot understand why ladies change
the fashions so often, and the men their ways of
doing things. They wonder why beards are
fashionable at one time, then moustaches long or
short at another, or smooth faces when razors are
cheap. Most fairies like to keep on doing the same
thing in the old way. They enjoy being like the

The Touch of Iron

mountains, which stand, or the sea, that rolls, or the sun, that rises and sets every day and forever. They never get tired of repeating tomorrow what they did yesterday. They are very different from the people that are always wanting something else.

That is the reason why the fairies did not like iron, or to see men wearing iron hats and clothes, called helmets and armour, when they went to war. They no more wanted to be touched by iron than by filth, or foul disease. They hated knives, stirrups, scythes, swords, pots, pans, kettles, or this metal in any form, whether sheet, barbed wire, lump or pig iron.

Now there was a long, pretty stretch of water, near which lived a handsome lad, who loved nothing better than to go out late on moonlight nights and see the fairies dance, or listen to their music. This youth fell in love with one of these fairies, whose beauty was dazzling beyond description. At last, unable to control his passion, he rushed into the midst of the fairy company, seized the beautiful one, and rushed back to his home, with his prize in his arms. This was in true cave-man fashion.

When the other fairies hurried to rescue her, they found the man's house shut. They dared not touch the door, for it had iron studs and bands, and was bolted with the metal they most abhorred.

The Touch of Iron

The young man immediately began to woo the fairy maid, hoping to win her to be his wife. For a long time she refused, and moped all day and night. While weeping many salt water tears, she declared that she was too homesick to live.

She was a smart fairy, and was sure she could outwit the man, even if he had every sort of iron everywhere in order to keep her as it were in a prison. So, pretending she loved him dearly, she said, "I will not be your wife, but, if you can find out my name, I shall gladly become your servant."

'Easily won,' thought the lover to himself. Yet the game was a harder one to play than he supposed. It was like playing 'Blind Man's Buff', or 'Hunt the Slipper'. Although he made guesses of every name he could think of, he was never 'hot' and got no nearer to the thing sought than if his eyes were bandaged. All the time, he was deeper and deeper in love with the lovely fairy maid.

But one night when he was returning home, he

saw a group of fairies sitting on a log. At once, he thought they might be talking about their lost sister. So he crept up close to them, and soon found that he had guessed right. After a long discussion, finding themselves still at a loss as to how to recover her, he heard one of them sigh and say, "Oh, Siwsi, my sister, how can you live with a mortal?"

"Enough," said the young man to himself. "I've got it." Then, crawling away noiselessly, he ran back all the way to his house, and unlocked the door. Once inside the room, he called out his servant's name, "Siwsi! Siwsi!"

Astonished at hearing her name, she cried out, "What mortal has betrayed me? For, surely no fairy would tell on me? Alas, my fate, my fate!"

But in her own mind, the struggle and the fear were over. She had bravely striven to keep her fairyhood, and in the battle of wits, had lost.

She would not be a wife, but what a wise, superb and faithful servant she made!

The Touch of Iron

Everything prospered under her hand. The house and the farm became models. Not twice, but three times a day, the cows, milked by her, yielded milk unusually rich in cream. In the market, her butter excelled, in quality and price, all others.

In the end, she agreed to become his wife – but only on one condition.

"You must never strike me with iron," she said. "If you do, I'll feel free to leave you, and go back to my relatives in the fairy family."

A hearty laugh from the happy lover greeted this remark. He thought that the condition was very easy to obey.

So they were married, and no couple in all the land seemed happier. Once, twice, the cradle was filled. It rocked with new treasures that had life, and were more dear than farm, or home, or wealth in barns or cattle, cheese and butter. A boy and a girl were theirs. Then the mother's care was contant.

Even though the happy father grew richer every

year, and bought farm after farm until he owned five thousand acres, he valued most his lovely wife and his two beautiful children.

Yet this very delight and affection made him less careful concerning the promise he had once given to his fairy wife, who still held to the ancient ideas of the fairy family in regard to iron.

One of his finest mares had given birth to a filly, which, when the day of the great fair came, he determined to sell at a high price.

So with a halter on his arm, he went out to catch the filly. But she was a spirited creature, so frisky that it was much like his first attempt to win his fairy bride. The lively and frolicsome beast scampered here and there, grazing as she stopped, as if she were determined to put off her capture as long as possible.

So, calling to his wife, the two of them together tried their skill to catch the filly. This time, leaving the halter in the house, the man took bit and bridle,

The Touch of Iron

and the two managed to get the pretty creature into a corner, but, when they had almost captured her, away she dashed again.

By this time, the man was so vexed that he lost his temper, and he who does that, usually loses the game, while he who controls the wrath within, wins. Mad as a flaming fire, he lost his brains also and threw the bit and bridle and the whole harness as far as he could, after the fleeting animal.

FAIRY HELPERS

Alas! Alas! The wife had started to run after the filly and the iron bit struck her on the cheek. It did not hurt, but he had broken his vow.

Now came the surprise of his life. It was as if, at one moment, a flash of lightning had made all things bright, and then in another second was inky darkness. He saw this lovely wife, one moment active and fleet as a deer. In another, in the twinkling of an eye, nothing was there. She had vanished. After this, there was a lonely home, empty of its light and cheer.

But by living with human beings, a new idea and form of life had transformed this fairy, and a new spell was laid on her. Mother-love had been awakened in her heart. Henceforth, though the law of the fairy world would not allow her to touch again the realm of earth, she, having once been wife and parent, could not forget the babies born of her body. So, making a grass raft, a floating island, she came up at night. And often, while these three mortals lived, this fairy mother would spend hours tenderly talking to her husband and her two children, who were now big boy and girl, as they stood on the lake shore.

Even today, good people sometimes see a little island floating on the lake, and point it out as the place where the fairy mother used to come and talk with her dear ones.

The Phantom Vessel

By Norman Hinsdale Pitman

*O*nce a ship loaded with pleasure seekers was sailing from North China to Shanghai. Stormy weather had delayed her, and she was still one week from port when a great plague broke out on board. The terrible illness attacked passengers and sailors alike until there were so few left to sail the vessel that it seemed as if she would soon be left to the mercy of winds and waves.

The Phantom Vessel

On all sides lay the dead, and the groans of the dying were most terrible to hear. Of that great company of travellers only one, a little boy named Ying-lo, had escaped. At last the few sailors, who had been trying hard to save their ship, were obliged to lie down upon the deck, a prey to the dreadful sickness, and soon they too were dead.

Ying-lo now found himself alone on the sea. For some reason – he did not know why – the gods or the sea fairies had spared him, but as he looked about in terror at the friends and loved ones who had died, he almost wished that he might join them.

The sails flapped about like great broken wings, while the giant waves dashed higher above the deck, washing many of the bodies overboard and wetting the little boy to the skin. Shivering with cold, he gave himself up for lost and prayed to the gods, whom his mother had often told him about, to take him from this dreadful ship and let him escape the fatal illness.

FAIRY HELPERS

As he lay there praying, he heard a slight noise in the rigging just above his head. Looking up, he saw a ball of fire running along a yardarm near the top of the mast. The sight was so strange that he forgot his prayer and stared with open-mouthed wonder. To his astonishment, the ball grew brighter and brighter, and then suddenly began slipping down the mast, all the time increasing in size. Nearer and nearer came the fireball. At last, when it reached the deck, to Ying-lo's surprise, something very, very strange happened. Before he had time to feel alarmed, the light vanished, and a funny little man stood in front of him peering anxiously into the child's frightened face.

"Yes, you are the lad I'm looking for," he said at last, speaking in a piping voice that almost made Ying-lo smile. "You are Ying-lo, and you are the only one left of this wretched company."

Although he saw that the old man meant him no harm, the child could say nothing, but waited in

184

silence, wondering what would happen next.

By this time the vessel was tossing and pitching so violently that it seemed every minute as if it would upset and go down beneath the foaming waves, never to rise again. Not many miles distant on the right, some jagged rocks stuck out of the water, lifting their cruel heads as if waiting for the helpless ship.

The newcomer walked slowly towards the mast and tapped on it three times with an iron staff he had been using as a cane. Immediately the sails spread, the vessel righted itself and began to glide over the sea so fast that the gulls were soon left far behind, while the threatening rocks upon which the ship had been so nearly dashed seemed like specks in the distance.

"Do you remember me?" said the stranger, turning and coming up to Ying-lo, but his voice was lost in the whistling of the wind, and the boy knew only by the moving of his lips that the old man was talking. The greybeard came close and whispered to Ying-lo, "Did you ever see me before?"

With a puzzled look, at first the child shook his head. Then as he gazed more closely there seemed to be something that he recognized about the wrinkled face. "Yes, I think so, but I don't know when."

With a tap of his staff the fairy stopped the blowing of the wind, and then spoke once more to his small companion, "One year ago I passed through your village. I was dressed in rags, and was begging my way along the street, trying to find someone who would feel sorry for me. Alas! No one answered my cry for mercy. Not a crust was thrown into my bowl. All the people were deaf, and fierce dogs drove me from door to door. I was almost dying of hunger when I began to feel that here was a village without one good person in it. Just then you saw my suffering, and brought me out food. Your heartless mother saw you doing this and beat you cruelly. Do you remember now, my child?"

FAIRY HELPERS

"Yes, I remember," he answered sadly, "and my mother is now lying dead. All are dead, my father and my brothers also. Not one is left of my family."

"Little did you know, my boy, to whom you were giving food that day. You took me for a lowly beggar, but, behold, it was not a poor man that you fed, for I am Iron Staff. You must have heard of me when they were telling of the fairies in the Western Heaven, and of their adventures here on earth."

"Yes, yes," answered Ying-lo, trembling half with fear and half with joy, "indeed I have heard of you many, many times, and all the people love you for your kind deeds of mercy."

"Alas! They did not show their love, my little one. Surely you know that if any one wishes to reward the fairies for their mercies, he must begin to do deeds of the same kind himself. No one but you in all your village had pity on me in my rags."

Ying-lo listened in wonder to Iron Staff, and when he had finished, the boy's face was glowing

The Phantom Vessel

with the love of which the fairy had spoken. "My poor, poor father and mother!" he cried, "they knew nothing of these beautiful things you are telling me. They were brought up in poverty. As they were knocked about in childhood by those around them, so they learned to beat others who begged them for help. Is it strange that they did not have hearts full of pity for you when you looked like a beggar?"

"But what about you, my boy? You were not deaf when I asked you. Have you not been whipped and punished all your life? How then did you learn to look with love at those in tears?"

The child could not answer, but looked sadly at Iron Staff. "Oh, can you not, good fairy, restore my parents and brothers, and give them another chance to be good and useful people?"

"Listen, Ying-lo, it is impossible unless you do two things first," he answered, stroking his beard gravely and leaning heavily upon his staff.

FAIRY HELPERS

"What are they? What must I do to save my family? Anything you ask of me will not be too much to pay for your kindness."

"First you must tell me of some good deed done by these people for whose lives you are asking. Name only one, for that will be enough, but it is against the rules of the fairies to help those who have done nothing."

Ying-lo was silent, and for a moment his face was clouded. "Yes, I know," he answered, brightening. "Last year when the foreigner rode through our village and fell sick in front of our house, they cared for him."

"How long?" asked the other sharply.

"Until he died the next week."

"And what did they do with the mule he was riding, his bed, and the money in his bag? Did they try to restore them to his people?"

"No, they said they'd keep them to pay for the trouble." Ying-lo's face turned scarlet.

The Phantom Vessel

"But you should try again, dear boy! Is there not one little deed of goodness that was not selfish? Think once more."

For a long time Ying-lo did not reply. At length he spoke in a low voice, "I think of one, but I fear it amounts to nothing."

"No good, my child, is too small to be counted when the gods are weighing a man's heart."

"Last spring the birds were eating in my father's garden. My mother wanted to buy poison from the shop to destroy them, but my father said no, that the little things must live, and he for one was not in favour of killing them."

"At last, Ying-lo, you have named a real deed of mercy, and as he spared the tiny birds from poison, so shall his life and the lives of your mother and brothers be restored from the deadly plague.

FAIRY HELPERS

"But remember there is one other thing that depends on you."

Ying-lo's eyes glistened gratefully. "Then if it rests with me, and I can do it, you have my promise."

"Very well, Ying-lo. What I require is that you carry out to the letter my instructions. Now it is time for me to keep my promise to you."

So saying, Iron Staff called on Ying-lo to point out the members of his family, and, approaching them one by one, with the end of his iron stick he touched their foreheads. In an instant each, without a word, arose. Looking round and recognizing Ying-lo, they stood back, frightened at seeing him with the fairy. Iron Staff beckoned all of them to listen. This they did willingly, too much terrified to speak, for they saw on all sides signs of the plague that had swept over the vessel, and they remembered the frightful agony they had suffered in dying. Each knew that he had been lifted by some magic power from darkness into light.

The Phantom Vessel

"My friends," began the fairy, "little did you think when less than a year ago you drove me from your door that soon you yourselves would be in need of mercy. As you look back through your wicked lives can you think of any reason why you deserved this rescue? No, there is no memory of goodness in your black hearts. Well, I shall tell you – it is this little boy, this Ying-lo, who many times has felt the weight of your wicked hands and has hidden in terror at your coming. To him alone you owe my help.

"If at any time you treat him badly and do not heed his wishes – mark you well my words – by the power of this magic staff which I shall place in his hands, he may enter at once into the land of the fairies, leaving you to die in your wickedness. This I command him to do, and he has promised to obey my slightest wish.

"This plague took you off suddenly and ended your wicked lives. Ying-lo has raised you from its grasp and his power can lift you from the bed of sin. No other hand than his can bear the rod which I am leaving. If one of you but touch it, instantly he will fall dead upon the ground.

"And now, my child, the time has come for me to leave you. First, however, I must show you what you are now able to do. Around you lie the corpses of sailors and passengers. Tap three times upon the mast and wish that they shall come to life." So saying he handed Ying-lo the iron staff.

Although the magic rod was heavy, the child lifted it as if it were a fairy's wand. Then, stepping forward to the mast, he rapped three times as he had been commanded. Immediately on all sides arose the bodies, once more full of life and strength.

"Now command the ship to take you back to your home port, for such sinful creatures as these are in no way fit to make a journey among strangers. They must first return and free their homes of sin."

Again rapping on the mast, the child willed the

194

The Phantom Vessel

great vessel to take its homeward course. No sooner had he moved the staff than the boat swung round and started on the return journey. Swifter than a flash of lightning it flew, for it had become a fairy vessel. Before the sailors and the travellers could recover from their surprise, land was sighted and they saw that they were entering the harbour.

Just as the ship was darting toward the shore the fairy suddenly changed into a ball of fire which rolled along the deck and ascended the spars. As it reached the top of the rigging it floated off into the sky, and all on board watched it until it vanished.

With a cry of thanksgiving, Ying-lo flung his arms about his parents and descended with them to the shore.

Farmer Mybrow
and the Fairies

By William H Barker

Farmer Mybrow was one day looking about for a suitable piece of land to convert into a field, for he wished to grow corn and yams. He discovered a fine spot, close to a great forest – which was the home of some fairies. He set to work at once to prepare the field.

Having sharpened his great knife, he began to cut down the bushes. No sooner had he touched

one than he heard a voice say, "Who is there,
cutting down the bushes?"

Mybrow was too much astonished to answer.
The question was repeated. This time the farmer
realized that it must be one of the fairies, and so
replied, "I am Mybrow, come to prepare a field."

Fortunately for him the fairies were in great good
humour. He heard one say, "Let us all help Farmer
Mybrow to cut down the bushes." The rest agreed.
To Mybrow's great delight, the bushes were all
rapidly cut down with very little trouble on his part.
He returned home, exceedingly well pleased with
his day's work, having resolved to keep the field a
secret even from his wife.

Early in January, when it was time to burn the
dry bush, he set off to his field, one afternoon, with
the means of making a fire. Hoping to have the
fairies' help once more, he struck the trunk of a tree
as he passed. Immediately came the question, "Who
is there, striking the stumps?"

FAIRY HELPERS

He promptly replied, "I am Mybrow, come to burn down the bush." Accordingly, the dried bushes were all burned down, and the field left clear in less time that it takes to tell it.

Next day the same thing happened. Mybrow came to chop up the stumps for firewood and clear the field for digging. In a very short time his firewood was piled ready, while the field was bare.

So it went on. The field was divided into two parts – one for maize and one for yams. In all the preparations – digging, sowing, planting – the fairies gave great assistance. Still, the farmer had managed to keep the whereabouts of his field a secret from his wife and neighbours.

The soil having been so carefully prepared, the crops promised exceedingly

Farmer Mybrow and the Fairies

well. Mybrow visited them from
time to time, and congratulated
himself on the splendid harvest he
would have.

One day, while maize and yams
were still in their green and milky
state, Mybrow's wife came to him.
She wished to know where his field
lay, that she might go and fetch
some of the firewood from it. At
first he refused to tell her. Being very
persistent, however, she finally
succeeded in obtaining the information –
but on one condition. She must not answer
any question that should be asked her. This she
readily promised, and set off for the field.

When she arrived there she was
utterly amazed at the wealth of the corn
and yams. She had never seen such
magnificent crops. The maize looked most

tempting – being still in the milky state – so she plucked an ear. While doing so she heard a voice say, "Who is there, breaking the corn?"

"Who dares ask me such a question?" she replied angrily, for she had quite forgotten her husband's command. Going to the field of yams she plucked one of them also.

"Who is there, picking the yams?" came the question again.

"It is I, Mybrow's wife. This is my husband's field and I have a right to pick." Out came the fairies.

"Let us all help Mybrow's wife to pluck her corn and yams," said they. And before the frightened woman could say a word, the fairies had all set to work with a will, and within a moment, all the corn and yams lay useless on the ground. They were not ready for picking, being all green and unripe, so the harvest was now utterly spoiled. The farmer's wife wept bitterly, but to no purpose. She returned slowly home, not knowing what to say to her

husband about such a terrible catastrophe. She decided to keep silence about the matter.

Accordingly, next day the poor man set off gleefully to his field to see how his fine crops were going on. His anger and dismay may be imagined when he saw his field a complete ruin. All his work and foresight had been absolutely ruined through his wife's forgetfulness of her promise.

MAGIC AND MISCHIEF

The Fairy Cure

By Patrick Kennedy

For nearly a year, Nora's daughter, Judy, had been confined to her bed by a sore leg, which neither she nor the neighbouring doctor could 'make any hand of.'

Now Nora's mother was a midwife, and one night she was summoned by a dark rider to help with a lady about to have a child. She was whisked away and brought to the door of a magnificent

The Fairy Cure

palace. In the hall she was surprised to see an old neighbour, who had long been spirited away from the haunts of his youth and manhood. He at once took an opportunity, when the dark man was not observing him, to warn Nora that if she ever wanted to return home, she must take no refreshment of any kind while under the roof of the fairy castle, and refuse money or any other reward in any form. The only exception he made was in favour of cures for diseases inflicted by evil spirits or by fairies.

She found the lady of the castle in a bed with pillows and quilts of silk, and in a short time (for Nora was a handy woman) there was a beautiful little girl sleeping peacefully with the delighted mother. All the fine ladies that were scattered through the large room now gathered round, and congratulated their queen, and paid many compliments to the lucky-handed Nora. "I am so pleased with you," said the lady, "that I shall be glad to see you take as much gold, and silver, and jewels,

out of the next room, as you can carry."

Nora stepped in out of curiosity and saw piles of gold and silver coins, and baskets of diamonds and pearls. Great heaps of treasure were lying about on every side, but she remembered her caution, and came out empty-handed.

"I'm much obliged to you, my lady," said she, "but if I took them guineas, and crowns, and jewels home, no one would ever call on me again to help his wife, and I'd be sitting and doing nothing but drinking tea, an' I'm sure I'd be dead before a year'd be gone by."

"Oh dear!" said the lady, "What an odd person you are! At any rate, sit down at that table, and help yourself to food and drink."

"Oh, ma'am, is it them jellies, an' custards, an' pastry you'd like to see me at? Lord love you! I would'n know the way to me mouth with the likes of them."

"Alas! Alas! Is there any way in which I can show

you how grateful I am for your help and your skill?"

"Indeed there is, ma'am. My girl, Jude, is lying under a sore leg for a twelvemonth, an' I'm sure that the lord or yourself can make her as sound as a bell if you only say the word."

"Ask me anything but that, and I shall see that you have it."

"Oh, lady, dear, that's giving me everything but the thing I want."

"You don't know the offence your daughter gave to us, I am sure, or you would not have asked me to cure her."

"Judy offend you, ma'am! Oh, it's impossible!"

"Not at all, and this is the way it happened. You know that all the fairy court enjoy their lives in the night only, and we frequently go through the country, and hold our feasts where the kitchen, and especially the hearth, is swept up clean. About a twelvemonth ago, myself and my ladies were passing your cabin, and one of the company liked the

207

appearance of the neat thatch, and the whitewashed walls, and the clean pavement outside the door, so much, that she persuaded us all to go in. We found the cheerful fire shining, the well swept hearth and floor, and the clean pewter and beautiful plates on the dresser, and the white table. We were so well pleased, that we sat down on the hearth, and laid our tea tray, and began to drink our tea as comfortably as could be. You know we can be any size we please, and there was a score of us settled before the fire.

"We were vexed enough when we saw your daughter come up out of your bedroom, and make towards the fire. Her feet, I acknowledge, were white and clean, but one of them would cover two or three of us, the size we were that night. On she came stalking, and just as I was raising my cup of tea to my lips, down came the soft flat sole on it, and spilled the tea all over me. I was very much annoyed, and I caught the thing that came next to

The Fairy Cure

my hand, and hurled it at her. It was the teapot, and the point of the spout is in her leg from that night till now."

"Oh, lady! How can you hold spite to the poor girl, that knew no more of you being there, nor of offending you, that she did of the night she was born?"

"Well, well, now that is all past and gone. Take this ointment. Rub it where you will see the purple mark, and I hope that your future thoughts of me may be pleasant."

Just then, a messenger came to say that the lord was at the hall door waiting for Nora, for the cockerels would be soon crowing. So she took leave of the lady, and mounted behind the dark man. The horse's back seemed as hard and as

thin as a hazel stick, but it bore her safely to her home. She was in a sleepy state all the time she was returning, but at last she woke up, and found herself standing by her own door. She got into bed as fast as she could, and when she woke next morning, she fancied it was all a dream. But she put her hand in her pocket, and there, for a certainty, was the box of ointment. She went to her daughter's room and without waking her, rubbed some of the stuff on her leg. In a few seconds she saw the skin bursting, and a tiny spout of a teapot working itself out.

When Judy awoke she wondered at the ease she felt in her leg. She rejoiced at her mother's story and soon regained her strength. From then on she always left the kitchen spotless at night, and took care never to let her feet stray after bedtime, for fear of giving offence to unseen visitors.

A French Puck

By Paul Sébillot

Among the mountain pastures and valleys that lie in the centre of France there dwelt a mischievous kind of spirit (whom we will call Puck), whose delight it was to play tricks on everybody, and particularly on the shepherds. They never knew when they were safe from him, as he could change himself into a man, woman or child, a stick, a goat or a ploughshare. Indeed, there was only one thing whose shape he could not take, and that was a needle. At least, he could transform himself into a needle, but he never was able to imitate the hole, so every woman would have found him out at once, and this he knew.

Puck was careful not always to play his tricks in the same place, but always moved on from one village to another, so that everyone trembled lest he should be the next victim.

One day he was told of a young couple who were going to the nearest town to buy all that they needed for setting up house. Quite certain that they would forget something which they could not do without, Puck waited patiently till they were jogging along in their cart on their return journey, and changed himself into a fly in order to overhear their conversation. For a long time it was very dull – all about their wedding day next month, and who would be invited. This led the bride to her dress, and she gave a cry of dismay.

A French Puck

"Oh how could I be so stupid? I have forgotten to buy the coloured reels of cotton to match my clothes!"

"Dear, dear!" exclaimed the young man. "That is unlucky, and didn't you tell me that the dressmaker was coming in tomorrow?"

"Yes, I did," and then she gave another little cry, which had quite a different sound from the first, and said, "Look!"

The bridegroom looked, and on one side of the road he saw a large ball of thread of all colours – of all the colours, that is, of the dresses that were tied on to the back of the cart.

"Well, that is a wonderful piece of good fortune," cried he, as he sprang out of the cart to get it. "One would think a fairy had put it there on purpose."

"Perhaps she has," laughed the girl, and as she spoke she seemed to hear an echo of her laughter.

For a moment she thought it was coming from the horse, but of course that was nonsense.

The dressmaker was delighted with the thread that was given her. It matched the clothes so perfectly, and never tied itself in knots, or broke perpetually, as most thread did. She finished her work much quicker than she expected and the bride invited her to come to the church and see her in her wedding dress.

There was a great crowd assembled to witness the ceremony, for the young people were immense favourites in the neighbourhood, and their parents were very rich. The doors were open, and the beautiful bride could be seen from afar, walking under the chestnut avenue.

"What a beautiful girl!" exclaimed the men. "What a lovely dress!" whispered the women. But just as she entered the church and took the hand of the bridegroom, who was waiting for her, a loud noise was heard – *Crick! Crack! Crick! Crack!* – and

the wedding garments fell to the ground, to the great confusion of the wearer.

Not that the ceremony was put off for a little thing like that! Cloaks were instantly offered to the young bride, but she was so upset that she could hardly keep from tears.

One of the guests, more curious than the rest, stayed behind to examine the dress, to find out the cause of the disaster. "The thread must have been rotten," she said to herself. "I will see if I can break it." But search as she would she could find none. The thread had vanished!

The Fairy Fluffikins

By Michael Fairless

*T*he Fairy Fluffikins lived in a warm woolly nest in a hole down an old oak tree. She was the sweetest, funniest little fairy you ever saw. She wore a little, soft dress, and on her head a little woolly cap. Fairy Fluffikins had red hair and the brightest, naughtiest, sharpest brown eyes imaginable.

What a life she led the animals! Fairy Fluffikins was a sad tease. She would creep into the nests

The Fairy Fluffikins

where the fat baby dormice were asleep in bed while mamma dormouse nodded over her knitting and papa smoked his little acorn pipe, and she would tickle the babies till they screamed with laughter.

One night she had fine fun. She found a little dead mouse in a field, and an idea struck her. She hunted about till she found a piece of long, strong grass, and then she took the little mouse, tied the piece of grass round its tail, and ran away with it to the big tree where the ancient owl lived. There was a little hole at the bottom of the tree and into it Fairy Fluffikins crept, leaving the mouse outside in the moonlight. Presently she heard a gruff voice in the tree saying, "I smell mouse, I smell mouse." Then there was a swoop of wings, and Fairy Fluffikins promptly drew the mouse into the little hole and stuffed its tail into her mouth so that she might not be heard laughing, and the gruff voice said angrily, "Where's that mouse gone? I smelt mouse, I know I smelt mouse!"

She grew tired of this game after a few times, so she left the mouse in the hole and crept away to a new one. She really was a very naughty fairy. She blew on the buttercups so that they thought the morning breeze had come to wake them up, and opened their cups in a great hurry. She buzzed outside the clover and made it talk in its sleep, so that it said in a cross, sleepy voice, "Go away, you stupid busy bee, and don't wake me up in the middle of the night."

She pulled the tail of the nightingale who was singing to his lady love in the hawthorn bush, and he lost his place in his song.

Next she took to tormenting the squirrels. She used to find their stores of nuts and carry them away and fill the holes with pebbles, and this, when you are a hard-working squirrel with a large family to support, is very trying to the temper. Then she would tie acorns to their tails, and she would clap her hands to frighten them, and pull the baby

The Fairy Fluffikins

squirrels' ears, till at last they offered a reward to anyone who could catch Fairy Fluffikins and bring her to be punished.

No one caught Fairy Fluffikins – but she caught herself, as you shall hear.

She was poking about round a haystack one night, trying to find something naughty to do, when she came upon a sweet little house with pretty wire walls and a wooden door standing invitingly open. In hopped Fluffikins, thinking she was going to have some new kind of fun. There was a little white thing dangling from the roof, and she laid hold of it. Immediately there was a bang, the wooden door slammed, and Fluffikins was caught.

How she cried and stamped and pushed at the door, and promised to be a good fairy and a great many other things! But all to no purpose, the door was tight shut, and Fluffikins was not like some fortunate fairies who can get out of anywhere.

There she had to remain, and in the morning one

of the labourers found her, and, thinking she was some kind of dormouse, he carried her home to his little girl, and if you call on Mary Ann Smith you will see Fairy Fluffikins there still in a little cage. There is no one to tease and no mischief to get into, so if there is a miserable little fairy anywhere it is Fairy Fluffikins, and I'm not sure it doesn't serve her quite right.

Iktomi and the Ducks

By Zitkala-sa

*I*ktomi is a spider fairy. He wears brown deerskin leggings with long soft fringes on either side, and tiny beaded moccasins on his feet. His long black hair is parted in the middle and wrapped with red, red bands. He even paints his funny face with red and yellow, and draws big black rings around his eyes. He wears a beautifully warm deerskin jacket, with bright coloured beads sewed tightly on it.

Iktomi and the Ducks

Indeed, Iktomi dresses like a real Dakota brave.

Iktomi is a wily fellow. He prefers to spread a snare rather than to earn the smallest thing with honest hunting. Why, he laughs outright with wide open mouth when some simple folk are caught in a trap, sure and fast.

Thus Iktomi lives alone in a cone-shaped wigwam upon the plain. One day he sat hungry within his teepee. Suddenly he rushed out, dragging his blanket after him. Quickly spreading it on the ground, he tore up dry tall grass with both his hands and tossed it fast into the blanket.

Tying all the four corners together in a knot, he threw the light bundle of grass over his shoulder.

Snatching up a slender willow stick with his free left hand, he started off with a leap. Soon he came to the edge of the great level land. On the hilltop he paused for breath. With a thin palm shading his eyes from the western sun, he peered far away into the lowlands.

"Ah ha!" grunted he, satisfied with what he saw.

A group of wild ducks were dancing and feasting in the marshes. With wings outspread, tip to tip, they moved up and down in a large circle. Within the ring, around a small drum, sat the chosen singers, nodding their heads and blinking their eyes. They sang in unison a merry dance-song, and beat a lively tattoo on the drum.

Following a winding footpath soon came along the bent figure of a Dakota brave. He bore on his back a very large bundle. With a willow cane he propped himself up as he staggered along beneath his burden.

"Ho! Who is there?" called out a curious old duck, still bobbing up and down in the strange circular dance.

"Ho, Iktomi! Old fellow, pray tell us what you carry in your blanket. Do not hurry off! Stop! Halt!" urged one of the singers.

"My friends, I must not spoil your dance. Oh,

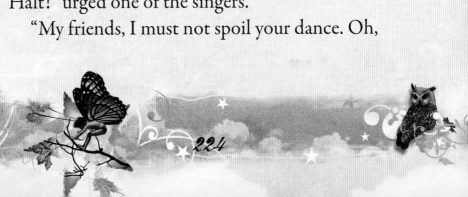

you would not care to see if you only knew what is
in my blanket. Sing on! Dance on! I must not show
you what I carry on my back," answered Iktomi.
Now all the ducks crowded about Iktomi.

"We must see what you carry! We must know
what is in your blanket!" they shouted in both his
ears. Some even brushed their wings against the
mysterious bundle.

Wily Iktomi replied, "My friends, it is only a
pack of songs I carry in my blanket."

"Oh, then let us hear your songs!" cried the
curious ducks.

At length Iktomi consented to sing his songs,
and with great delight all the ducks flapped their
wings and cried together, "Hoye! Hoye!"

Iktomi, with great care, laid down his bundle on
the ground.

"I will build first a round straw house, for I never
sing my songs in the open air," said he.

Quickly he bent green willow sticks, planting

both ends of each pole into the earth. These he covered thick with reeds and grasses. Soon the straw hut was ready. One by one the fat ducks waddled in through a small opening, which was the only entrance way.

In a strange low voice Iktomi began to sing his queer old tunes. All the ducks sat round-eyed in a circle about the mysterious singer. It was very dim inside the straw hut. All of a sudden his song burst into full voice. These were the words he sang:

Istokmus wacipo, tuwayatunwanpi kinhan ista nisasapi kta.

This means, 'With eyes closed you must dance. He who dares to open his eyes, forever red eyes shall have.'

Up rose the circle of seated ducks and holding their wings close against their sides began to dance to the rhythm of Iktomi's song and drum.

MAGIC AND MISCHIEF

With eyes closed they did dance! Iktomi ceased to beat his drum. He began to sing louder and faster. He seemed to be moving about in the centre of the ring. No duck dared blink a wink. Each one shut his eyes very tight and danced even harder.

At length one of the dancers could close his eyes no longer! It was a Skiska who peeped the least tiny blink at Iktomi within the centre of the circle.

"Oh! Oh!" squawked he in awful terror, "Run! Fly! Iktomi is twisting your heads and breaking your necks! Run out and fly! Fly!" he cried.

Hereupon the ducks opened their eyes. There beside Iktomi's bundle of songs lay half of their crowd – flat on their backs.

Out they flew through the opening Skiska had made as he rushed forth with his alarm.

But as they soared high into the blue sky they cried to one another, "Oh! Your eyes are red-red!"

"And yours are red-red!" For the warning words had proven true.

Iktomi and the Ducks

"Ah ha!" laughed Iktomi, untying the four corners of his blanket, "I shall sit no more hungry within my dwelling."

Homewards he trudged along with nice fat ducks in his blanket. He left the little straw hut for the rains and winds to pull down.

The Fairies and the Envious Neighbour

By Algernon Freeman-Mitford

Once upon a time there was a man, who, being overtaken by darkness among the mountains, was driven to seek shelter in the trunk of a hollow tree. In the middle of the night, a group of fairies assembled at the place. The man, peeping out from his hiding place, was frightened out of his wits. But after a while the fairies began to feast and drink wine, and to amuse themselves by singing and

The Fairies and the Envious Neighbour

dancing, until at last the man forgot all about his fright, and crept out of his hollow tree to join in the revels.

When the day was about to dawn, the fairies said to the man, "You're a jolly companion, and must come out and dance with us again. You must promise." Thinking to bind him to return, the fairies took a large wart that grew on the man's forehead and kept it as a pledge.

The man walked home, gleeful that he had passed a jovial night, and got rid of his wart into the bargain. He told the story to all his friends, who congratulated him warmly on being cured of his wart.

But he had a neighbour who was also troubled with a wart of long standing. Envious of his friend's luck, this man went to find the hollow tree, in which he passed the night.

Towards midnight the elves came, as expected, and began to feast and drink and sing and dance as before. As soon as he saw this, he came out of his hollow tree, and began dancing and singing as his neighbour had done. The elves, mistaking him for their former companion, were delighted to see him, and said, "You're a good fellow to recollect your promise, and we'll give you back your pledge."

So one of the elves pulled the pawned wart out of his pocket and stuck it onto the man's forehead, on top of the wart he already had.

The envious neighbour went home weeping, with two warts instead of one. This is a good lesson to people who cannot see the good luck of others without coveting it for themselves.

Drak,
the Fairy

By Kate Douglas Wiggin

*I*n the last century there lived in the little town of
Gaillac, in Languedoc, a young merchant named
Michael, who, having arrived at an age when he
wished to settle down in life, sought a wife.
Providing she was sweet-tempered, witty, rich,
beautiful, and of good family, he was not particular
about the rest. Unhappily, he could not see in
Gaillac one who appeared worthy of his choice. At

length he was told of a young lady in Lavaur with good qualities and a dowry of twenty thousand crowns. This sum was exactly that required by Michael to establish himself in business, so he instantly fell in love with the young lady of Lavaur. He obtained an introduction to the family, who liked his appearance, and gave him a good reception. But the young heiress had many suitors, from whom she hesitated to make a definite choice. After several discussions it was decided by her parents that the suitors should be brought together at a ball, and after having compared them a choice should be made.

On the appointed day Michael set out for Lavaur. His case was packed with his finest clothes – an apple-green coat, a lavender waistcoat, breeches of black velvet, silk stockings with silver trees, buckled shoes, powder box to powder his hair, and a satin ribbon for his pigtail. His horse was harnessed with gay trappings.

Drak, the Fairy

Furthermore, the prudent traveller, not having a pistol to put in his holsters, had slipped in a little bottle of wine and several slices of almond cake, in order to have something at hand to keep his courage up. For in reality, now that the day had come he was in a very anxious state, and when he saw in the distance the church of Lavaur he felt quite taken aback. He slackened the pace of his horse, then dismounted, and in order to reflect upon what he should do at the ball he entered a little wood and sat down on the turf. He drew from his holsters, to keep him company, the almond cake and the bottle. The latter he placed between his knees, so that without thinking of it he varied his reflections by sips of wine and mouthfuls of cake.

The sun having disappeared from the horizon he was about to pursue his journey, when he heard a sound behind him among the leaves, as of a multitude of little footsteps trampling the grass in tune to the music of a flute and cymbals.

MAGIC AND MISCHIEF

Astonished, he turned around, and by the light of the first stars, he perceived a troop of fairies, who were running, headed by the king, Tambourinet. In their rear, turning over and over like a wheel, was the buffoon of the little people – Drak, the fairy.

The fairies surrounded the traveller, and gave him a thousand welcomes and good wishes. Michael, who had drunk too freely not to be brave, began to crumble and throw his cake to them as one would to the birds. Each one had his crumb with the exception of Drak, who arrived when everyone had finished. King Tambourinet next asked what was in the bottle, and the fairies passed it from hand to hand till it reached the buffoon, who, finding it empty, threw it away.

Michael burst out laughing. "That is justice, my little man," said he to the fairy. "For those who arrive late, there remains nothing but regret."

"I will make you remember what you have just said," cried Drak in anger.

Drak, the Fairy

"And how?" asked the traveller. "Do you think, now, you are big enough to revenge yourself?"

Drak disappeared without answering, and Michael, after taking leave of Tambourinet, mounted his horse.

He had not gone a hundred paces, when the

saddle turned and threw him roughly to the ground. He arose a little stunned, rebuckled the straps, and mounted again. A little farther on, as he was going over a bridge, the right stirrup bent slightly, and he found himself thrown in the middle of the river. He got out again in a very bad humour, and fell the third time over the pebbles in the road, hurting himself so much that he could hardly proceed. He began to think that if he persisted in riding in the saddle he would be unable to present himself at all to the family of the young lady, so he decided to ride his horse barebacked, and take the saddle upon his shoulder. In this manner, he made his entry into Lavaur amid the laughter of the people who were sitting at their doors.

At length he reached the inn, where he alighted, and asked for a room in which to change his travelling clothes. Having obtained a chamber, he proceeded with much care to open his suitcase and lay out carefully on the bed the articles he needed.

Drak, the Fairy

His first consideration was whether he should powder his hair white or yellow. Having decided it should be white, he seized his swans-down powder puff, and commenced the operation on the right side. But the moment he had finished that side he saw that an invisible hand had powdered the other side yellow, so that his head had the appearance of a half-peeled lemon. Michael, stupefied, stretched out his hand toward the reel on which the ribbon for his pigtail was wound. The reel escaped from his fingers and fell to the ground.

Michael went to pick it up, but it seemed to roll before him. Twenty times he was about to seize it, and twenty times his impatient hands missed it. One would have said he looked like a kitten playing with a reel. At length, seeing that time was going, he lost patience and resigned himself to wearing his old ribbon.

He now hastened to put on his morocco shoes. He buckled the right, then having finished the left,

he stopped to admire them, but as he did so the right buckle fell to the ground. He replaced it, but no sooner had he done so than the left followed suit. Furious, he finished by putting on his travelling boots, and was about to put on his velvet breeches, when, immediately he approached the bed, the breeches began of their own accord to walk about the room.

Michael, petrified, stood mute, with his arm extended, watching this incongruous dance. But you may guess how he looked when he saw the vest, coat and hat join the breeches and form a sort of counterfeit of himself, which commenced to walk about and copy his movements.

Pale with fear Michael drew back to the window, but at this moment the peculiar figure turned towards him, and he saw, peering from beneath the brim of his own cocked hat, the mischevious face of Drak, the fairy.

Michael uttered a cry. "It is you, you villain, is it?

Drak, the Fairy

I'll make you repent of your insolence if you don't instantly give me back my clothes."

So saying, he rushed to take them, but the fairy, turning sharply around, ran to the other side of the room. Michael was beside himself with anger and impatience, and rushed again towards the fairy, who this time passed between his legs and rushed out on

to the staircase. Michael pursued him angrily up four flights of stairs till they arrived at the garret, where the fairy dodged round and round, and then skipped out of the window. Michael, exasperated, took the same route. The malicious fairy led him from roof to roof, dragging the velvet breeches, the vest, and coat in all the gutters, to Michael's despair.

The young gallant sat down upon the roof with a cry of despair, but rising immediately, said with resolution, "Well then, I'll go to the ball in my travelling dress."

"Hark!" interrupted the fairy.

The sound of a bell rang out from a neighbouring steeple. Midnight struck! Michael counted the twelve strokes, and could not restrain a cry. It was the hour designated by the parents when they would proclaim their daughter's choice for a husband. He wrung his hands in despair.

"Unhappy man that I am!" Michael cried. "By the time I arrive all will be over, and she and her

Drak, the Fairy

parents will laugh at me."

"And that would be justice, my big man," replied Drak. "For you have said yourself, 'For those who arrive late, there remains nothing but regret.' This time will serve you, I hope, as a lesson and prevent you another time from laughing at the feeble, for from henceforth you will know that the smallest are big enough to avenge themselves."

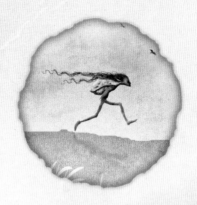

Iktomi and the Muskrat

By Zitkala-sa

*B*eside a white lake, beneath a large grown willow tree, sat Iktomi the fairy on the bare ground. With ankles crossed together around a pot of soup, Iktomi bent over some delicious boiled fish.

Fast he dipped his black horn spoon into the soup, for he was ravenous. Iktomi had no regular meal times. Often when he was hungry he went without food.

Iktomi and the Muskrat

"How, how, my friend!" said a voice out of the wild rice.

Iktomi started. He almost choked on his soup. He peered through the long reeds from where he sat with his long horn spoon in mid-air.

"How, my friend!" said the voice again, this time close at his side. Iktomi turned and there stood a dripping muskrat who had just come out of the lake.

"Oh, it is my friend who startled me. I wondered if among the wild rice some spirit voice was talking. How, how, my friend!" said Iktomi. The muskrat stood smiling. On his lips hung a ready 'Yes, my friend,' for when Iktomi would ask, 'My friend, will you sit down beside me and share my food?'

That was the custom of the plains people. Yet Iktomi sat silent. He hummed an old song and beat gently on the pot with his buffalo-horn spoon. The muskrat began to feel awkward before such lack of hospitality and wished himself under water.

245

MAGIC AND MISCHIEF

After many heart throbs Iktomi stopped
drumming with his spoon, and looking upward into
the muskrat's face, he said, "My friend, let us race to
see who shall win this pot of fish. If I win, I shall
not need to share it with you. If you win, you shall
have half of it." Springing to his feet, Iktomi began
at once to tighten the belt about his waist.

"My friend Iktomi, I cannot run a race with you!
I am not a swift runner, and you are nimble as a
deer," answered the hungry muskrat.

For a moment Iktomi stood with a hand on his
long protruding chin. The muskrat looked out of
the corners of his eyes without moving his head. He
watched the wily Iktomi concocting a plot.

"I shall carry a large stone on my back. That
will slacken my usual speed, and the race will be a
fair one."

Saying this he laid a firm hand upon the
muskrat's shoulder and started off along the edge of
the lake. When they reached the opposite side

Iktomi and the Muskrat

Iktomi pried about in search of a heavy stone.

At last he found one half-buried in the shallow water. Pulling it out upon dry land, he wrapped it in his blanket.

"Now, my friend, you shall run on the left side of the lake, I on the other. The race is for the boiled fish in yonder kettle!" said Iktomi.

The muskrat helped to lift the heavy stone upon Iktomi's back. Then they parted. Each took a narrow path through the tall reeds fringing the shore. Iktomi found his load a heavy one. Perspiration hung like beads on his brow. His chest heaved hard and fast.

He looked across the lake to see how far the muskrat had gone, but nowhere did he see any sign of him.

"Well, he is running low under the wild rice!" said he. Yet as he scanned the tall grasses on the lake shore, he saw not one stir as if to make way for the runner. "Ah, has he gone so fast ahead that the

disturbed grasses in his trail have quieted again?" exclaimed Iktomi. With that thought he quickly dropped the heavy stone. "No more of this!" said he, patting his chest with both hands.

Off with a springing bound, he ran swiftly towards the goal. Tufts of reeds and grass fell flat under his feet. Hardly had they raised

Iktomi and the Muskrat

their heads when Iktomi was many paces gone.

Soon he reached the heap of cold ashes. Iktomi halted stiff as if he had struck an invisible cliff. His black eyes showed a ring of white about them as he stared at the empty ground. There was no pot of boiled fish! There was no muskrat in sight!

"Oh, if only I had shared my food like a real Dakota, I would not have lost it all! Why did I not remember the muskrat would run through the water? He swims faster than I could ever run! That is what he has done. He has laughed at me for carrying a weight on my back while he shot hither like an arrow!"

"Ha! Ha! Ha!" laughed the muskrat. "Next time, say to a visiting friend, 'Be seated beside me, my friend. Let me share my food with you.'"

VISITORS TO FAIRYLAND

A Boy that Visited Fairyland

By William Elliot Griffis

Many are the places in Wales where the ground is lumpy with burial mounds. Among these sheep graze, donkeys bray, and cows chew the cud.

Here the ground is strewn with the ruins of Welsh strongholds, of old Roman camps, and of chapels and monasteries, showing that many different races of men have come and gone, while

A Boy that Visited Fairyland

the birds still fly and the flowers bloom.

Centuries ago, the monks of St David had a school where lads were taught Latin and good manners. One of their pupils was a boy named Elidyr. He was such a poor scholar and he so hated books and loved play, that in his case punishments were almost of daily occurrence. One day, though he was only twelve years old, the boy started on a long run into the country. The further he got, the happier he felt – at least for one day.

At night, tired out, he crept into a cave. When he woke up in the morning, he thought it was glorious to be as free as the wild asses. Like them, he quenched his thirst at the brook. But by noon he had found nothing to eat. His stomach seemed to enlarge with very emptiness, and his hunger grew every minute.

He dared not go out far and pick berries, for he saw that people were now out searching for him. He did not feel like going back to books, rods and scoldings, but the day seemed as long as a week and he was glad when darkness came. His bed was no softer in the cave. At dawn, the question in his mind was still whether to stay and starve, or to go home and get two thrashings – one from his father, and another from the monks. Finally, he came to a stern resolve. He set out, ready to face two whippings, rather than one death by starvation.

But he did not have to go home yet, for at the cave's mouth, he met two elves, who delivered a most welcome message. "Come with us to a land full of fun, play, and good things to eat."

All at once, his hunger left him. All desire to go home, or to risk either schooling or a thrashing, passed away also.

Into a dark passage all three went, but they soon came out into a beautiful country, where birds sang and flowers bloomed! All around could be heard the shouts of little folks at play. Never did things look so lovely.

Soon, in front of the broad path along which

A Boy that Visited Fairyland

they were travelling, there rose up before him a glorious palace. It had a splendid gateway, and the silver-topped towers seemed to touch the blue sky.

"What is this place?" asked the lad of his guides.

They made answer that it was the palace of the king of Fairyland. Then they led him into the throne room, where sat in golden splendour, a king of tiny stature but majestic presence, who was clad in resplendent robes. He was surrounded by

courtiers in rich apparel, and all about him was magnificence, such as the boy Elidyr had neither read about before nor even dreamed.

Yet everything was so small that it looked like Toy Land, and he felt like a giant among them, even though many of the little men around him were old enough to have whiskers on their cheeks and beards on their chins.

The king spoke kindly to Elidyr, asking him who he was, and whence he had come.

While they were talking the prince, the king's only son, appeared. He was dressed in white velvet and gold, and had a long feather in his cap. In the pleasantest way, he took Elidyr's hand and said, "Glad to see you. Come and let us play together."

That was just what Elidyr liked to hear. They played with golden balls, and rode little horses with silver saddles and bridles, but these pretty animals were no larger than small dogs, or greyhounds.

No meat was ever seen on the table, but plenty of

milk. They never told a lie, nor used bad language. They often talked about mortal men, but usually to despise them. To the elves, human beings were never satisfied, or long happy, even when they got what they wanted.

Everything in this part of Fairyland was lovely, but it was always cloudy. No sun, star or moon was ever seen, yet the little men did not seem to mind it and enjoyed themselves every day. There was no end of play, and that suited Elidyr.

Yet by and by, he got tired even of games and play, and grew very homesick. He wanted to see his mother. So he asked the king to let him visit his old home. He promised solemnly to come back after a few hours. His majesty gave his permission, but charged him not to take with him anything whatever from Fairyland, and to go with only the clothes on his back.

The same two elves who had brought him into Fairyland were chosen to conduct him back. When they had led him again through the underground passage into the sunlight, they made him invisible until he arrived at his mother's cottage.

She was overjoyed to find that no wolf had torn him to pieces, or wild bull had pushed him over a steep cliff. She asked him many questions, and he told her all he had seen, felt, or known.

When he rose up to go, she begged him to stay longer, but he said he must keep his word. So he made his mother agree not to tell – not even to his father – as to where he was, or what he was doing. Then he made off and reported again to his playmates in Fairyland.

The king was pleased at the lad's promptness in returning. As a reward for keeping his word so faithfully and telling the truth, he allowed Elidyr to go and see his mother as often as he wanted to do so. He even gave orders releasing the two little men from constantly guarding him and told them to let the lad go alone, and whenever he liked, for he

always kept his word – unlike other humans.

Many times did Elidyr visit his mother, and she loved to hear of his adventures in Fairyland. One day he spoke to her of the heavy yellow balls, with which he and the king's sons played, and how these rolled around.

Before leaving home, this boy had never seen gold, and did not know what it was, but his mother guessed that the yellow balls were made of the precious metal. So she begged him to bring one of them back to her.

This, Elidyr thought, would not be right, but after much argument, his parents being poor, and she telling him that out of hundreds in the king's palace, one single ball would not be missed, he decided to please her.

So one day he did not follow the princes to the throne room after play time. Instead Elidyr waited until he was alone, and then picked up one of the yellow balls and started off homeward.

But no sooner was he back on the earth, and in the sunlight again, than he heard footsteps behind him. Then he knew that he had been discovered.

He glanced over his shoulder and there were the two little men, who had formerly been his guards. They scowled at him as if they were mad enough to bite off the heads of nails. Then they rushed after him, and there began a race to the cottage.

A Boy that Visited Fairyland

But the boy had legs that were at least twice as long as the little men, and though they ran surprisingly fast he still managed to reach the

cottage door first. He now thought himself safe, but pushing open the door, he stumbled over the copper threshold, and the ball rolled out of his hand, across the floor of hardened clay, almost reaching the white-washed border which ran about the edges of the room. It stopped at the feet of his mother, whose eyes opened wide at the sight of the ball of shining gold.

As poor Elidyr lay sprawling on the floor, and before he could pick himself up, one of the little guardsmen leaped over him, rushed into the room, and, from under his mother's petticoats, picked up the ball.

The two fairies spat at the boy and shouted, 'traitor', 'rascal', 'thief', 'false mortal', 'fox', 'rat', 'wolf', and other bad names. Then they turned on their heels and sped out of the door and away, one of them holding the precious gold ball tightly.

Now Elidyr, though he had been a mischievous boy, often wilful, lazy, and never studying his books,

A Boy that Visited Fairyland

had always loved the truth. He was very sad because he had broken his word of honour to his fairy friends. So, almost mad with grief and shame, and from an accusing conscience, he went back to find the cave in which he had slept on the night he had run away. He knew in his heart that he should return to the king of the fairies, and ask his pardon, even if his majesty never allowed him to visit Fairyland again.

But though he returned often to that same place, and even spent whole days in searching those wild lands, he could never again discover the magical opening in the hills.

So, fully penitent, and resolving to live right, and become what his father wanted him to be, he went back to the monastery. There he plied his tasks so diligently that he excelled in all learning.

In time, he became one of the most famous scholars in Welsh history. When he died, he asked to be buried, not in the monk's cemetery, but with his father and mother, in the humble village churchyard. He had made a special request that no name, record, or epitaph be chiselled on his tomb, but only these words:

WE CAN DO NOTHING AGAINST THE TRUTH,
BUT ONLY FOR THE TRUTH.

The Fairy Wife

By Patrick Kennedy

This is one of the many stories in which a person is stolen away by the fairies, and another person hopes to rescue them, which usually takes great courage and steadfastness. In fairy stories from Ireland (where this tale is set), people who neglect their prayers or don't go to church are always at more risk of being stolen by the fairies. In this story, 'fairy man' means a man who claims to have skill in curing the illnesses and disorders that fairies cause.

There was once a little farmer and his wife living near Coolgarrow. They had three children, and my story happened while the youngest was a baby. The wife was a good woman, but her mind was always on her family and her farm. She worked so hard that she hardly ever had time to pray before falling asleep, and she thought the time spent in the chapel was twice as long as it need be. So one day, she let her husband and her two children go ahead of her to Mass, while she called to consult a fairy man about a disorder one of her cows had. She was late at the chapel, and was sorry all the day after, for her husband was in grief about it.

Late one night the farmer was wakened up by the cries of his children calling out, "Mother! Mother!"

When he sat up and rubbed his eyes, he found there was no wife by his side, and he asked the little ones what had become of their mother. They answered that they had seen the room full of nice little men and women, all dressed in clothes of white and red and green, and their mother in the middle of them, going out by the door as if she was walking in her sleep.

The farmer leapt out of bed, and searched

The Fairy Wife

everywhere round the house and down the road, but neither tale nor tidings did he get of her for many a day.

Well, the poor man was miserable enough, for he was as fond of his wife as she was of him. It used to bring the salt tears down his cheeks to see his poor children neglected and dirty, as they often were, and they would have been in an even worse state if it hadn't been for a kind neighbour that used to look in whenever she could spare time.

About six weeks after – just as the farmer was going out to his work one morning – a neighbour that used to mind women when they were ill came up to him, and kept step by step with him to the field. On the way, she told him, "Just as I was falling asleep last night, I heard a horse's tramp on the grass and a knock at the door, and there, when I came out, was a fine-looking dark man, mounted on a black horse. He told me to get ready in all haste, for a lady was in great want of me.

"As soon as I put on my cloak and things, he took me by the hand, and before I knew it I was sitting behind him. 'Where are we going, sir?' said I.

"'You'll soon know,' said he, and he drew his

The Fairy Wife

fingers across my eyes, and not a ray could I see.

"I kept a tight grip of him, and I little knew whether we were going backwards or forwards, or how long we were about it, till my hand was taken again, and I felt the ground under me. The fingers went the other way across my eyes, and there we were before a castle door, and in we went through a big hall and great rooms all painted in fine green colours, with red and gold bands and ornaments, and the finest carpets and chairs and tables and window curtains, and beautiful ladies and grand gentlemen walking about.

"At last we came to a bedroom, with a beautiful lady in bed, with a fine bouncing boy beside her. The lady clapped her hands, and in came the dark man and kissed her and the baby, and praised me, and gave me a bottle of green ointment to rub the child all over.

"Well, the child I rubbed, sure enough, but my right eye began to smart, and I put up my finger and

gave it a rub. And then I stared, for never in all my life was I so frightened. The beautiful room was really a big, rough cave, with water oozing over the edges of the stones and through the clay, and the

The Fairy Wife

lady, and the lord, and the child were weazened, poverty-bitten creatures – nothing but skin and bone – and the rich dresses had turned to old rags. I didn't let on that I found any difference, and after a bit the dark man said, 'Go before me to the hall door, and I will be with you in a few moments, and see you safe home.'

"Well, just as I turned into the outside cave, who should I see watching near the door but your poor wife Molly. She looked round all terrified, and said to me in a whisper, 'I'm brought here to nurse the child of the king and queen of the fairies, but there is one chance of saving me. All the court will pass the cross near Templeshambo next Friday night, on a visit to the fairies of Old Ross. If my husband John can catch me by the hand or cloak when I ride by, and has courage not to let go his grip, I'll be safe. Here's the king. Don't open your mouth to answer.'

"The dark man didn't once cast his eye towards Molly, and he seemed to have no suspicion of me.

When we came out I looked about me, and saw that we were in the dyke of the Rath of Cromogue. I was on the horse again, which was nothing but a big ragweed, and I was in dread every minute I'd fall off, but nothing happened till I found myself in my own cabin.

"The king slipped five guineas into my hand as soon as I was on the ground, and thanked me, and bade me good night. I hope I'll never see his face again. I got into bed, and couldn't sleep for a long time, and when I examined my five guineas this morning, which I left in the table drawer last night, I only found five withered leaves of oak – bad luck to the giver!"

Well, you may imagine the fright, and the joy, and the grief the poor man was in when the woman finished her story. They talked and they talked, till Friday night came, when both were standing where the mountain road crosses the one going to Ross. There they stood, looking towards the bridge of

The Fairy Wife

Thuar, in the dead of the night, with a little moonlight shining.

At last the woman gave a start, and said, "Here they come, bridles jingling and feathers tossing!" He looked, but could see nothing, and she stood trembling and her eyes wide open, looking down the way to the ford of Ballinacoola.

"I see your wife," said she, "riding on the outside. We'll walk on quietly, as if we suspected nothing, and when we are passing I'll give you a shove. If you don't do your duty then, woe be with you!"

Well, they walked on easy, their poor hearts beating hard, and though he could see nothing, he heard a faint jingle and trampling and rustling, and at last he got the push that she promised. He spread out his arms, and there was his wife's waist within them, and he could see her plain, but such a hullabulloo rose as if there was an earthquake, and he found himself surrounded by horrible-looking things, roaring at him and striving to pull his wife away. But he made the sign of the cross and bid them begone in God's name, and held his wife as if his arms were made of iron. In one moment everything was as silent as the grave, and the poor woman lay in a faint in the arms of her husband and her good neighbour. Well, all in good time she was minding her family and her business again, and I expect, after the fright she got, she spent more time praying, and avoided fairies all the days of the week, and particularly on Sunday.

Billy Beg, Tom Beg, and the Fairies

By Sophia Morrison

ot far from Dalby, two humpback cobblers called Billy Beg and Tom Beg lived together on a lonely farm. Billy Beg was cleverer than Tom Beg, who was always at his command. One day Billy gave Tom a staff, and said, "Tom Beg, go to the mountain and fetch home the white sheep."

Tom took the staff and went to the mountain, but he could not find the white sheep. At last, when he was far from home, and dusk was coming on, he began to think that he had best go back. The night was fine, and stars and a small crescent moon were in the sky. Tom was hastening home, and had almost reached Glen Rushen, when he lost his way in a grey mist. When it cleared, Tom found himself in a green glen he had never seen before, though he knew every glen within five miles of him. He was wondering where he could be, when he heard a faraway sound drawing nearer to him.

"Aw," said he to himself, "there's more than myself afoot on the mountains tonight."

The sound grew louder. First, it was like the humming of bees, then like rushing water, and last it was like the marching of a crowd. All of a sudden the glen was full of fine horses and little people riding on them, with the lights on their red caps shining like the stars above. There was the blowing of horns, the waving of flags, and the playing of music. Tom thought that he had never seen anything so splendid as all he saw there. In the midst of the drilling and dancing, he saw coming towards him the grandest little man he had ever set eyes upon, dressed in gold and silver silk, shining like a raven's wing.

"It is a bad time you have chosen to come this way," said the little man, who was the king.

"It is not here that I'm wishing to be," said Tom.

The king said, "Are you one of us tonight, Tom?"

"I am surely," said Tom.

"Then," said the king, "it will be your duty to take the password. You must stand at the foot of the glen, and as each regiment goes by, you must take the password – it is: 'Monday, Tuesday, Wednesday, Thursday, Friday, Saturday.'"

"I'll do that with a heart and a half," said Tom.

At daybreak the fiddlers took up their fiddles, the fairy army set itself in order, the fiddlers played before them out of the glen, and sweet that music was. Each regiment gave the password to Tom as it went by, "Monday, Tuesday, Wednesday, Thursday, Friday, Saturday."

Last of all came the king, and he, too, gave it, "Monday, Tuesday, Wednesday, Thursday, Friday, Saturday."

Billy Beg, Tom Beg, and the Fairies

Then he called to one of his men, "Take the hump from this fellow's back," and before the words were out of his mouth the hump was whisked off Tom Beg's back and thrown into the hedge.

How proud was Tom, who now found himself the straightest man in the Isle of Man! He went back down the mountain and came home early in the morning with a light heart and an eager step. Billy was amazed when he saw Tom standing so straight and strong, and when Tom had rested and refreshed himself he told his story about how he had met the fairies who came every night to Glen Rushen to drill.

The next night Billy set off along the mountain road and came at last to the green glen. About midnight he heard the trampling of horses, the lashing of whips, and a great hullabaloo, and, behold, the fairies and their king all at drill in the glen as Tom had said.

When they saw the humpback they all stopped.

One came forward and crossly asked his business.

"I am one of yourselves for the night, and should be glad to do you some service," said Billy.

So he was set to take the password, 'Monday, Tuesday, Wednesday, Thursday, Friday, Saturday.' And at daybreak the King said, "It's time for us to be off," and up came regiment after regiment giving Billy the password, "Monday, Tuesday, Wednesday, Thursday, Friday, Saturday."

Last of all came the king with his men. and gave the password also, "Monday, Tuesday, Wednesday, Thursday, Friday, Saturday."

"And Sunday," said Billy, thinking himself clever. Then there was a great outcry.

"Get the hump that was taken off that fellow's back last night and put it on this man's back," said the king, with flashing eyes, pointing to the hump that lay under the hedge.

Before the words were well out of his mouth the hump was clapped onto Billy's back.

Billy Beg, Tom Beg, and the Fairies

"Now," said the king, "be off, and if ever I find you here again, we will clap another hump onto your front!"

And they all marched away with one great shout, and left poor Billy standing where they had found him, with a hump growing on each shoulder. And he came home next day dragging one foot after another, with a wizened face as cross as two sticks, with his two humps on his back, and if they are not off they are there still.

Fairy Ointment

By Joseph Jacobs

Dame Goody was a nurse who looked after sick people, and minded babies. One night she woke up at midnight, and when she went downstairs, she saw a strange, little old fellow, who asked her to come to his wife who was too ill to mind her baby. Although Dame Goody didn't like the look of the old fellow, she decided that business is business, so she popped on her things, and went

Fairy Ointment

down to him. And when she got down to him, he whisked her up on to a large coal-black horse with fiery eyes, that stood at the door, and soon they were going at a rare pace, Dame Goody holding on to the old fellow like grim death.

They rode and they rode, till at last they stopped before a cottage door. There they got down and went in and found the good woman in bed with the children playing about, and the baby, a fine bouncing boy, beside her.

Dame Goody took the baby, which was as fine a boy as you'd wish to see. The mother, when she handed the baby to Dame Goody to mind, gave her a box of ointment, and told her to stroke the baby's eyes with it as soon as it opened them.

After a while it began to open its eyes. Dame Goody saw that it had eyes just like its father. So she took the box of ointment and stroked its two eyelids with it. But she couldn't help wondering what it was for, as she had never seen such a thing

done before. So she looked to see if the others were looking, and, when they were not noticing, she stroked her own right eyelid with the ointment.

No sooner had she done so, than everything seemed changed about her. The cottage became elegantly furnished. The mother in the bed was a

Fairy Ointment

beautiful lady, dressed up in white silk. The little baby was still more beautiful than before, and its clothes were made of a sort of silvery gauze.

Its little brothers and sisters around the bed were flat-nosed imps with pointed ears, who made faces at one another, and scratched their heads. In fact, they were up to all kinds of mischief, and Dame Goody knew that she had got into a house of fairies. But she said nothing, and as soon as the lady was well enough to mind the baby, she asked the old fellow to take her back home. So he came round to the door with the coal-black horse with eyes of fire, and off they went as fast as before till they came to Dame Goody's cottage, where the strange fellow lifted her down and left her, thanking her civilly enough, and paying her more than she had ever been paid before for such service.

Now next day happened to be market day, and as Dame Goody had been away from home, she wanted many things in the house, and trudged off to get them at the market. As she was buying the things she wanted, who should she see but the strange fellow who had taken her on the coal-black horse. And what do you think he was doing? Why he went about from stall to stall taking things from each – here some fruit, and there some eggs, and so on – and no one seemed to take any notice.

Now Dame Goody did not think it her business to interfere, but she thought she ought not to let so good a customer pass without speaking. So she went up to him, bobbed a curtsey and said, "Good day, sir, I hope your good lady and the little one are as well as—"

But she couldn't finish what she was saying, for the funny old fellow started back in surprise, and he said to her, "What! Do you see me today?"

"See you," said she, "why, of course I do, as plain as the sun in the skies, and what's more," said she, "I see you are busy, too, into the bargain."

"Ah, you see too much," said he, "now, pray, with

which eye do you see all this?"

"With the right eye to be sure," said she, as proud as can be to find him out.

"The ointment! The ointment!" cried the old fairy thief. "Take that for meddling with what don't concern you – you shall see me no more." And with that he struck her on the right eye, and she couldn't see him anymore, and, what was worse, she could no longer see with her right eye from that hour until this.

Murdoch's Rath

By Juliana Horatia Gatty Ewing

A rath is an ancient hillfort, which looks like a grassy mound on top of a high bank. They are scattered all over Ireland and fairies are believed to live inside them.

There was not a nicer boy in all Ireland than Pat, and clever at his trade too, if only he'd had one.

But from his cradle he learnt nothing (small blame to him with no one to teach him!), so when he grew old enough to make his own decisions, he earned his living by running errands for his neighbours. Pat proved that he could always be trusted to make the best of a bad bargain, and bring back all the change, for he was the soul of honesty and good nature.

It's no wonder then that he was beloved by everyone, and got as much work as he could do, and if the pay had fitted the work, he'd have been mighty comfortable. But as it was, what he got wouldn't have kept him in shoe leather, if it wasn't for the fact that he made ends meet by keeping his shoes in his pocket, except when he was in the town and obliged to look genteel for the credit of the place he came from.

Well, all was going on as peacefully as could be, till one market day, when business (or it may have been pleasure) detained him till the very end of the evening, and by nightfall, when he began to make the journey home, he never thought to leave off his shoes, but tramped on just as if shoe leather were made to be knocked to bits on the king's highway.

And as he walked this was what he was saying to himself: "A dozen hanks of grey yarn for Mistress Murphy, three gross of bright buttons for the tailor, half an ounce of throat drops for Father Andrew, and an ounce of snuff for his housekeeper," and so on, over and over. For these were what he went to the town to fetch, and he was afraid one of the lot might have slipped his memory.

Now everybody knows there are two ways home from the town – the highway, and the way by Murdoch's Rath.

Murdoch's Rath was a pleasant enough spot to stroll along during the daytime, but not many people cared to walk past it when the sun was down. And in all the years Pat was walking backwards and forwards, he never once came home except by the high road till this unlucky evening, when, just at the place where the two roads part, he got, as one may say, into a sort of confusion. How far he walked he never could tell, before all of a sudden the moon shone out from behind the clouds as bright as day, and Pat found himself in Murdoch's Rath. And this was only the smallest part of the wonder, for the Rath was full of fairies.

When Pat saw them they were dancing round and round in circles. It made his feet tingle to look at them, for he was a good dancer himself. As he sat on the side of the Rath, and snapped his fingers to mark the time, the dancing stopped, and a little man came up to Pat. He wore a tall black hat and a fine green coat, with white stockings, and red shoes on his tiny feet.

"Won't you take a turn with us, Pat?" said he, bowing till he nearly touched the ground. And, indeed, he had not far to go, for he was barely two feet high.

"You don't need to say it twice, sir," said Pat. "I will be proud to take to the the floor with ye," and before you could look round, there was Pat in the circle dancing away with all his might.

At first his feet felt like feathers for lightness, and it seemed as if he could have gone on forever. But at last he grew tired, and would have liked to stop, but the fairies would not, and so they danced on and on. Pat tried to think of something good to say, that he might free himself from the spell, but all he could think of was, 'A dozen hanks of grey yarn for Mistress Murphy, three gross of bright buttons for the tailor, half an ounce of throat drops for Father Andrew, and an ounce of snuff for his housekeeper,' and so on.

And it seemed to Pat that the moon was on the one side of the Rath when they began to dance, and on the other side when they left off, but he could not be sure after all that going round. One thing was plain enough. He danced every bit of leather off the soles of his feet, and they were blistered so that he could hardly stand, but all the little folk did was

to stand and hold their sides with laughing at him.

At last the one who spoke before stepped up to him. "Don't break your heart about it, Pat," said he. "I'll lend you my shoes till the morning, for you seem to be a good natured boy."

Well, Pat looked at the fairy man's shoes, which were the size of a baby's, and he looked at his own feet, but not wishing to be uncivil, "Thank ye kindly, sir," said he. "And if you'll be good enough to put them on for me, maybe you won't spoil the shape." For he thought to himself, 'Small blame to me if the little gentleman can't get them to fit.'

With that he sat down on the side of the Rath, and the fairy man put on the shoes for him. As soon as they touched Pat's feet they became altogether a convenient size, and fitted him like wax. And, more than that, when he stood up, he didn't feel his blisters at all.

"Bring 'em back to the Rath at sunrise, Pat, my boy," said the little man. And as Pat was climbing over the ditch, "Look round, Pat," said he. And when Pat looked round, there were jewels and pearls lying at the roots of the bushes on the ditch, as thick as peas.

"Will you help yourself, or take what's given ye, Pat?" said the fairy man.

"Did I ever learn manners?" said Pat. "Would you have me help myself before company? I'll take what your honour pleases to give me, and I'll be thankful for it."

The fairy man picked a lot of yellow blossoms from the bushes, and filled Pat's pockets.

"Keep 'em for love, Pat, me darling" said he.

Pat would have liked some of the jewels, but he put the blossoms by for love.

"Good evening to your honour," said he.

"And where are you going, Pat, dear?" said the fairy man.

"I'm going home," said Pat. And if the fairy man didn't know where that was, small blame to him.

"Just let me dust them shoes for ye, Pat," said the fairy man. And as Pat lifted up each foot he breathed on it, and dusted it with the tail of his green coat.

"Home!" said he, and when he let go, Pat was at his own doorstep before he could look round, and his parcels safe and sound with him.

Next morning he was up with the sun, and carried the fairy man's shoes back to the Rath. As he came up, the little man looked over the ditch.

"The top of the morning to your honour," said Pat, "here's your shoes."

"You're an honest boy, Pat," said the little gentleman. "It's inconvenienced I am without them, for I have only the one pair. Have you looked at the

yellow flowers this morning?" he said.

"I have not, sir," said Pat, "I'd be loth to deceive you. I came off as soon as I was up."

"Be sure to look when you get back, Pat," said the fairy man, "and good luck to ye."

With that he disappeared, and Pat went home. He looked for the blossoms, as the fairy man told him, and there's not a word of truth in this tale if they weren't all pure gold pieces.

Well, now Pat was so rich, he went to the shoemaker to order another pair of brogues. Being a kindly, gossiping boy, the shoemaker soon learnt the whole story of the fairy man and the Rath. This stirred up the shoemaker's greed, and he resolved to go the next night himself, to see if he could not dance with the fairies, and have the same luck.

He found his way to the Rath, and sure enough the fairies were dancing, and asked him to join. He danced the soles off his brogues, as Pat did, and the fairy man lent him his shoes, and sent him home in a twinkling.

As he was going over the ditch, he looked round, and saw the roots of the bushes glowing with precious stones as if they had been glow worms.

"Will you help yourself, or take what's given ye?" said the fairy man.

"I'll help myself, if you please," said the cobbler, for he thought, 'If I can't get more than Pat brought home, my fingers must all be thumbs.'

So he drove his hand into the bushes, and if he didn't get plenty, it wasn't for want of grasping.

When he got up in the morning, he went straight to look at the jewels. But not a stone of the lot was more precious than roadside pebbles. "I ought not to look till I come back from the Rath," said he. "It's best to do like Pat."

But he made up his mind not to return the fairy man's shoes. "Who knows the virtue that's in them?" he said. So he made a small pair of red leather shoes, as like as could be to the pair he had borrowed, and

he blacked the others upon his feet, so that the fairies might not know them, and at sunrise he went to the Rath.

The fairy man was looking over the ditch, just as he had done before.

"Good morning to you," said he.

"The top of the morning to you, sir," said the cobbler. "Here's your shoes." And he handed him the pair that he had made, making sure that his face was as grave as a judge.

The fairy man looked at them, but he said nothing, though he did not put them on. "Have you looked at the things you got last night?" said he.

"I'll not deceive you, sir," said the cobbler. "I came to see you as soon as I was up. Not a peep I took at them."

"Be sure to look when you get back," said the fairy man. And just as the cobbler was getting over the ditch to go home, he said, "If my eyes don't deceive me," said he, "there's a little dirt on your left shoe. Let me dust it with the tail of my coat."

'That means home in a twinkling,' thought the cobbler, and he held up his foot.

The fairy man dusted it, and muttered something the cobbler did not hear. "It's the dirty pastures that you've come through," said he, "for the other shoe's as bad."

So the cobbler held up his right foot, and the fairy man rubbed that with the tail of his green coat.

When all was done the cobbler's feet seemed to tingle, and then to itch, and then to smart, and then to burn. And at last he began to dance, and he danced all round the Rath (the fairy man laughing and holding his sides), and then round and round again. And he danced till he cried out with weariness, and tried to shake the shoes off. But they stuck fast, and the fairies drove him over the ditch, and through the bushes, and he danced away.

Where he danced to, I cannot tell you. Whether he ever got rid of the fairy shoes, I do not know. The

Murdoch's Rath

jewels never were more than wayside pebbles, and
they were swept out when his cabin was cleaned,
which was not too soon, you may be sure.

All this happened long ago, but there are those
who say that the covetous cobbler dances still,
between sunset and sunrise, round Murdoch's Rath.

I WISH, I WISH

Beautiful as the Day

From *Five Children and It*
by E Nesbit

*T*he house was three miles from the station, but
before the dusty hired carriage had rattled
along for five minutes the children began to put
their heads out of the window to say, "Aren't we
nearly there?" And every time they passed a house,
which was not very often, they all said, "Oh, is *this*
it?" But it never was, till they reached the very top of
the hill, just past the chalk quarry and before you

Beautiful as the Day

come to the gravel pit. And then there was a white house with a green garden and an orchard beyond, and mother said, "Here we are!"

"How white the house is," said Robert.

"And look at the roses," said Anthea.

"And the plums," said Jane.

"It is rather decent," Cyril admitted.

The baby said, "Wanty go walky."

Everyone got their legs kicked or their feet trodden on in the scramble to get out of the carriage that very minute, but no one seemed to mind. The children had explored the gardens and the outhouses thoroughly before they were caught and cleaned for tea, and they saw quite well that they were certain to be happy at the White House. The best part of it all was that there were no rules about not going to places and not doing things. In London almost everything is labelled 'You mustn't touch', and though the label is invisible, it's just as bad, because you know it's there.

I WISH, I WISH

Now that I have begun to tell you about the place, I feel that I could go on and make this into a most interesting story about all the ordinary things that the children did – just the kind of things you do yourself, you know – and you would believe every word of it. But children will believe almost anything, and I daresay you will find it quite easy to believe that before Anthea and Cyril and the others had been a week in the country they had found a fairy. At least they called it that, because that was what it called itself, but it was not at all like any fairy read about.

It was at the gravel pits. Father had to go away suddenly on business, and mother had gone away to stay with Granny, who was not very well. They both went in a great hurry, and when they were gone the house seemed dreadfully quiet and empty. It was Cyril who said, "I say, let's take our spades and go and dig in the gravel pits. We can pretend we're all at the seaside."

Beautiful as the Day

"Father said it was once," Anthea said, "he says there are shells there thousands of years old."

So they went. Of course they had been to the edge of the gravel pit and looked over, but they had not gone down into it for fear father should say they mustn't play there.

Each of the children carried its own spade, and took it in turns to carry the Lamb. He was the baby, and they called him that because 'Baa' was the first thing he ever said. They called Anthea 'Panther',

which sounds silly when you read it, but when you say it it sounds a little like her name.

First the children built a castle, of course, but castle-building is rather poor fun when you have no hope of the tide ever coming in to fill the moat.

Cyril wanted to dig out a cave to play smugglers in, but the others thought it might bury them alive, so it ended in all spades going to work together to dig a hole to Australia. The children dug and they dug and they dug, and their hands got sandy and hot and red, and their faces got damp and shiny. The Lamb had tried to eat the sand, and had cried so hard when he found that it was not – as he had supposed – brown sugar, that he was now tired out, and was lying asleep in a warm fat bunch in the middle of the half-finished castle. This left his brothers and sisters free to work really hard, and the hole that was to come out in Australia soon grew so deep that Jane (who was called Pussy for short) begged the others to stop.

Beautiful as the Day

Cyril and Anthea knew that Australia was not quite so near as all that, but they agreed to stop using the spades and go on with their hands. This was quite easy, because the sand at the bottom of the hole was very soft and fine and dry, like sea sand.

The party were just making up their minds that sand makes you thirstier when it is not by the seaside, and someone had suggested going home for lemonade, when Anthea suddenly screamed, "Cyril! Come here! Oh, come quick! It's alive! It'll get away! Quick!"

They all hurried back.

"Perhaps it is a snake," said Jane, shuddering.

"Oh, don't be silly!" said Anthea, "it's not a snake. It's got feet, I saw them, and fur! No – not the spade. You'll hurt it! Dig with your hands."

But Cyril merely observed that his sister must have gone off her nut, and he and Robert dug with spades while Anthea sat on the edge of the hole, jumping up and down with hotness and anxiety.

I WISH, I WISH

They dug carefully, and presently everyone could see that there really was something moving in the bottom of the hole.

Then Anthea cried out, "*I'm* not afraid. Let me dig," and fell on her knees and began to scratch like a dog does when he has suddenly remembered where it was that he buried his bone.

"Oh, I felt fur," she cried, half laughing and half crying. "I did indeed! I did!" Suddenly a dry husky voice in the sand made them all jump back, and their hearts jumped nearly as fast as they did.

"Leave me alone," it said. Everyone heard the voice and looked at the others to see if they had too.

"But we want to see you," said Robert bravely.

"I wish you'd come out," said Anthea, also taking courage.

"Oh, well – if that's your wish," the voice said, and the sand stirred and spun, and something brown and furry came rolling out into the hole and the sand fell off it, and it sat there yawning.

Beautiful as the Day

"I believe I must have dropped asleep," it said, stretching itself.

The children stood round the hole in a ring, looking at the creature they had found. It was certainly worth looking at. Its eyes were on long horns like a snail's eyes, and it could move them in and out like telescopes. It had ears like a bat's ears, and its tubby body was shaped like a spider's and

covered with thick soft fur. Its legs and arms were furry too, and it had hands and feet like a monkey's.

"What on earth is it?" Jane said in amazement. "Shall we take it home?"

The thing turned its long eyes to look at her, and said, "Does she always talk nonsense, or is it only the rubbish on her head that makes her silly?"

It looked scornfully at Jane's hat as it spoke.

"She doesn't mean to be silly," Anthea said gently, "We none of us do, whatever you may think. Don't be frightened."

It said. "*Me* frightened? Upon my word! Why, you talk as if I were nobody in particular." All its fur stood out like a cat's when it is going to fight.

"Well," said Anthea, still kindly, "perhaps if we knew who you are in particular we could think of something to say that wouldn't make you cross."

"You don't know?" it said. "Well, I knew the world had changed – but – well, really – do you mean to tell me seriously you don't know a

Beautiful as the Day

Psammead when you see one? Or, in plain English, then, a *sand-fairy*. Don't you know a sand-fairy when you see one?"

Of course no one could think of anything to say, but at last Robert thought of 'How long have you lived here?' and he said it at once.

"Oh, ages – several thousand years," replied the Psammead.

"Was the world like this then?"

It stopped digging.

"Not a bit," it said, "it was nearly all sand where I lived, and coal grew on trees. We sand-fairies used to live on the seashore, and the children used to come with their little flint-spades and flint-pails and make castles for us to live in. That's thousands of years ago, but I hear that children still build castles on the sand. It's hard to break yourself of a habit."

"Why did you stop living in castles?" asked Robert, with interest.

"It's a sad story," said the Psammead gloomily.

I WISH, I WISH

"It was because they *would* build moats to the castles, and the nasty wet bubbling sea used to come in, and of course as soon as a sand-fairy got wet it caught cold, and generally died. And so there got to be fewer and fewer."

"And did *you* get wet?" Robert inquired.

The sand-fairy shuddered. "Only once," it said, "the end of the twelfth hair of my top left whisker – I feel the place still in damp weather. I scurried away to the back of the beach, and dug myself a house deep in warm dry sand, and there I've been ever since. And the sea changed its lodgings afterwards. And now I'm not going to tell you another thing."

"Just one more, please," said the children. "Can you give wishes now?"

"Of course," said it, "didn't I give you yours a few minutes ago? You said, 'I wish you'd come out,' and I did."

"Oh, please, mayn't we have another?"

"Yes, but be quick about it. I'm tired of you."

314

Beautiful as the Day

I daresay you have often thought what you would do if you had three wishes given you. These children had often talked this matter over, but, now the chance had suddenly come to them, they could not make up their minds.

"Quick," said the sand-fairy crossly.

No one could think of anything. Only Anthea did manage to remember a private wish of her own and Jane's which they had never told the boys. "I wish we were all as beautiful as the day," she said in a great hurry.

The children looked at each other, but each could see that the others were not any better looking than usual. The Psammead pushed out its long eyes, and seemed to be holding its breath and swelling itself out till it was twice as fat and furry as before. Suddenly it let its breath go in a long sigh.

"I'm really afraid I can't manage it," it said apologetically, "I must be out of practise."

The children were horribly disappointed.

"Oh, *do* try again!" they said.

"Well," said the sand-fairy, "the fact is, I was keeping back a little strength to give the rest of you your wishes with. If you'll be contented with one wish a day amongst the lot of you I daresay I can screw myself up to it. Do you agree to that?"

"Yes, oh yes!" they all agreed.

It stretched out its eyes farther than ever, and swelled and swelled and swelled.

"I do hope it won't hurt itself," said Anthea.

"Or crack its skin," Robert said anxiously.

Everyone was very much relieved when the sand-fairy, after getting so big that it almost filled up the hole in the sand, suddenly let out its breath and went back to its proper size.

"That's all right," it said, panting heavily. "It'll come easier tomorrow. It'll last till sunset."

"Did it hurt much?" asked Anthea.

"Only my whisker, thank you," said he.

And with a hurried 'Good day!' the sand-fairy

Beautiful as the Day

scratched suddenly with its hands and feet, and disappeared in the sand. Then the children looked at each other, and each child suddenly found itself alone with three strangers, all radiantly beautiful.

They stood for some moments in perfect silence. Each thought that its brothers and sisters had wandered off, and that these strange children had stolen up while it was watching the sand-fairy.

Anthea spoke first, "Excuse me," she said very politely to Jane, who now had enormous blue eyes and a cloud of russet hair, "but have you seen two little boys and a little girl anywhere about?"

"I was just going to ask you that," said Jane.

And then Cyril cried, "Why, it's *you*! I know the hole in your pinafore! You *are* Jane, aren't you? Crikey! The wish has come off, after all. I say, am I as handsome as you are?"

"If you're Cyril, I liked you better before," said Anthea decidedly. "You look like the picture of the young chorister, with your golden hair, you'll die

317

young, I shouldn't wonder. And if that's Robert, he's like an Italian organ grinder."

"You two girls are like silly Christmas cards, then – that's all," said Robert angrily.

"Well, it's no use finding fault with each other," said Anthea, "let's get the Lamb and lug it home to dinner. The servants will admire us most awfully, you'll see."

Baby was just waking when they got to him. The children were relieved to find that he was not as beautiful as the day, but just the same as usual.

"I suppose he's too young to have wishes," said Jane. "We shall have to mention him specially next time."

Anthea ran forward and held out her arms.

Beautiful as the Day

"Come to own Panther, ducky," she said.

The Baby looked at her disapprovingly, and put a sandy pink thumb in his mouth.

"G'way long!" said the Baby.

"Come to own Pussy," said Jane.

"Wants my Panty," said the Lamb dismally.

"Here, come on, Veteran," said Robert, "come and have a yidey on Yobby's back."

"Yah, narky narky boy," howled the Baby, giving way altogether. Then the children knew the worst: *The baby did not know them!*

319

I WISH, I WISH

They all looked at each other in despair, and it was terrible to each, in this dire emergency, to meet only the beautiful eyes of perfect strangers, instead of the merry, friendly, little eyes of its own brothers and sisters.

"This is most truly awful," said Cyril. "I can't carry him home with him screaming like that. Fancy having to make friends with our own baby! It's just too silly."

That, however, was exactly what they had to do. It took them over an hour to persuade the Lamb that they were not dangerous strangers. This difficult task was not rendered any easier by the fact that he was by this time as hungry as a lion and as thirsty as a desert.

At last he consented to allow these peculiar people to carry him home by turns, but as he refused to hold on to such new acquaintances he was a dead weight and most exhausting.

"Thank goodness, we're home!" said Jane,

320

staggering through the iron gate to where Martha, the nursemaid, stood at the front door shading her eyes with her hand and looking out anxiously. "Here! Do take baby!"

Martha snatched the baby from her arms.

"Thanks be, *he's* safe back," she said. "Where are the others, and whoever to goodness gracious are all of you?'

"We're *us*, of course," said Robert.

"And who's *us*, when you're at home?" asked Martha scornfully.

"I know we *look* diffcrent, but I'm Anthea, and we're so tired, and it's long past dinner time."

"Then go home to your dinners, whoever you are, and if our children put you up to this play-acting you can tell them from me they'll catch it, so they know what to expect!"

With that she did bang the door, leaving them all outside. Cyril rang the bell violently. No answer. Presently cook put her head out of a bedroom

window and said, "If you don't take yourselves off, I'll go and fetch the police." And she slammed down the window.

"It's no good," said Anthea. "Oh, do, do come away before we get sent to prison!"

The boys said it was nonsense, and the law of England couldn't put you in prison for just being as beautiful as the day, but all the same they followed the others out into the lane.

"We shall be our proper selves after sunset, I suppose," said Jane.

It was a horrible afternoon. There was no house near where the children could beg a crust of bread or even a glass of water. They were afraid to go to the village, because they had seen Martha go down there with a basket, and there was a local constable. True, they were all as beautiful as the day, but that is a poor comfort when you are as hungry as a hunter and as thirsty as a sponge.

It came at last to their sitting down in a row

under the hedge, with their feet in a dry ditch, waiting for sunset.

At last hunger and fright and crossness and tiredness – four very nasty things – all joined together to bring one nice thing, and that was sleep. The children lay asleep in a row, with their beautiful eyes shut and their beautiful mouths open. Anthea woke first. The sun had set, and the twilight was coming on.

"Wake up," she said, almost in tears of joy, "it's all right. Oh, Cyril, how nice and ugly you do look, with your old freckles and your brown hair and your little eyes. And so do you all!" she added, so that they might not feel jealous.

When they got home they were very much scolded by Martha, who told them about the strange children.

"A good-looking lot, I must say, but that impudent."

"I know," said Robert, who knew by bitter

experience how hopeless it would be to try to explain things to Martha.

"And where on earth have you been all this time, you naughty little things, you?"

"In the lane."

"Why didn't you come home hours ago?"

"We couldn't because of *them*," said Anthea. "They wouldn't let us go."

"'Who?"

"The children who were as beautiful as the day. They kept us there till after sunset. We couldn't come back till they'd gone. You don't know how we hated them! Oh, do, do give us some supper – we are so hungry."

"Hungry! I should think so," said Martha angrily, "out all day like this. Well, I hope it'll be a lesson to you not to go picking up with strange children – down here after measles, as likely as not! Now mind, if you see them again, don't you speak to them – not one word."

Beautiful as the Day

"If ever we *do* see them again we'll tell you,"
Anthea said, and Robert, fixing his eyes fondly on
the cold beef that was being brought in on a tray by
cook, added in heartfelt undertones, "And we'll take
jolly good care we never *do* see them again."

And they never have.

Christmas
Every Day

By W D Howells

*T*he little girl came into her papa's study and
asked for a story. He tried to beg off, for he
was busy, but she would not let him. So he began,
"Well, once there was a little pig—"

But the little girl said that she had heard pig
stories till she was sick of them.

"Well, what kind of story shall I tell, then?"

"About Christmas. It's getting to be the season.

Christmas Every Day

After all, it's past Thanksgiving already."

"It seems to me," her papa argued, "that I've told as often about Christmas as I have about little pigs."

"Christmas is more interesting."

"Well, then, I'll tell you about the little girl that wanted it to be Christmas every day in the year. How do you like the sound of that?"

"First-rate!" said the little girl, and she nestled into a comfortable shape in his lap, ready for listening.

"Once there was a little girl who liked Christmas so much that she wanted it to be Christmas every day. As soon as Thanksgiving was over she began to send letters to the Christmas Fairy to ask if she could make it so, and – the day before Christmas – she got a letter from the fairy, telling her that she would grant her wish to have Christmas every day for a year, and they could see how they got on.

"The little girl was a good deal excited already, preparing for the old-fashioned, once-a-year Christmas that was coming the next day, and perhaps the fairy's promise didn't make such an impression on her as it would have made at some other time. She just resolved to keep it to herself, and surprise everybody with it as it kept coming true, and then it slipped out of her mind altogether.

"She had a splendid Christmas. She went to bed early, so as to let Santa Claus have a chance at the stockings, and in the morning she was up the first of anybody and went and felt them, and found hers all lumpy with packages of candy, and oranges and grapes, and books and rubber balls, and all kinds of small presents. Then she waited around till the rest of the family were up, and she was the first to burst into the library when the doors were opened, and

look at the large presents laid out – books, and
boxes of stationery, and dolls, and little stoves, and
skates, and photograph-frames, and little easels, and
boxes of water-colours, and Turkish paste, and
nougat, and candied cherries, and dolls' houses –
and the big Christmas tree, lighted and standing in
a basket in the middle.

"She had a splendid Christmas all day. She ate so
much candy that she did not want any breakfast,
and she went round giving the presents she had got
for other people, and came home and ate turkey and
cranberry for dinner, and plum-pudding and nuts
and raisins and oranges and more candy, and then
went out sledging, and came in with a stomach-
ache, crying, and her papa said he would see if his
house was turned into that sort of fool's paradise
another year, and they had a light supper, and pretty
early everybody went to bed cross.

"The little girl slept very heavily, and she slept
very late, but she was wakened at last by the other

children dancing round her bed with their stockings full of presents in their hands.

"'What is it?' said the little girl, and she rubbed her eyes and tried to sit up in bed.

"'Christmas! Christmas! Christmas!' they all shouted, and waved their stockings.

"'Nonsense! It was Christmas yesterday.'

"Her brothers and sisters just laughed. 'We don't know about that. It's Christmas today, anyway. You come into the library and see.'

"Then all at once it flashed on the little girl that the fairy was keeping her promise, and her year of Christmases was beginning. She was dreadfully sleepy, but she sprang up like a lark – a lark that had overeaten itself and gone to bed cross – and darted into the library. There it was again! Books, and boxes of stationery..."

"'You needn't go over it all, papa, I guess I can remember just what was there," said the little girl.

"Well, and there was the Christmas tree blazing

away, and the family picking out their presents, but looking pretty sleepy, and her father perfectly puzzled, and her mother ready to cry.

"'I don't see how I'm to dispose of all these things,' said her mother, and her father said it seemed to him they had had something just like it the day before, but he supposed he must have dreamt it. This struck the little girl as the best kind joke, and so she ate so much candy she didn't want breakfast, and went round carrying presents, and had turkey and cranberry for dinner, and then went out sledging, and came in with a..."

"Papa!"

"Well, what now?"

"What did you promise, you forgetful thing?"

"Oh! Oh yes!

"Well, the next day, it was just the same thing over again, but everybody getting crosser, and at the end of a week's time so many people had lost their tempers that you could pick up lost tempers anywhere, they perfectly strewed the ground. Even when people tried to recover their tempers they usually got somebody else's, and it made the most dreadful mix.

"The little girl began to get frightened, keeping the secret all to herself. She wanted to tell her mother, but she didn't dare to, and she was ashamed to ask the fairy to take back her gift, it seemed ungrateful and ill-bred, and she thought she would try to stand it, but she hardly knew how she could, for a whole year. So it went on and on, and it was Christmas on St Valentine's Day and Washington's birthday, just the same as any day, and it didn't skip even the first of April, though everything was counterfeit that day, and that was some little relief.

"After a while turkeys got to be about a thousand dollars apiece and they got to passing off almost anything for turkeys – half-grown humming-birds, and even rocs out of the Arabian Nights – the real turkeys were so scarce. And cranberries – well, they asked a diamond apiece for cranberries. All the woods and orchards were cut down for Christmas trees, and where the woods and orchards used to be it looked just like a stubble field, with the stumps.

"After a while they had to make Christmas trees out of rags, and stuff them with bran, like old-fashioned dolls, but there were plenty of rags, because people had all got so poor, buying presents for one another, that they couldn't get any new clothes, and they just wore their old ones to tatters. They got so poor that everybody had to go to the poorhouse, except the confectioners, and the shopkeepers, and the picture-book sellers, and they all got so rich and proud that they would hardly wait upon a person when he came to buy. It was perfectly shameful!

"Well, after it had gone on for about three or four months, the little girl, whenever she came into the room in the morning and saw those great ugly, lumpy stockings dangling at the fireplace, and the disgusting presents around everywhere, used to just sit down and burst out crying. In six months she was perfectly exhausted. She couldn't even cry anymore. About the beginning of October she took to sitting down on dolls wherever she found them because she hated the sight of them so much, and by Thanksgiving she was crazy, and just slammed her presents across the room.

"By that time people didn't carry presents around nicely any more. They flung them over the fence, or through the window, or anything, and they used to write in the gift books, 'Take it, you horrid old thing!' and then go and bang it against the front door. Nearly everybody had built barns to hold their presents, but very soon the barns overflowed, and then people just let their presents lie out in the rain, or anywhere. Sometimes the police used to come and tell them to shovel their presents off the sidewalk, or they would arrest them.

"Well, before Thanksgiving came it had leaked

out who had caused all these Christmases. The little girl had suffered so much that she had talked about it in her sleep, and after that hardly anybody would play with her. People just perfectly despised her, because if it had not been for her greediness it wouldn't have happened

"When it came to Thanksgiving, and she wanted everybody to go to church, and have squash-pie and turkey, and show their gratitude, everyone said that all the turkeys had been eaten up for her old Christmas dinners, and if she would only put a stop to the Christmases, they would see about the gratitude. Wasn't it dreadful?

"And the very next day the little girl began to write letters and send them to the Christmas Fairy, and then telegrams, asking her to stop it. But it didn't do any good. And then she got to calling at the fairy's house, but the girl that came to the door always said, 'Not at home,' or 'Engaged,' or 'At dinner,' or something like that.

Christmas Every Day

"And so it went on till it came to the old once-a-year Christmas Eve. The little girl fell asleep, and when she woke up in the morning..."

"She found it was all nothing but a dream," suggested the little girl.

"No, indeed!" said her papa. "The situation was every bit as true and dreadful as it had been when she went to bed!"

"Well, what did she find out, then?"

"Why, that it wasn't Christmas at last, and wasn't

ever going to be, any more. And now it's time for us
to have breakfast."

The little girl held her papa fast around the neck.
"You shan't go if you're going to leave it so!"

"How do you want it left?"

"Christmas once a year."

"All right," said her papa, and he went on again...

"Well, there was the greatest rejoicing all over the
country, and it extended clear up into Canada. The
people met together everywhere, and hugged and
kissed and cried for joy. The city carts went around
town and gathered up all the chocolates and sweets
and raisins and nuts, and dumped them into the
river, and it made the fish perfectly sick, and the
whole United States, as far out as Alaska, was one
blaze of bonfires, where the children were burning
up their gift books and presents of all kinds. They
had the best time!

"The little girl went to thank the fairy because
she had stopped it being Christmas, and she said

she hoped she would keep her promise and see that Christmas never came again. Then the fairy frowned, and asked her if she was sure she knew what she meant. The little girl asked why, and the fairy said that now she was behaving as greedily as ever, so she'd better look out.

"This made the little girl think it all over carefully again, and then she said she would be willing to have it Christmas about once in a thousand years, and then she said a hundred, and then she said ten, and at long last she got down to one. The fairy said that was the good old way that had pleased people ever since Christmas began, and she agreed.

"Then the little girl said, 'What are your shoes made of?' And the fairy said, 'Leather.' And the little girl said, 'Bargain's done forever,' and skipped off, and hippity-hopped the whole way home, she was so glad.

"How will that do?" asked the papa.

"First-rate!" said the little girl, but she hated to have the story stop, and was rather quiet. However, her mamma put her head in at the door, to ask her papa, "Are you two never coming to breakfast? What have you been telling that child?"

"Oh, just a moral tale."

The little girl caught him around the neck again. "We know! Don't you tell what, papa! Don't you tell what!"

Under the Sun

By Juliana Horatia Gatty Ewing

*O*nce upon a time there lived a farmer who was so greedy and miserly, and so very hard in all his dealings that, as folks say, he would skin a flint. It is needless to say that he made it a rule never to give nor lend.

Now, by thus scraping, and saving, and grinding for many years, he had become almost wealthy, though, indeed, he did not enjoy it – in fact, he was no better fed and dressed than if he had not a single penny to bless himself with. But what vexed him sorely was that his neighbour's farm prospered in every matter much better than his own, and this, although the owner was as generous as our farmer was stingy.

Now on the lands of the generous farmer (whose name was Merryweather) there lived a fairy or hillman, who made a wager that he would both beg and borrow of the envious farmer, and out-bargain him as well.

So the fairy went one day to the mean farmer's house, and asked him if he would kindly give him half a stone of flour to make hasty pudding with. He added that if the farmer would lend him a bag to carry it into the hill, this should be returned clean and in good condition.

The farmer recognized with half an eye that this was the fairy who lived on his neighbour's estate. He had always laid the good fortune of the

generous farmer to his being favoured by the fairies (rather than hard work and consideration for others), so he resolved to himself that he would treat the little man with all politeness.

"Look you," said he quietly to his wife, "this is no time to be saving half a stone of flour when we may make our fortunes at one happy stroke. I have heard my grandfather tell of a man who once lent a sack of oats to a party of fairies, and when he got it back it was filled with gold pieces. And as good measure as he gave of oats so he got of gold." Saying which, the farmer took a canvas bag to the flour bin, and began to fill it.

The fairy had sharper ears than the farmer imagined, and he smiled from ear to ear at the thought of the fun he could have. He leapt up to sit in the larder window and cried, "Give us good measure, neighbour, and you shall have anything under the sun that you like to ask for."

When the farmer heard him say this he was

nearly out of his wits with delight, and his hands shook so much that the flour spilled all about the larder floor.

"Thank you, dear sir," he said, "It's a bargain, and I agree to it. My wife hears us agree, and is witness. Wife! Wife!" he cried, running into the kitchen, "I am to have anything under the sun that I choose to ask for. I think first of asking for neighbour Merryweather's estate, but this is a chance never likely to happen again, and I should like to make a wise choice."

"You will be given a week to think it over in," said the fairy, who had come into the kitchen behind him. "I must be off now, so give me my flour, and come to the hill behind your house seven days hence at midnight."

"Not for seven days, did you say, sir? You know, dear sir, when amongst each other we men have to wait for the settlement of an account, we expect something over and above the exact amount.

Interest we call it, my dear sir."

"And you want me to give you something extra for waiting a week?" asked the fairy. "And what do you expect?"

"Oh, my dear sir, I will leave it entirely to you," said the farmer, thinking himself generous.

"I will give you something over and above what you shall choose," said the fairy, "but, as you say, I shall decide what it is to be." And with this pronouncement he shouldered the flour-sack, and went his way.

For the next seven days, the farmer had no peace for thinking and scheming how to get the most out of his one wish. His wife made many suggestions to which he did not agree, but he was careful not to quarrel with her, "For," he said, "we will not be like the foolish couple who wasted three wishes on black puddings."

And so, after a week of anxious thinking, he came back to what had been his very first thought, and resolved to ask for his neighbour's estate.

At last the night came. It was full moon, and the farmer looked anxiously about, fearing the fairy might not be true to his appointment. But at midnight he appeared, with the flour bag neatly folded in his hand.

"You will keep the bargain," said the farmer, "of course. I am to have anything under the sun I ask for, and I am to have it right now."

"Indeed you shall – ask away," replied the fairy.

"I want my neighbour Merryweather's whole estate," said the farmer.

"What, all this

land below here, that joins on to your own farm?"

"Every acre," said the farmer.

"Unfortunately for you, Farmer Merryweather's fields are under the moon at present," said the fairy, coolly, "and thus not within the terms of the agreement. You must choose again."

But the farmer could choose nothing that was not then under the moon, though he thought with all his might. At once he realized that he had been outwitted, and his rage knew no bounds at the trick the fairy had played on him.

"Give me my bag, at any rate," he screamed, "and the string – and your own extra gift that you promised. For half a loaf is better than no bread," he muttered to himself, "and I may yet come in for a few gold pieces."

"There's your bag," cried the fairy, gleefully clapping it over the old miser's head like an extinguisher, "it's clean enough for a nightcap. And there's your string," he added, tying it tightly round the farmer's throat. "And, for my part, I'll now give you exactly what you deserve."

Saying which he gave the mean farmer such a hearty kick that he rolled straight down from the very top of the hill to his own back door.

"And if all that does not satisfy you, I'll give you as much again," shouted the fairy after him, and as the farmer made no reply, he went chuckling back to his hill.

The Laird and the Man of Peace

By Juliana Horatia Gatty Ewing

In Scotland, fairies were often called Daoiné Shi *(pronounced dheen-ya-shee), meaning 'men of peace'. A laird is an important landowner, always known by the name of his estate. Cairngorms are a type of smoky quartz, much prized for making jewellery, especially in Scotland, where kilt pins are often decorated with them.*

*I*n the Highlands of Scotland there once lived a Laird of Brockburn, who would not believe in fairies. Not that he bore any ill-will to the Good People, or spoke uncivilly of them. Indeed he always

The Laird and the Man of Peace

denied any feeling of disrespect towards them if they existed, saying that he was a man of peace himself, and anxious to live peaceably with whatever neighbours he had, but that till he had seen one he could not believe in them.

Now one afternoon, between Hallowmas and Yule, it chanced that the laird, being out on the hills looking for some cattle, got parted from his men and dogs and was overtaken by a mist, in which, familiar as the country was to him, he lost his way.

In vain he raised his voice high, and listened low, but no sound of man or beast came back to him through the thickening vapour.

Then night fell, and darkness was added to the fog, so that Brockburn could barely see to place his feet on a path in the gloom.

Suddenly light footsteps pattered beside him, then something brushed against him, then ran between his legs. The delighted laird was sure that his favourite collie had found him once more.

"Wow, Jock, man!" he cried, "but ye needn't run about – ye near threw me on my face. What's got into ye this night, that you should lose your way in a bit of mist?"

To this a voice from the level of his elbow replied, in piping but patronizing tones, "Never did I lose my way in a mist since the night that Finn crossed over to Ireland in the dawn of history. Eh, laird! I'm well acquainted with every little path on the hillside these hundreds of years, and I'll guide ye safe home, never fear!"

At the sound of the voice, the hairs on Brockburn's head all stood up on end, and a cold, damp chill broke out all over him that was not the fog. But, despite all that, he stoutly resisted the evidence of his senses, and only felt about him in the darkness for the collie's head to pat, crying, "Bark! Jock, my mannie, bark! Then I'll recognize your voice, ye ken. It's not canny to hear ye speak like a Christian, my wee doggie."

The Laird and the Man of Peace

"I'm nae your doggie, I'm a man of peace," was the swift reply. "Don't miscall your betters, Brockburn – why will ye not believe in our existence, man?"

"Seeing's believing," said the laird, stubbornly, "but the mist's a good deal too thick for seeing this night, ye ken."

"Turn round to your left, man, and ye'll see," said the dwarf, and catching Brockburn by the arm, he twisted him swiftly round three times. When the laird stopped spinning he saw a sudden blaze of bright light pouring through the mist, and it revealed a crag of the mountain well known to the laird, and which he now recognized to be a kind of turret, or tower.

Lights shone gaily through the crevices or windows of the tower, and sounds of fiddling came forth from within. Blinded by the light, and amazed at what he saw, the laird staggered, and was silent. Then stepping up to the door of the tower, the

I WISH, I WISH

strange man stood so that the light from within fell full upon him, and the astonished laird saw a tiny, well-proportioned man, with delicate features, and golden hair flowing over his shoulders. He wore a cloak of green cloth, lined with daisies. His beautiful face quivered with amusement at the laird's surprise, and he cried triumphantly, "D'ye see me? D'ye see me now, Brockburn?"

"Aye, aye," said the laird, "and seeing's believing."

"Then round with ye!" shouted the man of peace, and once more seizing the laird by the arm, he turned him swiftly round – this time, to the right – and at the third turn the light vanished, and Brockburn and the man of peace were once more alone together in the mist.

"Aweel, Brockburn," said the man of peace, "I'll allow ye're honest, and have a convincible mind. I'm not ill disposed towards ye, and ye shall get safe home, man."

As he spoke he stooped down, and picking up half-a-dozen big stones from the mountainside, he gave them to the laird, saying, "If your good wife asks ye about the stones, say ye got them as a compliment."

Brockburn put them into his pocket, briefly

I WISH, I WISH

saying, "I'm obliged to ye," but as he followed the
man of peace down the hillside, he found the
obligation so heavy, that from time to time he threw
a stone away, unobserved, as he hoped, by his

companion. When the first stone fell, the man of peace looked sharply round, saying, "What's that?"

"It'll be my feet striking upon the ground," said the laird.

"You're mad," said the man of peace, and Brockburn felt sure that he knew the truth, and was displeased. But as they went on, the stones were so heavy, and bumped his side so hard, that he threw away a second, dropping it as gently as he could. But the sound of its fall did not escape the ears of the man of peace, who cried as before, "What's that?"

"It's just a nasty cough that I have," said the laird.

"Man, you're daft," said the dwarf, with contempt, "that's what ails ye."

The laird now resolved to be prudent, but the heaviness of his burden was so great that after a while he resolved to risk the displeasure of the man of peace once more, and gently slipped a third stone to the ground.

'Third time's lucky,' he thought. But the proverb

failed him, for the dwarf turned as before, shouting, "What's that?"

"It'll be my new shoes that ye hear stumbling upon the big stones," said the laird.

"Ye're drunk, Brockburn, I tell ye so. Ye're drunk!" growled the man of peace, angrily, and the laird dared not drop any more of the gifts. After a while his companion's good humour seemed to return, and he became talkative and generous.

"Ye shall not have to say that ye've been with the Daoiné Shi and are not the better for it," he said. "I'm thinking I'll grant ye three wishes. But choose wisely, man, and don't throw them away."

The laird at once began to cast about in his mind for three wishes sufficiently comprehensive to secure his lifelong prosperity, but the more he beat his brains the less could he satisfy himself.

How many miles he wandered thus, the dwarf keeping silently beside him, he never knew, before he sank exhausted on the ground, saying, "I'm thinking, man, that if ye could bring home to me, in place of bringing me home, I'd doubt your powers no more. It's a far cry to Loch Awe, ye know, and it's a weary long road to Brockburn."

"Is this your wish?" asked the man of peace.

"This is my wish," said the laird.

The words had just scarcely fell from his lips when the whole homestead of Brockburn, the house and all the farm buildings, was planted upon the bleak hillside.

The astonished laird now began to bewail the rash wish which had removed his home from the sheltered and fertile valley where it originally stood to the barren side of a bleak mountain.

The man of peace, however, would not take any hints as to undoing his work of his own accord. All he said was, "If ye wish it away, so it'll be. But then ye'll only have one wish left."

"To leave the steading in such a spot is no to be thought on," sighed the laird, as he spent his second

wish in undoing his first. But he cannily added the provision, "And ye may take me with it."

The words were no sooner spoken than the homestead was back in its place, and Brockburn himself was lying in his own bed, with Jock, his favourite collie, barking and licking his face for joy.

"Whisht, whisht, Jock!" said the laird, angrily. "Ye would not bark when I begged, so ye may hand your peace now."

And pushing the collie from him, he sat up in bed and looked anxiously but vainly round the chamber for the man of peace.

"Lie down, lie down," cried his good wife from beside him. "Ye're surely out of your wits. Would ye go wandering about the country again tonight?"

"Where is he?" cried the laird.

"There's not a soul here but your lawful wife and your own dear doggie. Was there anybody that ye expected?" asked his wife.

"The man o' peace, woman!" cried Brockburn.

The Laird and the Man of Peace

"I've one of my wishes to get yet, and I must have it."

"The man's mad!" was his good wife's comment. "Ye've surely forgotten yourself. Ye never believed in the Daoiné Shi before."

"Seeing's believing," said the laird. "I forgathered with a man of peace tonight on the hill, and I wish I just saw him again."

As the laird spoke the window of the chamber was lit up from without, and the man of peace appeared sitting on the window ledge in his daisy-lined cloak, his feet hanging down into the room, the silver shoes glittering as they dangled.

"I'm here, Brockburn!" he cried. "But eh, man! Ye've had your last wish."

And even as the stupefied laird gazed, the light slowly died away, and the man of peace vanished with it.

On the following morning the laird was roused from sleep by loud cries of surprise and admiration.

His wife had been stirring for some hours, and in

emptying the pockets of her good man's coat she had found huge cairngorms of exquisite tint and lustre. Brockburn thus discovered the value of the gifts he had thrown away.

But no subsequent visits to the hillside led to their recovery. Many a time did the laird bring home a heavy pocketful of stones, at his thrifty wife's bidding, but they only proved to be the common stones of the mountainside. The tower could never be distinguished from any other crag, and the Daoiné Shi were visible no more.

Yet it is said that the Laird of Brockburn prospered and throve thereafter, in acre, stall, and steading, as those seldom prosper who have not the good word of the people of peace.

The Laird and the Man of Peace

Peter's Two Wishes

From *Peter Pan in Kensington Gardens*
by J M Barrie

*Peter Pan is a human boy who was left behind in a famous London park
called Kensington Gardens by mistake. He has lived there ever since, a
friend of the fairies. During the day, the fairies hide away from humans,
but they come out to play at night time when the park is locked up.*

*I*t is frightfully difficult to know much at all
about the fairies – indeed, almost the only thing
we know for certain is that there are fairies wherever
there are children. Long ago children were

Peter's Two Wishes

forbidden in the Gardens, and at that time there was not a fairy in the place. Then the children were admitted, and the fairies came trooping in that very evening. They can't resist following the children, but you seldom see them, partly because they live in the daytime behind the railings – where you are not allowed to go – and also partly because they are so very cunning.

You remember a good deal about fairies in your babyhood, which it is a great pity you can't write down, for gradually you forget, and I have heard of children who declared that they had never once seen a fairy. Very likely if they said this in the Kensington Gardens, they were standing looking at a fairy all the time. The reason they were cheated was that she pretended to be something else. This is one of their best tricks. They usually pretend to be flowers, because the court sits in the Fairies' Basin, and there are so many flowers there, and all along the Baby Walk, that a flower is the thing least likely

to attract attention. They dress exactly like flowers, and change with the seasons, putting on white when lilies are in and blue for bluebells, and so on.

They like crocus and hyacinth time best of all, as they are partial to a bit of colour, but tulips (except white ones, which are the fairy cradles) they consider garish, and they sometimes put off dressing like tulips for days, so that the beginning of the tulip weeks is almost the best time to catch them.

Peter's Two Wishes

When they think you are not looking they skip along pretty lively, but if you look, and there is no time to hide, they stand quite still pretending to be flowers. Then, after you have passed without knowing that they were fairies, they rush home and tell their mothers they have had such an adventure.

I WISH, I WISH

Numbers of them can also be found along the Baby Walk, which is a famous gentle place (as spots frequented by fairies are called). Once, twenty-four of them had an extraordinary adventure. They were a girls' school out for a walk with the governess, and all wearing hyacinth gowns, when she suddenly put her finger to her mouth, and then they all stood still on an empty bed and pretended to be hyacinths. Unfortunately what the governess had heard was two gardeners coming to plant flowers in that very bed. They were wheeling a handcart with flowers in it, and were surprised to find the bed occupied.

"It's a pity to lift them hyacinths," said the younger of the two men.

"Duke's orders," replied the other, and, having emptied the cart, they dug up the boarding school and put the poor, terrified things in it in five rows. Of course, neither the governess nor the girls dared let on that they were fairies, so they were carted far away to a potting shed, out of which they escaped in the night without their shoes, but there was a great row about it among the parents, and the school's reputation was ruined.

As for their houses, it is no use looking for them, because they are the exact opposite of our houses. You can see our houses by day but you can't see them by dark. Well, you can see their houses by dark, but you can't see them by day, for they are the colour of night, and I never heard of any one yet who could see night in the daytime. This does not mean that they are black, for night has its colours just as day has, but ever so much brighter.

Their blues and reds and greens are like ours with light behind them. Their palace is entirely built of many-coloured glasses, and is the loveliest of all royal residences, but the queen sometimes complains because the common people will peep in to see what she is doing. They are very inquisitive folk, and press quite hard against the glass, and that is why their noses are mostly snubby.

I WISH, I WISH

One of the great differences between the fairies and us is that they never do anything useful. When the first baby laughed for the first time, his laugh broke into a million pieces, and they all went skipping about. That was the beginning of fairies. They look tremendously busy, as if they had not a moment to spare, but if you were to ask them what they are doing, they could not tell you in the least. They are frightfully ignorant, and everything they do is make-believe. It is a very noticeable thing that, in fairy families, the youngest is always chief person, and usually becomes a prince or princess.

The fairies are exquisite dancers, and hold their great balls in the open air, in what is called a fairy ring. For weeks afterwards you can see the ring on the grass. It is not there when they begin, but they make it by waltzing round and round. Sometimes you will find mushrooms inside the ring, and these are fairy chairs that the servants have forgotten to clear away. The chairs and the rings are the only signs these little people ever leave behind, and they would remove even these were they not so fond of dancing that they continue to make merry till the very moment of the opening of the park gates.

If on such a night we could remain behind in the gardens, we might see delicious sights. One of the grandest is when hundreds of fairies hasten to the ball, the married ones wearing their wedding rings round their waists, the gentlemen, all in uniform, holding up the ladies' trains, and linkmen running in front carrying winter cherries, which are the fairy lanterns. The supper table, with Queen Mab at the head, glows with the light of one hundred fireflies, and behind the queen's chair stands the Lord Chamberlain, who carries a dandelion on which he blows when her majesty wants to know the time.

The tablecloth varies according to the seasons, and in May it is made of chestnut blossom. The way the fairy servants make them is this: Scores of the men climb up the trees and shake the branches, and

the blossom falls like snow. Then the lady servants sweep it together by whisking their skirts until it is exactly like a tablecloth, and that is how they get their tablecloth.

Peter Pan is the fairies' orchestra. He sits in the middle of the ring, and they would never dream of having a smart dance nowadays without him. They are grateful little people, too, and at the coming-of-age ball of the princess (they come of age on their second birthday and have a birthday every month) they agreed to grant him the wish of his heart.

The queen ordered him to kneel, and then said that for playing so beautifully she would give him the wish of his heart. Then all the fairies gathered round Peter in order to hear what the wish of his heart was, but for a long time he hesitated, for he was not quite certain what it was himself.

"If I chose to go back to mother," he asked at last, "could you give me that wish?"

Now this question vexed them, for were he to

Peter's Two Wishes

return to his mother they should no longer have his music, so the queen tilted her nose and said, "Pooh, you should ask for a much bigger wish than that."

"Is that quite a little wish?" he inquired.

"As little as this," the queen answered, putting her hands near each other.

"What size is a big wish?" he asked.

She measured it off on her skirt and it was a very handsome length.

Then Peter thought, and said, "Well, I think I shall have two little wishes instead of one big one."

Of course, the fairies felt they could not say no to his request, though his cleverness in asking rather shocked them. He told them that his first wish was to go back to his dear mother, but with the right to return to his home and friends in Kensington Gardens if he found her to be disappointing. His second wish he decided he would hold in reserve until he thought of something that was really worth wishing for.

They tried to dissuade him, and even put obstacles in the way. "I can give you the power to fly to her house," the queen said, "but I can't open the door for you."

"The window I flew out at will be open," Peter said confidently. "Mother always keeps it open in the hope that I may fly back."

"How do you know?" they asked, quite surprised, and, really, Peter could not explain how he knew.

"I just know," he said.

So as he persisted in his wish, they had to grant it. The way they gave him power to fly was this: They all tickled him on the shoulder, and soon he felt a funny itching in that part, and then up he rose higher and higher, and flew away out of the Gardens and over the housetops.

It was so delicious that instead of flying straight to his own home he skimmed away over St Paul's to the Crystal Palace and back by the river and

Peter's Two Wishes

Regent's Park, and by the time he reached his mother's window he had quite made up his mind that his second wish should be to become a bird.

The window was wide open, just as he knew it would be, and in he fluttered, and there was his mother lying asleep. Peter alighted softly on the

wooden rail at the foot of the bed and had a good look at her. She lay with her head on her hand, and the hollow in the pillow was like a nest lined with her brown wavy hair. He remembered, though he had long forgotten it, that she always gave her hair a holiday at night. How sweet the frills of her nightgown were! He was very glad she was such a pretty mother.

But she looked sad, and he knew why she looked sad. One of her arms moved as if it wanted to go round something, and he knew what it wanted to go round.

"Oh, mother," said Peter to himself, "if you just knew who is sitting on the rail at the foot of the bed at this very moment."

Very gently he patted the little mound that her feet made, and he could see by her face that she liked it. He knew he had but to say 'Mother' ever so softly, and she would wake up. They always wake up at once if it is you that says their name. Then she

Peter's Two Wishes

would give such a joyous cry and squeeze him tight.
How nice that would be to him, and how
exquisitely delicious it would be to her. That, I am
afraid, is how Peter regarded it. In returning to his
mother he never doubted that he was giving her the
greatest treat a woman can have. Nothing can be
more splendid, he thought, than to have a little boy
of your own. How proud of him they are! And very
right and proper, too.

But why does Peter sit so long on the rail, and
why does he not tell his mother that he has come
back to her?

I quite shrink from the truth, which is that he sat
there in two minds. Sometimes he looked longingly
at his mother, and sometimes he looked longingly at
the window. Certainly it would be pleasant to be
her boy again, but on the other hand, what times
those had been in the Gardens! Was he so sure that
he should enjoy wearing clothes again? He popped
off the bed and opened some drawers to have a look

at his old garments. They were still there, but he could not remember how you put them on. The socks, for instance, were they worn on the hands or on the feet? He was about to try one of them on his hand, when he had a great adventure. Perhaps the drawer had creaked – at any rate, his mother woke up, for he heard her say 'Peter,' as if it was the most lovely word in the language. He remained sitting on the floor and held his breath, wondering how she knew that he had come back. If she said 'Peter' again, he meant to cry 'Mother' and run to her. But she spoke no more, she made little moans only, and when he next peeped at her she was once more asleep, with tears on her face.

It made Peter very miserable, and what do you think was the first thing he did? Sitting on the windowsill, he played a beautiful lullaby to his mother on his pipe. He had made it up himself out of the way she said 'Peter,' and he never stopped playing until she looked happy.

Peter's Two Wishes

I WISH, I WISH

He thought this so clever of him that he could scarcely resist wakening his mother to hear her say, 'Oh, Peter, how exquisitely you play.' However, as she now seemed comfortable, he again cast looks at the window.

You must not think that he meditated flying away and never coming back. He had quite decided to be his mother's boy once more, but hesitated about beginning tonight. It was the second wish which troubled him. He no longer intended to make it a wish to be a bird, but not to ask for a second wish seemed wasteful, and, of course, he could not ask for it without returning to the fairies. Also, if he put off asking for his wish too long it might go bad.

And in the end, you know, he flew away. Twice he came back from the window, wanting to kiss his mother, but he feared the delight of it might waken her, so at last he played her a lovely kiss on his pipe, and then he flew back to the gardens.

Peter's Two Wishes

Many nights and even months passed before he asked the fairies to grant his second wish, and I am not sure that I quite know why it was that he delayed so long. One reason was that he had so many goodbyes to say, not only to his particular friends, but to a hundred favourite spots. Then he had his last sail, and his very last sail, and his last sail of all, and so on.

But, mind you, though Peter was so slow in going back to his mother, he was quite decided to go back. The best proof of this was his caution with the fairies. They were most anxious that he should remain in the gardens to play to them, and to bring this to pass they tried to trick him into making such a remark as 'I wish the grass was not so wet,' and some of them danced out of time in the hope that he might cry, 'I do wish you would keep time!' Then they would have said that this was his second wish. But though on occasions he began, "I wish," he always checked himself in time.

I WISH, I WISH

So when at last he said to them bravely, "I wish now to go back to mother for ever and always," they had to tickle his shoulders and let him go.

He went in a hurry in the end because he had dreamt that his mother was crying, and he knew the great thing she cried for, and that a hug from her splendid Peter would be the only thing to quickly make her to smile. Oh, he felt sure of it, and so eager was he to be nestling in her arms that this time he flew straight to the window, which was always to be left open for him.

But when at last he reached the window he found that it was closed, and there were strong iron bars upon it. And when he peered inside he saw his mother sleeping peacefully with her arm round another little boy.

Peter called, "Mother! Mother!" but she heard him not. In vain he beat his little limbs against the iron bars. He had to fly back, sobbing, to the Gardens, and he never saw his dear mother again.

Peter's Two Wishes

What a glorious boy he had meant to be to her. Ah, Peter, we who have made the great mistake, how differently we should all act at the second chance. But there is no second chance, not for most of us. When we reach the window it is Lock-out Time. The iron bars are up for life.

The End